T0311997

SPORT HISTORY

This is a fundamental text for the study of sport history. It answers the 'why,' 'how,' and 'what' questions, introducing the key principles and practices of sport history and walking the reader through the fascinating stories, debates, issues, and national and international narratives that constitute the history of sport.

The book provides an overview of the field and the various professional roles assumed by practitioners, such as researchers, academics, and public historians. It is brief, crisp, and to the point. The main general topics of interest within the field – gender, race, nationalism, religion, sport and leisure, and megaevents – are covered with introductory vignettes, stories of interest, a wide variety of theoretical frameworks, and relevant historiography in the most current and timely text of its kind. Each chapter provides a list of further readings for more in-depth study. Students are taught how to conduct research and present their findings in a variety of mediums, and teaching and publication tips are offered for educators.

Sport History: The Basics is essential reading for any student on a sport-related degree course or with an interest in social and cultural history. It is also fascinating reading for anybody with a general interest in sport.

Gerald R. Gems is Professor Emeritus at North Central College, USA. He is past president of the North American Society for Sport History, past vice president of the International Society for the History of Physical Education and Sport, and an international Fulbright Scholar.

THE BASICS

The Basics is a highly successful series of accessible guidebooks which provide an overview of the fundamental principles of a subject area in a jargon-free and undaunting format.

Intended for students approaching a subject for the first time, the books both introduce the essentials of a subject and provide an ideal springboard for further study. With over 50 titles spanning subjects from artificial intelligence to women's studies, *The Basics* are an ideal starting point for students seeking to understand a subject area.

Each text comes with recommendations for further study and gradually introduces the complexities and nuances within a subject.

For a full list of titles in this series, please visit
www.routledge.com/The-Basics/book-series/B

SPORT HISTORY

THE BASICS

Gerald R. Gems

LONDON AND NEW YORK

First published 2021
by Routledge
2 Park Square, Milton Park, Abingdon, Oxon OX14 4RN

and by Routledge
52 Vanderbilt Avenue, New York, NY 10017

Routledge is an imprint of the Taylor & Francis Group, an informa business

British Library Cataloguing-in-Publication Data
A catalogue record for this book is available from the British Library

Library of Congress Cataloging-in-Publication Data
Names: Gems, Gerald R., author.
Title: Sport history: the basics / Gerald R. Gems.
Description: Abingdon, Oxon; New York, NY: Routledge, 2021. |
Series: The basics | Includes bibliographical references and index.
Identifiers: LCCN 2020043098 | ISBN 9780367543945 (hardback) |
ISBN 9780367543921 (paperback) | ISBN 9781003089094 (ebook)
Subjects: LCSH: Sports–History. | Sports–Historiography. |
Sports–Research–Methodology. | Sports–Social aspects. |
Sports–Political aspects.
Classification: LCC GV571 .G46 2021 | DDC 796.09–dc23
LC record available at https://lccn.loc.gov/2020043098

ISBN: 978-0-367-54394-5 (hbk)
ISBN: 978-0-367-54392-1 (pbk)
ISBN: 978-1-003-08909-4 (ebk)

Typeset in Bembo
by Newgen Publishing UK

For my brother, lifelong friend, confidant, and inspiration.

CONTENTS

WHY STUDY SPORT HISTORY?

In 2020, the death of a black man at the hands of police in the United States erupted into a national protest rally for social justice and an end to systemic racism. Celebrated athletes assumed leadership roles within the movement, which soon became an international crusade to address the wrongs of the historical past. In order to fully understand how and why this campaign occurred and the role of athletes in it, one must know the historical efforts to affect a better future in the United States, including the relevant social, cultural, racial, and sport histories.

Sport history is a subdiscipline of history that analyzes the various factors that compose the record of human development. It involves the recording of past events as well as analysis and explanation of practices and meanings to develop a better understanding of all cultures and societies. It provides a means to measure change over time and offers insights into the transitions in politics, economics, education, and technology. Sport provides a different lens through which to study such factors as race, ethnicity, gender, social class, religion, identity, migration, and nationalism. It can be used to examine current issues and to provide a comparative analysis across time periods and different societies. Historian Wray Vamplew states that 'Sports history is a counter to nostalgia, myth, and invented tradition. It can be considered the sports memory of a nation; without sports history there is sporting amnesia' (2017: 15). In other words, sport history can tell us who we are as individuals, groups, communities, and nations.

The distinguished historian Peter Stearns adds that the 'really big point in sports history is to help us figure out why sports have become so important in so many modern societies, in serving so many different functions and rousing such obvious and often highly entertaining passions' (2010: xi).

Many people have an intense interest in sport, and they express a passion for it as athletes, fans, and consumers. For some, it provides immense pleasure as they immerse themselves in the pursuit of greater knowledge about sporting activities. It can even become a career, one in which you are paid to indulge in what would otherwise be a hobby. That is the life of a sport historian.

While many sport historians pursue their craft within academia, they might also engage in other related occupations. Some are professional researchers who may be freelance operators paid commissions for their time spent gaining information for others. Some may be journalists who need such information or procure historical sport records or materials to augment their own work. Archivists also need a working knowledge of sport to accommodate the increasing number of requests for historical records, materials, and artifacts relative to the pursuit of sport knowledge. Like archivists, museum curators, particularly those who create exhibits in the ever-growing number of sport museums, must have a command of knowledge relative to their particular sport forms. One can hardly think of a sport that does not have its own museum, hall of fame, or memorial, all of which have buttressed the burgeoning sport tourism business. Secondary school teachers, like university professors, have found that sport is a means to engage their students in almost any other educational discipline. Math, language arts, history, sociology, business, economics, marketing, biology, civics, science, art, and music can all be tailored to use sports to increase students' interest in the subject matter. One need not be in the teaching profession to study sport or use it in this way. Public historians who engage the populace on economic, political, or social matters can use sport as a segue to discussion. Similarly, independent authors need not have a university affiliation to write a book on sport. Popular sport history books generally sell in greater numbers than those produced by academics. Authors also need editors who must be familiar with the subject matter in order to acquire, polish, and produce their work. The study of sport history thus lends itself to a variety of occupations.

Regardless of one's chosen path as a sport historian, particular characteristics are required in this role. Sport historians must research their subject matter and, thus, must be able to work independently. They should be able to critically analyze their sources and scholarly interpretations of the subject matter. They must be organized in order to present their findings in a comprehensive manner. They must possess good communication skills in order to transmit the knowledge gained. If one pursues a career within academia, flexibility is important, as job placement will likely require relocation. Academics must be ambitious, for the process of attaining tenure and promotion is a competitive one. At university level, professors are expected to add to the current state of knowledge by presenting and publishing their research, which requires self-confidence as well as a good deal of fortitude, as critical peer review and editorial rejection are normal and regular parts of the process.

A HISTORIOGRAPHY OF SPORT HISTORY

Written sport history has a long chronology of its own. Archeologists provided the evidence of sport in ancient times. Pottery, stone carvings, and documents retrieved from ancient Chinese dynasties indicated dancers, acrobats, runners, and wrestlers between 8000 BCE and 2000 BCE. In succeeding years, horse racing became a prominent activity, and polo was played by both men and women as a favorite sport of the nobility. Both men and women also played a sport known as cuju, similar to soccer in that players kicked a ball. Other artifacts provided knowledge relative to gymnastics and horse racing during the Han dynasty (206 BCE–220 CE). Touhu, involving tossing arrows into a vase, was another game played in this period. During the Yuan dynasty (618–907 CE), awards were given to the top finishers in a 90-kilometer cross-country run, which qualified them to become royal bodyguards. At this time, Wushu, the practice of martial arts, included swordplay. Weightlifting contests, swimming, and dragon boat racing also appeared, and the latter remains a popular sport today. During the Tang dynasty (618–907 CE), women played a game called buda or chuiwan, similar to golf, in which players used sticks to hit a ball into a hole. During the same period, professional wrestlers entertained imperial audiences, and a national wrestling tournament ensued in the Song dynasty (960–1279 CE). In northern China, people took to sledding and skating on the ice (Gems, 2014b).

In other Asian countries, among the oldest civilizations, archeology and historical research unearthed other evidence of early sport. In Japan, archery was practiced by the seventh century BCE, and sumo wrestling appeared by 23 BCE. The rise of the samurai class in the twelfth century CE required archery and fencing skills. In India during 1400–1000 BCE, people swam, lifted weights, honed their archery skills, wrestled, and fought with swords. In later years, there was a greater emphasis on meditation and mental rather than physical development, especially after the rise of Buddhism after 483 BCE. Polo, played by the Persians by the sixth century CE, soon spread to India, where the British adopted the game in the nineteenth century. Kabbadi, a popular Indian game in which players try to invade the territory of opponents without being captured, spread to other Asian and some western counties. In Mesopotamia, the land between the Tigris and Euphrates rivers (now comprised of Iraq and parts of Iran, Syria, and Turkey), friezes and surviving documents provided evidence of early chariot racing, archery, boxing, and wrestling as early as 4000–3000 BCE (Gems 2014b).

Like the archeological digs of Asia, ancient artifacts revealed much about Egyptian life. The Egyptians had developed an early form of picture writing known as hieroglyphics. This was undecipherable in modern times until 1799 when Napoleon's troops discovered the Rosetta Stone, a tablet that included a Greek translation of its hieroglyphic message, enabling European scholars to interpret the hieroglyphic script. Hieroglyphic inscriptions on monuments and murals on royal tomb walls could then be understood. These revealed wrestlers, weightlifters, runners, jumpers, swimmers, rowers, fishermen, archers, gymnasts, boxers, equestrians, and people engaged in ball games. Women also played ball-and-stick games. Religious festivals included running events, and even the pharaohs had to demonstrate their fitness to rule by displaying their running prowess (Gems 2014b).

We know much about the athletic activities of the ancient Greeks due to an abundance of archeological, artistic, and literary sources. The *Iliad* and the *Odyssey*, poems attributed to Homer, provide details of funeral games that took place during the Trojan War, including chariot and foot racing, boxing, wrestling, jumping, javelin and discus throwing, archery, and dancing. Greek city-states were often at war with each other or with the Persian Empire. Athens, a democracy, fostered the education of well-rounded individuals taught in a gymnasium that included physical development of male youth. Sparta, the preeminent warriors, trained both boys and girls in running, wrestling, discus, and javelin in preparation for battle. Spartans reasoned that strong women would produce strong men. Weak babies faced infanticide. Spartans exemplified stoicism to endure pain and never admit defeat (Gems 2014b). The film *300* (2006, dir. Z. Snyder) commemorates the role of King Leonidas and his Spartan warriors, who held off an entire Persian army at the Battle of Thermopylae in 480 BCE.

The Greeks did unite in the practice of their polytheistic religion, incorporating sport in their spiritual festivals. The most notable, the Olympic Games, honored Zeus, the chief god, and were held every four years. Other festivals worshiped the gods Apollo and Poseidon, while women, who were not allowed to attend the Olympic Games, had their own festival devoted to Hera, the wife of Zeus. Competition permeated Greek life, and the festivals not only included athletic events, but also recognized winners in music, art, speech, poetry, drama, and singing. Greek colonies throughout the Mediterranean sent competitors to the festivals, and athletes began to specialize in particular events. Some became professionals selling their abilities to the highest bidder. The Olympic Games have a recorded history that goes back to at least 776 BCE. By the fourth century BCE, the Olympic stadium seated 40,000, and the hippodrome, which hosted chariot and horse races, was double or triple the size of the athletic site. Greeks recognized their athletic heroes with classical statues, many of which are now housed in European museums. Archeologists have uncovered the Greek columns and statues on which victors inscribed their feats. One describes dual wins by Kyniska, a Spartan princess, in the chariot races of 396 BCE and 392 BCE. Although women were denied entry and she did not drive the chariots, like horse racing today, it was the owner who got the prize. The athletic competitions also showcased the extent of Greek technology, which featured starting blocks, starting gate, and designated lanes in the running events (Gems 2014b).

Greek judges were adamant that the rules be enforced. False starts in the sprints might result in a whipping. Perhaps the most unusual case resulted from a boxing match circa 400 BCE at the Nemean Games, held every two years in honor of Zeus. Damoxenes of Syracuse and Kreugas of Epidamnos had engaged in a long and brutal match with no clear winner when they agreed to allow one undefended blow to be delivered by each fighter. Kreugas struck a powerful blow to the head of Damoxenes, but it did not result in a knockout. Damoxenes then told his opponent to cover his own head before he retaliated. When he did so, Damoxenes delivered a karate-like thrust to Kreugas's abdomen, piercing the skin and even extracting his intestines. Kreugas died on the spot. But the judges ruled that Damoxenes's blow was illegal because his five fingers constituted *five* blows rather than the agreed-upon *one*, and they thereby awarded the victory to the body of Kreugas (Gems 2014b).

Rome showed the influence of Sparta in its devotion to the martial endeavors that built its empire. At the Campus Martius in the city of Rome, soldiers trained in archery, swordfighting, spear throwing, equestrian skills, ball games, and hand-to-hand combat. Hikes and swimming exercises simulated the experiences of military campaigns. At the Circus Maximus, an immense stadium that seated 200,000, the Romans staged chariot races. Four districts within the city each fielded their own teams with rabid fans and team colors (see Alan Cameron's *Circus Factions: Blues and Greens at Rome and Byzantium*, 1976). Spectacular crashes excited fans, not unlike the NASCAR (in full, the National Association for Stock Car Auto Racing) races of today. In the Roman Colosseum, wealthy citizens staged violent gladiatorial bouts for the general populace, as men and even women faced each other, or even wild animals, in mortal combat. Gladiators often specialized in particular weapons, learning their trade in schools that taught such skills. The special edifices constructed for such spectacles predate the modern stadiums of today's professional teams. As well as being a form of entertainment, gladiator fights served a social and political function – the social control of the populace by keeping them amused, thus curtailing any uprising against the ruling class. In 107 CE, the Emperor Trajan offered 123 days of such violence, involving 10,000 gladiators and resulting in the deaths of 11,000 animals (Gems 2014b).

With the rise of Christianity, gladiatorial spectacles and the Olympic Games were both banned. The medieval period promoted spirituality over corporeal strength. While folk games persisted, the only remnants of athletic spectacle emerged in the jousting tournaments of the warrior class. Knights engaged in melees as practice for warfare; but these could sometimes turn deadly. A French knight is credited with organizing the first jousting tournament in 1066. In tournaments, the knight could practice his skills by knocking an opponent from his horse. Such a defeated knight, or at least his horse and armor, might be held for ransom. William Marshal became one of the richest men of England, even serving as regent, through his jousting expertise (Johnson, n.d.). King Richard I (the Lionheart), in an early form of sports franchising, required the licensing of tournaments in 1194. A century later, in 1292, King Edward I tried to limit the injuries incurred in such trials by requiring blunted lance tips in charges; and after 1400, a timber barrier separated the knights in their approach, to avoid collisions. In the era of chivalry, jousting tournaments became ever larger and more spectacular festivals, with knights often acting as champions for the ladies of the court, designated by the knight wearing an article of the lady's clothing upon their helmet. When sponsored by royalty, the tournaments evolved into opulent pageants. The invention of firearms in the sixteenth century forecast the eventual end of jousting, but not before King Henry II of France was killed in a tournament in 1559 when a splinter from a lance pierced his eye and entered his brain (Cavendish 2009).

Sport assumed greater meaning during the Renaissance period in Europe as upper-class males sought to develop the whole person, mentally and physically. Baldassare Castiglione's *Il Cortegiano* (The Courtier), published in 1528 (see Castiglione 1974), 'became the standard reference on proper education throughout all of Europe and included physical activity as a necessity' (Gems 1980: 11). Physical activities included vaulting onto one's horse, rather than simply mounting it, as a means to impress others. Only three years after the release of Castiglione's work, Sir Thomas Elyot published a similar tome entitled *The Boke Named the Governour* (1531) in England, which went through eight printings by 1580. Written in the vernacular, it was accessible to a wide variety of readers beyond the scholars trained in Latin. Elyot advocated exercise as a means to improve fitness, digestion, strength, agility, and speed. Archery proved a particular necessity for recreation as well as war. Swimming, running, riding, fencing, tennis, wrestling, weightlifting, and dancing constituted part of the curriculum suggested for the training of young gentlemen (Gems 1980).

In 1545, Roger Ascham, tutor to the future Queen Elizabeth I, published *Toxophilus*, a vernacular treatise on archery, which might be considered the first sport book (see Ascham 2016). The book, which went through three printings, covered the history of the sport, its prominence in military victories, and its role as a recreational activity, as an educational tool with instructional techniques, and for competitive purposes. Archery was a required activity in England, a necessity for military needs. Each family had to provide a bow for male children when they reached the age of 7, and the father or male guardian was responsible for instruction in its use. The English longbow reached a length of six feet, and its use required considerable strength as well as skill. The sport also provided economic benefits, as it supported bowyers, fletchers, stringers, and arrowhead makers. The government enacted price controls to insure that bows and arrows might be easily purchased. The prestigious archery clubs also enjoyed privileges, such as immunity when accidental deaths occurred. That proved to be important, as a stray arrow once pierced the hat of Dame Alice Owen when she chanced too close to a mark (Gems 1980). Even though the introduction of gunpowder to England eventually resulted in the discontinuance of archery, an assembly of archers for a two-day meet in 1583 still numbered 3,000.

Robert Dover's *Annalia Dubrensia*, consisting of 35 poems celebrating Dover's annual folk parody of the ancient Olympics, was published in 1636. Dover's escapade originated during the reign of King James I (1603–1625) in defiance of the Puritan prohibitions relative to sport. The games consisted of a wide variety of entertainments: cudgel (stick) fighting, wrestling, running, jumping, throwing, football, skittles, quoits, shovelboard, horse races, sack races, hunt-ing, dancing, and even bell-ringing. Periodically resurrected over the years, the frivolities continued into the nineteenth century with don-key races, cockfights, and backsword contests (sticks used for fencing practice) until they were eventually banned and the traditional site on Cotswold Hill was enclosed in 1853–1854 (Dover 1636).

In both the United Kingdom and the United States, antiquar-ians who studied relics and ancient works of art had begun to write about sport by the nineteenth century, and sport history rested largely their hands until the twentieth century. For example, Joseph Strutt, an antiquarian but not a trained historian, published *The Sports and Pastimes of the People of England* (1801), an early but unreliable historical source. Pierce Egan's *Boxiana*, published in 1813, presented a lively account of the history of bare-knuckle pugilism in England during the eighteenth and early nineteenth centuries (see Egan 1997). Egan's coverage of the fighters, their sponsors, the fights, the fans, the gamblers, and the social context captured the spirit of the times. John Nyren's *The Cricketeers of My Time*, published in 1833, provided insight into the sport in the late eighteenth century. In the United States, *Athletic Sports for Boys* was published in 1866 as a compendium of physical activities suitable for middle-class youth.

In the early twentieth century, scholars began to turn their atten-tion to sport. In 1910, historian E. Norman Gardiner published *Greek Athletic Sports and Festivals*, an ode to the amateur ideal. Gardiner's intellectual disciple H. A. Harris continued the glorification of ancient athletes in *Greek Athletes and Athletics* in 1964. Sport histori-ans of the 1970s challenged such idealistic portrayals by exposing the negative aspects of the Olympic Games. Others forged new paths, such as the German scholar Wolfgang Decker with *Sports and Games of Ancient Egypt* in 1987 and Michael Poliakoff's *Combat Sports in the Ancient World: Competition, Violence and Culture* in the same year. Since that time, scholars such as David C. Young (*The Olympic Myth of Greek Amateur Athletics*, 1984) Stephen G. Miller (*Ancient Greek Athletics*, 2004), Nigel B. Crowther (*Athletika: Studies in the Olympic Games and Greek Athletics*, 2004), and Donald G. Kyle (*Sport and Spectacle in the Ancient World*, 2007) have added further insights and rectifications relative to ancient sport practices.

The study of modern sport began to assume greater importance when Frederic Paxson, a prominent historian, published an article entitled 'The Rise of Sport' in 1917. In the article, he envisioned sport as the new American frontier, an agent of social change. In 1938, Dutch historian Johan Huizinga published *Homo Ludens*, which recognized play as an essential element in the development of culture. A year later, German sociologist Norbert Elias published *The Civilizing Process*, a work that covered more than 1,000 years of European social development, including the harnessing of physical violence to eventually produce modern sport (see Elias 2000). French sociologist Roger Caillois's publication *Man, Play, and Games* in 1961 challenged Huizinga's notions of competition as theoretical application assumed greater importance in the study of sport. In 1978, American literary scholar Allen Guttmann authored *From Ritual to Record* in which he analyzed the development of modern sport and the ways in which it shaped modern life.

This brief history of the development of the field shows the interdisciplinary nature of its lineage. That was not always the case as sport historians battled for academic acceptance in the latter twentieth century. Even within the subdiscipline, scholars debated whether one was a *historian of sport* or a *sport historian*. Mark Dyreson notes the distinction in the following:

> Historians of sport seek to explain how American sport illuminates larger issues in the nation's development, from the nature and practice of political and social reform to the role of class, race, and gender in shaping culture. Sport historians, on the other hand, are in some ways commanded to do the opposite. Their particular audience is far more interested in the nature of sport and other forms of physical activity in human societies than they are in the particularities of historical experience.
>
> (2010, 608)

Historians of sport were more likely to work in history departments and sport historians in physical education or kinesiology departments. That distinction may be largely semantic, as scholarship has coalesced around more inclusive themes.

After Frederic Paxson's 1917 journal article, sport history in the United States languished. John Allen Krout published *Annals of American Sport* in 1929, followed by Jennie Holliman's *American Sports,*

1785–1835 in 1931. Nearly a decade passed before Foster Rhea Dulles offered *America Learns to Play: A History of Popular Recreation 1607–1940* (1940). In the post-World War II years, Frederick Cozens and Florence Stumpf conducted anthropological studies on the sporting practices of people in New Zealand and Fiji, published in *Research Quarterly* in 1947 and 1949, respectively, followed by Helen Dunlap's (1951) inquiry into Samoan culture and William Goellner's (1953) work on Mayan ball games in Mexico and Central America (Dyreson 2010). Anthropologist Clifford Geertz's essay on Balinese cockfights in *The Interpretation of Cultures* in 1973 had important meanings for, and continues to influence, sport historians. John Rickards Betts's dissertation thesis of 1951 did not reach publication until 1974, as *America's Sporting Heritage, 1850–1950* (Dyreson 2010). Well before that time, Seward C. Staley, a distinguished professor of physical education and dean of the college at the University of Illinois, had called for the training of sport historians, stating that 'sport has a long usage by civilized man [and] during recent years that activity has had increasingly significant interrelationships with many other aspects of life' (1962: 133). A year later, in England, Peter McIntosh published *Sport in Society*, which became a standard text in school programs (McIntosh 1963). Dennis Brailsford's *Sport and Society: Elizabeth to Anne* followed in 1969, offering a history of social life, physical education, and sport in seventeenth-century England.

The civil rights and feminist movements of the mid-twentieth century fostered a greater interest in social history. In England, E.P. Thompson's *The Making of the English Working Class* and C.L.R. James's *Beyond a Boundary*, a study of cricket in the West Indies, both published in 1963, analyzed social class and race as major factors in sport and society. James's work can be considered a watershed in sport history as he

> opened the field of sports to a complicated and interdisciplinary realm in which sports became a transom for so much more. James frames his study of cricket using techniques of memoir, cultural theory, and social analysis, making it a benchmark in cultural history writ large.
>
> (Bass 2014: 152)

Historical journals also began to feature sport-related articles, such as Keith Thomas's 'Work and Leisure in Pre-Industrial Society,' in *Past and Present* in 1964, and Gareth Stedman Jones's 'Working Class Culture and Working Class Politics in London, 1870–1900,' in the *Journal of Social History* in 1974. This extended the scope of sport history studies.

German historians also produced a number of sport histories, some particularly focused on the nationalistic Turner movement. By the 1960s, East German scholars introduced class studies based on their Marxist ideology.

Case histories and urban studies soon followed. Dale Somers's *The Rise of Sport in New Orleans, 1850–1900* in 1972 initiated a host of similar books that varied in content as well as theoretical frameworks that are still used in analysis of the role of sport in urban centers. Robert Malcolmson's *Popular Recreations in English Society* (1973) addressed the history of working-class pastimes, and James Walvin's *The People's Game: The History of British Football*, published in 1975, accounted for the historical roots and global expansion of soccer. The publication of Tony Mason's *Association Football and English Society, 1863–1915* in 1980 marked the clear arrival of sport history in British academia.

The growth of sport history became apparent with the establishment of the International Committee for the History of Physical Education and Sport (ICOSH) at a conference in Prague in 1967. The *Canadian Journal of History of Sport and Physical Education* (later renamed *Sport History Review*), pioneered by Professor Alan Metcalfe of the University of Windsor in 1970, provided the first sport-specific scholarly journal for historians. In 1972, Metcalfe became one of the founding members of the North American Society for Sport History (or NASSH), largely established by American professors of physical education. The organization began holding annual conferences in 1973 and initiated publication of its *Journal of Sport History* in 1974. As the study of sport history gradually gained increasing acceptance in academic circles, the British Society of Sports History (known as the BSSA), organized by social historians, followed in 1982. *The International Journal of the History of Sport* began publication in 1984. The Australian Society for Sports History (or ASSH) followed a year after the establishment of the BSSA and produced its own journal, *Sporting Traditions*. In 1989, the International Association for History of Physical Education and Sport merged with ICOSH to become the International Society for the History of Physical Education and Sport (or ISHPES), which has held annual international conferences thereafter. The European Committee for Sport History (known as CESH), evolved from a conference forum in 1991 and reached full realization in 1995. A succession of national and regional sport history associations followed over the next two decades. The success of such enterprises resulted in a proliferation of sport-related publications and annual conferences where scholars presented their work (Dyreson 2019).

By the 1990s, largely influenced by labor historians, British sport history was largely focused on urban studies and particular sports, with an emphasis on soccer and cricket. Jeffrey Hill's assessment of the field in 1996 lamented the absence of media, military, and gender studies; although Kathleen McCrone's *Sport and the Physical Emancipation of Women, 1870–1914* in 1988 and Jennifer Hargreaves's *Sporting Females: Critical Issues in the History and Sociology of Women's Sports* in 1994 gave impetus to the latter.

In the United States, a proliferation of sport studies ensued, largely focused on team sports such as baseball and American football. With the rise of postmodernism in the 1990s, alternative theoretical frameworks appeared and feminism enjoyed a greater voice, initiated by Patricia Vertinsky's *The Eternally Wounded Woman* in 1990.

Australian sport historians published a wealth of urban studies centered around the surf lifesaving culture in following years (Brawley 1995, 1996; Booth 2001; Jaggard 2002). The Australians were among the first to champion the movement toward postmodern and multidisciplinary approaches to the study of sport history. In Great Britain, the scholarship moved beyond England to include studies of Scotland and Wales, and Ireland was also represented with the work of Mike Cronin having particular prominence (see, for example, Cronin 1999).

In the United States, S. W. Pope edited an anthology in 1997 that showcased the broad scope of research in American sport history at that time. The 17 chapters by leading sport historians covered four particular topics: national culture; gender and the body; class, race, and ethnicity; and markets and audiences (Pope 1997). During the

1990s, sport history began to take a cultural turn to postmodern approaches, becoming more introspective and personal and questioning the nature of truth, texts, language, and meanings. While this caused a rupture with more traditional historians, Douglas Booth, a convert to the postmodern approach, argued that too many sport historians had 'a tendency toward conformity and a stifling of experimentation' (2005b: 221).

In 2017, co-editors Linda Borish, David Wiggins, and Gerald Gems published *The Routledge History of American Sport*, an 'examination of the rich field of the history of American sport from various historical approaches' (2017: 2). Comprehensive in nature, this volume consisted of 33 essays covering theory and methods, teaching, school sports, race, ethnicity, social class, gender, the business of sport, film, sport tourism, material culture, sport training and technology, the military, politics, alternative sports, globalization, and the future of sport history. In Jaime Schultz's (2017) assessment of the latter, she acknowledges the continued need for sport history to find full acceptance within academia. She notes that 'it is imperative that historians view sport as "something capable of exerting social and cultural influence; of being a process, a language, a system of meaning through which we know the world."' (Schultz 2017: 21, quoting British historian Jeffrey Hill (2003: 361)). Canadian sport historian Colin Howell adds, 'if history does not have emancipatory potential then what is its value?' (2007: 461). Hill, once again, supplies the answer: 'If the study of sport and leisure is not "political" in the broadest sense of the term, then it isn't worth a damn' (2002: 187). Amy Bass concludes her assessment of the 'state of the field' by proclaiming that 'the work of sport historians is important, contributing across many fields while maintaining its distinct lines of identity, and as it continues to develop, its legitimacy and significance will continue to follow and thrive' (Bass 2014: 172).

There is still much work to be done. For those who might wish to contribute, De Montfort University in Leicester has offered a master's degree in Sports History and Culture since 1996. Bachelor's, master's, and doctoral degrees can be obtained at several universities in Europe, the United States, and Canada.

FURTHER READING

Amy Bass (2014) 'State of the Field: Sports History and the "Cultural Turn,"' *Journal of American History* 101:1, 148–172.

Linda J. Borish, David K. Wiggins, and Gerald R. Gems, eds. (2017) *The Routledge History of American Sport*. New York: Routledge.

Robert Colls (2015) 'British Sports History,' *History Today* 65:4, at https://www.historytoday.com/archive/british-sports-history (accessed 24 March 2020).

Mike Cronin (2014) *Sport: A Very Short Introduction*. New York: Oxford.

Gerald R. Gems (2014) *Blood and Guts to Glory: A History of Sports* [e-book]. Oslo: Total Health Publications.

Jeffrey Hill (1996) 'British Sport History: A Postmodern Future?' *Journal of Sport History* 23:1, 1–19.

Richard Holt (2014) 'Historians and the History of Sport,' *Sport in History* 34:1, 1–33.

Mike Huggins (2008) 'Sport and the British Upper Classes *c*.1500–2000: A Historiographic Overview,' *Sport in History* 28:3, 364–388.

Martin Johnes (2004) 'Putting the History into Sport: On Sport History and Sport Studies in the U.K.,' *Journal of Sport History* 31:2, 145–160.

Ross McKibbin (2011) 'Sports History: Status, Definitions and Meanings,' *Sport in History* 31:2, 167–174.

Martin Polley (2007) *Sports History: A Practical Guide*. New York: Palgrave Macmillan.

S. W. Pope (1997) *The New American Sport History: Recent Approaches and Perspectives*. Urbana: University of Illinois Press.

Jaime Schultz (2017) 'New Directions and Future Considerations in American Sport History,' in Linda J. Borish, David K. Wiggins, and Gerald R. Gems, eds., *The Routledge History of American Sport*. New York: Routledge, 17–29.

2

THE WORK OF A SPORT HISTORIAN

In 1831, Charles Darwin embarked on a voyage to circumnavigate the globe aboard the HMS *Beagle*. The trip took five years, during which Darwin studied plants, birds, and fossils. In 1859, he published his theory of evolution in a book entitled *The Origin of Species by Means of Natural Selection*. Darwin's belief that species survived via adaptation overturned the biblical version of creationism that had been prevalent for centuries. Darwin's theory, based on science, changed the world.

THEORY

Theory provides a framework for analysis, a means to test a hypothesis. While early sport histories were largely narrative accounts of events, scholars have increasingly adopted a wide variety of theoretical frameworks in which to present their findings. Frontier theory, first expressed by Frederick Jackson Turner at the 1893 World's Fair held in Chicago, claims that the American frontier created a culture that values individualism, self-reliance, democracy, and economic mobility. This perception of uniqueness became known as American exceptionalism. Frederic Paxson declared sport to be the new frontier in 1917. Turner's thesis has since come into disrepute for several reasons, among them the fact that most countries can also claim a frontier experience, relatively few people lived on the American frontier compared to the general population, and Turner failed to address the experiences of women and social class differences.

American historian Herbert Bolton pioneered the borderlands theory as early as 1921. Bolton studied the southern American borderlands from the eastern state of Florida to the west coast of California and noted the merging of social, religious, economic, linguistic, architectural, and legal elements of the seemingly disparate cultures. Relative to sport, rodeo originated as a contest of work skills among the Mexican *vaqueros* (cowboys). Borderlands in general are considered to be peripheral, dynamic regions where people, lifestyles, ideas, languages, identities, etc. clash in contested relationships, resulting in cultural exchange and often adaptation. Studies of such areas offer new insights into transnational comparisons and continue to have relevance. Two excellent examples are offered by Colin Howell and Daryl Leeworthy in their examination of the South Wales border with England and the Cape Breton area of Canada near the northeastern United States (Howell and Leeworthy 2010).

Functionalism, employed by early sport historians and sport sociologists, assumed that sport is good and beneficial to society in that it contributes to the assimilation of immigrant groups and produces positive character traits in participants. This structuralist approach gained greater sophistication with the advent of modernization theory, that drew from the works of sociologists Max Weber, Norbert Elias, and Eric Dunning. Allen Guttmann's (1978) *From Ritual to Record: The Nature of Modern Sports* is a landmark study in the field of sport history for its application of modernization theory in which he identifies the characteristics of modern sport as secularity, equality, bureaucratization, specialization, rationalization, and quantification. Melvin Adelman's (1986) *A Sporting Time: New York City and the Rise of Modern Athletics, 1820–70* adds urbanization and commercialization to Guttmann's list. Neil Tranter's (1998) *Sport, Economy, and Society in Britain, 1750–1914* ties the rise of modern sport to the industrialization process and social class. Stefan Szymanski (2008) claims that modern sport emanated from the formation of clubs in Europe and the United States, an assertion that resulted in a special forum of dissent in the *Journal of Sport History*. Mike Huggins (2020) disputes

Szymanski's interpretation and gives his own thesis in 'Associativity, Gambling, and the Rise of Protomodern British Sport, 1660–1800,' contending that gambling fostered the transition to modern sport.

Sport historians buttressed their studies of urban and modern sport with economic analysis. Wray Vamplew's (1988) *Pay Up and Play the Game, 1863–1915* is an award-winning quantitative economic analysis of gambling, crime, and violence rooted in four early sports as they began to commercialize and professionalize in the late nineteenth century. Steven Riess's (1989) *City Games: The Evolution of American Urban Society and the Rise of Sports* includes tables, maps, and comparisons in a social, cultural, and economic interdisciplinary study. Michael Lomax's (2003) *Black Baseball Entrepreneurs, 1860–1901: Operating by Any Means Necessary* is not only a business history, but also one of racial migration, urbanization, and the hardships of segregation and lack of full inclusion in the white economy.

Social class assumed much greater importance with the publication of E. P. Thompson's *The Making of the English Working Class* in 1963, a Marxist analysis. Marxism took hold among sport historians thereafter, as it proposed a direct conflict with the functionalist interpretations. Marxism assumes that capitalists, usually the social and economic upper classes, act in their own self-interests to the detriment of the working class. Labor history merged with sport history by the 1970s and, rather than the social conformity seen by the functionalists, scholars found alienation, aggression, violence, nationalism, sexism, and materialism among the masses. Alan Metcalfe became an early proponent of Marxism in his studies of Montreal, Canada (1976, 1978). Cary Goodman's (1979) *Choosing Sides: Playground and Street Life on the Lower East Side*, a case study of New York, found that capitalists organized play for the immigrant masses to counteract the negative influences of street life in order to produce complacent workers. British Marxists Eric Hobsbawm and Terence Ranger (1983) determined that the upper classes even 'invented traditions' that were easily adapted to sports in order to meet their own desires.

Marxist studies provided new insights into power relationships in societies and inequalities relative to social class, race, gender, and ethnicity; but they focused largely on economic analyses within the capitalist system that belied the agency of the working class to determine its own outcomes. Neo-Marxist approaches allowed for such human agency, based on the works of Italian philosopher Antonio Gramsci, imprisoned by the fascist government of Benito Mussolini for his revolutionary doctrine. Gramsci languished in prison for nearly a decade before succumbing to a variety of illnesses; but he left a compendium of works in his *Prison Notebooks*, in which he contended that 'the state is the instrument for conforming civil society to the economic structure' (Hoare and Smith 1971: 208). In Gramsci's conception, each society has a dominant group that sets the norms, standards, and tastes of the community. All other members who are not part of the dominant group have choices: to accept or reject the dominant group's mandates or to adopt or adapt them to their own needs. Within groups, there may be what he calls 'organic intellectuals' that might act as intermediaries between factions. Welsh academic Raymond Williams (1977) further adds that hegemony involved a constant power struggle between the dominant and subordinate groups (see also Ingham and Hardy 1993). Stephen Hardy's (1982) *How Boston Played: Sport Recreation, and Community, 1865–1915* provides an early introduction to the hegemony genre among sport historians, examining how the local elites contended with the immigrant working class over the use of recreational spaces.

John Hargreaves (1986a) employs hegemony theory in *Sport, Power, and Culture: A Social and Historical Analysis of Popular Sport in Britain*, as does Lois Bryson (1987) in 'Sport and the Maintenance of Masculine Hegemony,' her study of gender relations in Australia. An American example of this approach is Gerald Gems's (1997) case study *Windy City Wars: Labor, Leisure, and Sport in the Making of Chicago*, in which the power struggle between the capitalists and their workers resulted in some measure of adaptation.

> Within one lifetime the city of Chicago virtually erupted from a frontier outpost to a city of more than a million inhabitants of various racial and ethnic groups, each with their own interests and values. ... Change often occurred in a volatile fashion.
>
> [...] Sport, as a common interest, provided a less overt means to infuse a particular ideology, allayed tensions, and brought some accommodation between divergent interests. Sport proved to be an integral part of the popular culture that merged shared interests as it allowed for pluralistic values. It transcended the lines of race, class, ethnicity, religion, and gender.
>
> (Gems 1997: xv, xix)

Steven W. Pope's anthology, *The New American Sport History: Recent Approaches and Perspectives* (1997), is an exemplary model of sport history that examines broader social issues and power relationships, employing the context of cultural studies but rejecting modernization theory. Pope draws upon the works of Stephen Hardy (1990) in the development of a new framework for analysis, which is influenced by the *longue durée* (long term) of the French Annales School, most notably the work of Fernand Braudel, whose work on the Mediterranean departed from traditional historiography to include the importance of the economy, geography, and the environment to determine change in trends or patterns over time. Pope's other contributors demonstrate the Marxist influences of Antonio Gramsci and Raymond Williams.

The rise of cultural studies in the 1980s broadened the scope of sport history and introduced deconstructionism, which became known as postmodernism. Such revolutionary ideas challenged conventional practices, concepts, and narrative histories of the past, which were deemed to be too Eurocentric. Sport historians, the postmodernists claimed, lacked self-reflection. Their version of the truth could only be one part of the whole story. Deconstructionists favored speculation and conjecture over various meanings rather than any absolute historical truth. The postmodernists invoked French philosopher Michel Foucault's notion of discourse that can have contested meanings, thus challenging traditional historians who based their arguments on accurate and 'truthful' sources (Phillips 2001, 2006; Booth 2005b). For example, the word 'sport' has had very different meanings across different historical periods. An early example of the postmodernist approach is Synthia Sydnor's (1998) 'A History of Synchronized Swimming.'

Other French scholars provided additional material for the historiographical debate. Pierre Bourdieu's examination of social class provided the concepts of fields, habitus, social, economic, and cultural capital as well as the power of language. Fields, in which individuals or teams compete for position, may be vertical or horizontal. Grad students may compete with other job applicants who are already in the field (vertical, a step above) or within their own class (horizontal). Soccer teams compete within their own league for advancement and to avoid relegation (vertical, a step below). Habitus refers to the taste or preferences that have been learned and established based on the social class in which one was raised. For example, among the working class, physicality or physical prowess is held in high esteem; therefore, sports such as boxing hold appeal, while the elite might gravitate toward polo. Among the working class, disputes are often settled by physical force, whereas the upper classes might hire a lawyer to settle matters in court. Economic capital provides an advantageous position for those with financial resources. Social or symbolic capital accrues to one who is honored with prestige or attention, such as a celebrity. One who holds a higher position in society may engage in symbolic violence, a nonphysical assault on someone else, such as a public insult or disparagement. A teacher who publicly berates a student in class would be engaging in symbolic violence. Social capital, however, may be temporary and does not necessarily provide economic or cultural capital. The boxer may carry social capital within his local community, but enjoy little prestige among the wider populace. Cultural capital results when one possesses certain skills or assets valued by the community, such as education or knowledge, that garner wholesale respect (Bourdieu 1977, 1984).

The critiques of the postmodernists caused some sport historians to meld examination of discourse with their more conventional methods. Patricia Vertinsky's (1990) *The Eternally Wounded Woman* is a successful adaptation that focuses on the authority of nineteenth-century medical doctors, based on their presumably superior knowledge, to shape an inferior status for women. Michael Oriard's (1993) *Reading Football* is another important addition to the new genre, as he adopts the anthropological approach of Clifford Geertz to ascertain various ways in which the media constructed narratives of the American version of football. Jeffrey Hill's (2006) *Sport and the Literary Tradition* utilizes novels to show how creative fiction can offer insights into the nature of sport in the latter twentieth century.

The advent of cultural studies spawned new interdisciplinary research on sport. Dan Nathan's (2003) *Saying It's So: A Cultural History of the Black Sox Scandal* provides a thorough, interdisciplinary interpretation of the varied narratives surrounding a major baseball catastrophe in the United States when several members of one team agreed to purposely lose the national championship series after being bribed by gamblers in 1919. Nathan's study makes innovative use of secondary sources to examine the development of collective memory and cultural meanings over time.

Historians and sociologists have often been at odds over the cultural turn and its ramifications for scholarship and presentation; but the two disciplines need not be antithetical. In 1995, sport sociologist Joe Maguire established 'Links Between Sports History, Sports Geography, and the Sociology of Sport,' in a *Sporting Traditions* article. Both sport historians and sociologists of sport might find some benefit in Ben Carrington and Ian McDonald's (2008) *Marxism, Cultural Studies and Sport*, which covers theory, economics, media, class, race, and gender. Louise Mansfield and Dominic Malcolm (2010) propose additional possibilities in their essay on 'Sociology' in the *Routledge Companion to Sports History*. They cite numerous interdisciplinary journals that publish articles in both subdisciplines. The collaborations of Hilary Beckles and Brian Stoddart (1995) on *Liberation Cricket: West Indies Cricket Culture*, Jennifer Hargreaves and Patricia Vertinsky (2006) on *Physical Culture, Power and the Body*, as well as Gerald Gems and Gertrud Pfister (2009) on *Understanding American Sports* hold promise for the future.

Tatiana Ryba and Handel Kashope Wright (2005) published an article entitled 'From Mental Game to Cultural Praxis: A Cultural Studies Model's Implications for the Future of Sport Psychology' in *Quest* considering the topics of identity, agency, and justice, which have also gained the attention of sport historians. Though not prolific, studies of the relationship between sport and music have gained some attention. See S. W. Pope's (2006) 'Decentering "Race" and (Re)presenting "Black" Performance in Sport History: Basketball and Jazz in American Culture, 1920–50.' John Bale and Anthony Bateman (2009) offer a more comprehensive and global treatment of the subject in *Sporting Sounds: Relationships Between Sport and Music*.

The merger of sport and economics is noticeable in the work of many scholars. Among them, the works of Wray Vamplew and Steven Riess have previously been cited. Tony Collins's (2013) *Sport in a Capitalist Society* traces the growth of capitalism and its sporting enterprises from the eighteenth century through its intersections with nationalism and militarism to the role of neoliberal politics of the late nineteenth century in the globalization of sport. Sport historians have also integrated with legal studies, as shown by Sarah Fields's (2005) *Female Gladiators: Gender, Law, and Contact Sport in America*, which followed girls' and women's quest for gender equity in the American courts. Sam Regalado and Sarah Fields's (2014) anthology, *Sport and the Law: Historical and Cultural Intersections*, expanded such investigations to examine social and legal issues that changed the nature of American sport and politics.

Simon Inglis, one of the first to address sporting architecture, wrote a series of books aimed at a popular audience in the late twentieth and early twenty-first centuries. More scholarly works followed with Robert Trumpbour's (2007) *The New Cathedrals: Politics and Media in the History of Stadium Construction*, in which the title indicates the interdisciplinary nature of the presentation. Trumpbour and Kenneth Womack (2010) followed with *The Eighth Wonder of the World: The Life of Houston's Iconic Astrodome,* which extends the analysis beyond architecture to show the birth of stadiums as year-round entertainment centers and the effects of gentrification. Benjamin Flowers's (2011) essay 'Stadiums: Architecture and the Iconography of the Beautiful Game' indicates the role of stadiums in the enhancement of an urban identity. Sean Dinces's (2018) award-winning study of the Chicago Stadium, Bulls Markets: Chicago's Basketball Business and the New Inequality, addresses the pitfalls of gentrification, the political and social networking, and the social and economic repercussions of stadium building. Architecture is only one of the factors considered by Gerald Gems (2020) in *Sport and the Shaping of Civic Identity in Chicago*, which covers economics, aesthetics, race, ethnicity, social class, and gender – all topics to be covered in subsequent chapters.

In 2004 Patricia Vertinsky and Sherry McKay produced an anthology entitled *Disciplining Bodies in the Gymnasium*, that analyzes the ways in which buildings and the sport spaces within them are arranged or used in ways that reinforce gender inequities. The interdisciplinary study of sport and space was furthered by Natalie Koch's (2017) *Critical Geographies of Sport: Space, Power and Sport in Global Perspective*, which examines the political uses of space in both urban and national contexts in Europe, Asia, Africa, the Middle East, and the Americas.

While sport historians still grapple over the relevance of traditional empirical history or the reflexivity of the postmodern cultural turn, the general topic of sport still maintains a mass of unstudied material for future researchers. French sport historian Thierry Terret maintains that 'the future of sport history lies with a diversity of approaches' (2008: 305). Canadian sport historian Colin Howell urges sport historians to 'engage critically with the theoretical discourses that shape our historical understandings and to contemplate intellectual trends that cut across disciplinary boundaries' (2007: 461). If past history is an indication, surely new theories await to be discovered by future scholars.

RESEARCH

When carrying out research, sport historians must first develop a research question to analyze; but for most new professors, the dissertation will provide a decade's worth of additional questions for analysis. A typical research question might be does sport assimilate ethnic migrant groups? Assuming that the expected answer is yes, follow-up questions would include: How long does the process take? Do all sports have assimilative functions? If not, which ones do or do not? Why?

In order to determine the answers to such questions, the researcher must compile relevant information and data. Where can such data be found? Depending on the chronological limits of the study, the researcher might check official public documents housed in archives, museums, newspaper repositories, magazines, private papers, artwork, material culture artifacts, films, photos, books, and journal articles contemporary to the era of study as well as later publications or media sources that reflect upon that era. Interviews with people who actually experienced the phenomenon being studied can provide more insight.

Once sufficient data is gathered, it must be analyzed. Are some sources better than others? Why? Primary sources are generally considered to be better than secondary sources. Primary sources are those composed during the period under study and, therefore, closer to the subject matter. For example, if the period of study is 1900–1920, a newspaper article about an ethnic soccer team in 1920 would likely be a better source than a secondary source such as a reflective piece about the same team written by a journalist in 2020.

Sport historian Martin Polley states that

we need primary evidence so that we know what happened in the past, and so that we can get an insight to what people thought was happening. Primary evidence not only takes us into the events of the past, but can also give us a sense of the feelings, perceptions, and ideas of the people who lived in the past, and how they interpreted and perceived events.

(2007: 78)

While primary sources are considered to be closer to the truth, the researcher must carefully dissect all accounts to determine any particular biases on the part of the writer and take those into account. Melvin Adelman cautions that 'journalists were not neutral observers'; they often expressed their own social class and ethnic prejudices as well as sensationalizing events (1986: 369). Thus, analysis and evaluation of all relevant information gathered during the research phase is a must. Moreover, 'Absence of evidence, as any historian or archaeologist will tell you, is not evidence of absence' (Goodman 2018: 210). In other words, the story can never be complete, and one scholar's version may contradict that of another due to the use of different sources or different interpretations.

Scholars therefore must support their arguments with evidence. In a recent study, students enrolled in an American history class that required them to use primary sources indicated they had developed interpretive skills by 'analyzing and establishing the credibility of primary sources, and determining the causes and consequences of events. … [It] taught them to think critically about credibility, authorship, and potential bias' (Ford et al. 2020: 1007).

As illustration of the effort by researchers to assess sources of evidence, while historians of the ancient Greek sport used anecdotal evidence of the athletic activities in limited literary sources, in making their case, they supplemented this evidence through archeological digs that uncovered artifacts depicting pictorials of athletes as well as the inscribed stelae and statues of Olympic heroes.

Secondary sources that might lend additional support can be found in books, journals, encyclopedias and other reference works, media reports, and websites. In the age of information overload supported by ever-growing technological capabilities, the historian must judge the reliability and validity of all sources.

Stephen Hardy (2014) offers an example that he uses in his own classes in discussing Title IX, the 1972 US federal law relative to gender equity that is generally credited with the promotion of women's sport in the country. Hardy assigns his students several accounts that differ in perspective and source material, including the *NCAA News* (a bulletin produced by the male-dominated National Collegiate Athletic Association), the account of a sport historian opposed to the NCAA, and that of another sport historian who researched the Association for Intercollegiate Athletics for Women (AIAW – a rival to the NCAA). Each source tells a different story, and the students must realize that the 'truth is dependent on evidence,' which can be contradictory and incomplete (Hardy 2014: 125).

THE PROCESS OF PUBLICATION

Most academic appointments will require publication of scholarly research. Whereas the publication of a book or books would be one of the criteria for tenure and promotion in the past, many universities now prefer a number of peer-reviewed articles in the top journals, which are ranked by their impact factor (average number of citations).

Most journals require online submission via the publication's website. The author should submit an abstract, which generally has a word limit, and a designated number of keywords that describe the article. The entire article must adhere to word limits, proper format, and style. Submissions that do not adhere to such guidelines are automatically rejected. Upon successful submission, the editor and usually two to three expert reviewers will read and assess the value of the article and make recommendations: accepted for publication; accepted with reservations (necessary rewrites); or rejection. In each case, the author should receive descriptive and helpful feedback regarding the reasons for the decision and the ways in which the article might be improved. This process usually takes two to three months, but may take longer depending on the availability and punctuality of the reviewers. Upon final acceptance of the revised article, the author might expect publication within a year if the journal meets its publication schedule. No royalties are paid for the publication of journal articles. Some journals require a publication fee, which may be substantial; although this is not generally the case in sport history journals. All authors should be wary of predatory publishers that contact academics by email, promising publication within a few weeks and including a large publication fee. Some reputable open access journals (free online to readers) may charge a fee for publication.

Getting published is not easy, especially with one's first attempt. Graduate students may ease that process by establishing a publication record and a measure of name recognition by volunteering to write reviews of books, films, museums, and media reviews. Such short pieces are usually limited to two or three pages and are not sent out for peer review, but judged by the reviews editor. They are published quickly and signed by the author. Reviews editors often call for voluntary reviewers and may be willing to accept unsolicited reviews if approved beforehand.

Book publication is a more daunting task requiring a full proposal. Such a document would include the author's qualifications for the project, a full description of the content, the theoretical framework, the contribution to knowledge, how the book differs from others that cover the same topic, the sources used, the intended audience (whether academic, general public, or both), and the expected number of pages. The author may be asked to supply marketing information and whether illustrations or photos will be included; the latter must meet publication requirements. A timeline for expected completion is expected. The publisher may require one or more sample chapters to assess the writing style and value. Like the article review process, the full manuscript will be reviewed by the acquisitions editor and two or three peer reviewers, who will deliver judgment and feedback. The value of a book publication rather than an article is in the royalties paid: the author will receive a percentage of the profits based on the number of books sold.

Academic scholars may also gain tenure and promotion based on the amounts and nature of grants received from organizations, institutions, or government agencies. Although rare for sport history research projects, they may be granted for large governmental studies such as European Union studies or Fulbright Awards from the

US government, which provides for teaching and research exchanges between American scholars and their foreign counterparts who travel to host sites for periods of up to one year. Museums and other archival depositories may also offer smaller, competitive research grants, that may cover residence and expenses. The role of museums is emphasized in the following:

> Sport history has become a popular form of public history in Europe, Australia and North America as urban museums increasingly mount sport-related exhibitions. The Australian National Museum … offered an exhibit on the history of lifesaving and the National Portrait Gallery at the Smithsonian Institute in Washington, DC presented a display on a variety of athletes. The USA has two museums for sporting art, and all major sports and many minor ones in America have museums dubbed as 'international,' 'national,' or local repositories of sporting heritage … even small villages now attempt to attract visitors with sport artifacts, photos, documents and local guides who act as interpreters and keepers of the past knowledge.
>
> (Gems 2010: 58)

Gary Osmond and Murray Phillips contend that

> to ignore museums as sources and to focus mainly on their documentary collections risks missing opportunities to understand how museums manufacture knowledge about the past and to bridge the chasm between 'what sports scholars do and what the larger public consumes and conceives of sports history'.
>
> Consideration of pedagogical and memory practices utilized by and in museums can enable sports historians to investigate how the organization, demarcation and structural forms of museum displays, both physical and virtual, shape understandings of the past. Key questions concern how objects, labels, audiovisual material, interactive components as well as lighting, sound and spacing are combined in a pedagogical environment to create memories and meanings.
>
> (2010: 44–45)

Work in such an environment requires one to become a scholar, researcher, teacher, director, producer, arranger, and engineer conducting a theatrical play, perhaps an exciting profession without the tensions of the academic tenure process. (See Howard 2018 for a detailed account of public sport history).

TEACHING

As indicated in Chapter 1, sport historians might find employment in several professions; but the most likely career path is in academia. At the university level, sport historians are required to teach classes to undergraduate and graduate students, advise graduate students relative to their theses or dissertations, and publish their own research. The teaching load varies by each school dependent upon the level of research or administrative duties incurred by the professor. Research funded by external groups, such as a grant for a European Union project, or administrative duties, such as chairing a department, might gain release time from teaching. At smaller schools, such as private schools in the United States, teaching may carry greater weight than one's publication record.

Teaching is a boon for most sport historians, as they are getting paid for something they do anyway in their leisure time – that is, talking about sports. Regardless of one's placement in a variety of academic departments, sport history is interdisciplinary and amenable to different approaches. For example, a sport historian in a sport management program could adapt his/her syllabus to include the history of franchises, labor issues, sport venues, team economics, past and present management styles, the history and growing importance of sport media, and the attraction of fans, among a host of other possibilities.

Teaching can, and should be, a very rewarding process. Historian Rob Ruck contends that

> the underlying strength of sports history is its capacity to reach people and subvert how they look at society and the past. Sport historians write and teach about topics and questions that interest many people, some of whom would otherwise ignore history altogether. That creates opportunities to talk about deeper issues as we establish context and back story. The capacity to expand an audience might be sport's biggest contribution to the historical profession.
>
> (2014: 193)

Expanding an audience – that is, recruitment of students to fill classes – is never a problem for sport historians. So many are attracted to the subject that classes of 150 seated in large auditoriums is the norm at some universities. Limiting class sizes to manageable levels is more likely the case and requires skill in negotiating with the school administration.

Sport history teachers may reside in a variety of academic departments: history, physical education, kinesiology, sport management, or American studies; but regardless of their placement, the job requirements will be similar in nature. Teachers spend a major part of their time preparing their lesson plans. They must construct a class syllabus that will include learning objectives, readings, and class assignments. They will create and grade quizzes, tests, or examinations and read assigned essays. Traditional sport history teachers continue to present lectures; although research shows that this is not the best method for providing students with the analytical skills required to become sport historians (Swanson 2014). In elective classes, however, given that class sizes are often large, this negates opportunities for individual attention. Teachers must also consider the variety of learning styles among students. Most teachers will accompany lectures with PowerPoint presentations, as many students are visually oriented. Relevant films can help to convey teaching points in a manner more suitable to some students' learning styles. Some students may respond well to class discussions, which can be spontaneous or based on prepared topics or questions. A question can generate debate – for example: Who is more important, Muhammad Ali or Michael Jordan? This debate would have to consider issues well beyond athletic ability and include the historical eras of each sportsman, considering social justice, economic issues, and legacy. Other students may work well in small group projects or independently. In addition to assigned class readings, there are good sport history websites and blogs that can promote discussion or additional learning outside of the classroom.

Digital sources have become more commonplace in all classes. A good example is Stephen Townsend, Gary Osmond, and Murray G. Phillips's (2019) study entitled 'Clay vs. Ali,' which analyzed nearly 38,000 digitized newspaper articles to determine changing attitudes relative to the boxer's name change. See Ari de Wilde's (2017) 'Revisiting "Ghosts of the Garden": Sport History, Modernizing Technology, and the Promise and Perils of Digital Vizualization,' in the *Journal of Sport History* on the construction of a multimedia history accessible to the general public. Jennifer Sterling, Murray Phillips, and Mary McDonald's (2017) 'Doing Sport History in the Digital Present' is also helpful.

The 2020 COVID-19 coronavirus pandemic forced the closure of many schools and necessitated online teaching for many professors. Such remote delivery systems may become the norm in the future. There are a number of video platforms that allow for such transmission, such as Zoom and Google. Regardless of the chosen system, professors should consider the particular mechanics of teaching online. Check with the school tech staff to avoid or fix potential problems. In order to facilitate online sessions, it is a good idea to initiate a practice class beforehand. Students should be provided with an email before the practice session and all scheduled class sessions as well as being informed of the expectations on them. While teachers may conduct their usual lectures online, such classes are not conducive to passive learning. Students should be expected to engage in the subject matter through reflection and discussion. Real-time chat responses to students' questions, concerns, and issues are most helpful, and feedback on class assignments is essential. Class sessions should be recorded, archived, and accessible for students who missed the class (a useful resource is provided by Wiley (n.d.)).

In addition to teaching, professors are required to advise both undergraduate and graduate students. That duty becomes more intense among graduate students, who require and seek guidance relative to the selection of topics, research, writing, and editing of master's theses or doctoral dissertations. Professors are also evaluated relative to their ability to guide students through the process to completion of their chosen degree in a timely fashion. In some European universities, doctoral students may submit a number of published journal articles and a public defense of their research in lieu of a dissertation to meet the requirements for the Doctor of Philosophy degree. Often the faculty advisor will serve as a coauthor on such publications. The research should present new knowledge or a new interpretation of previous knowledge that will add to the collective scholarship on the topic.

In addition to coaching students through their required tasks, professors must present their own work in publications and public performances. In the United States, tenure, usually granted after six years of employment, and promotion in faculty rank are competitive processes often dependent on one's publication record and/or the ability to obtain funded research.

Professors are not the only teachers who benefit from sport history. Coaches, school administrators, and, above all, parents are among the most important teachers. Children who lack interest in other topics but who are drawn to sport can, through application of principles relevant in sport, be taught valuable lessons about science (velocity, swing dynamics, effect of weather), geometry (proper angles, field coverage), math (analytics, scoring percentages), and virtually any other subject in a more interesting way.

FURTHER READING

Brad Austin and Pamela Grundy, eds. (2019) *Teaching U.S. History through Sports*. Madison: University of Wisconsin Press.

Douglas Booth (2005) *The Field: Truth and Fiction in Sport History*. London: Routledge.

Mark Dyreson (2019) 'Looking Backward and Forward from the 24-Million-Word Mark: A Managing Editor's Perspective on *The International Journal of the History of Sport* in Transition,' *The International Journal of the History of Sport* 36:17–18, 1487–1500.

Josh Howard (2018) 'On Sport, Public History, and Public Sport History,' *Journal of Sport History* 45:1, 24–40.

Gary Osmond and Murray G. Phillips, eds. (2015) *Sport History in the Digital Era*. Urbana: University of Illinois Press.

Murray G. Phillips (2001) 'Deconstructing Sport History: The Postmodern Challenge,' *Journal of Sport History* 28:3, 327–343.

Murray G. Phillips, ed. (2006) *Deconstructing Sport History: A Postmodern Analysis*. Albany, NY: SUNY Press.

Martin Polley (2007) *Sports History: A Practical Guide*. New York: Palgrave Macmillan.

Michael Silk, David Andrews, and Holly Thorpe, eds. (2017) *Routledge Handbook of Physical Culture Studies*. London: Routledge.

Duncan Stone, John Hughson, and Rob Ellis (2017) *New Directions in Sport History*. London: Routledge.

Stephen Townsend, Gary Osmond, and Murray G. Phillips (2019) 'Clay vs. Ali: Distant Reading, Methodology, and Sport History,' *Journal of Sport History* 46:3, 380–395.

Wray Vamplew (2017) *Numbers and Narratives: Sport, History and Economics*. London: Routledge.

Wray Vamplew and Dave Day, eds. (2017) *Methodology in Sport History*. London: Routledge.

3

GENDER

In 1973, Bobby Riggs, a 55-year-old former tennis champion and self-proclaimed male chauvinist, set out to prove the inferiority of female athletes. He challenged Australian Margaret Court, ranked #1 among women tennis players, to a match on Mother's Day, which he won easily, 6-2 and 6-1. His win was intended to check the feminist movement within the women's tour. Billie Jean King, a top American player, also accepted his challenge. They met in the much publicized 'Battle of the Sexes' before more than 30,000 spectators and a global television audience. King dominated 6-4, 6-3, 6-3 to make an emphatic statement about the rightful place of women in sport and to salvage the feminist movement.

A HISTORY OF GENDER AND POWER

Women have long been perceived as and labeled the 'weaker sex,' largely because history has been written by men who assumed their physical and mental superiority. While this faulty perception continues to hold prominence in most cultures, even a cursory examination reveals the contrary. Sport has been likened to war, and females have certainly proved adept in both activities. In ancient China, the Empress Lu Zhi reigned for 15 years between 195 BCE and 180 BCE during the Han dynasty. She proved to be as domineering and ruthless as any male ruler, killing off rivals to consolidate her power; but she also advocated books and reading to improve oneself. Another woman, Wu Zetian, assumed de facto leadership of the Chinese Empire in 665 CE during the Tang dynasty, claiming the throne for herself in 690 CE. She brutally imposed her power on male subordinates as she led the empire to greater prosperity. Empress Cixi, the concubine of a weak and sickly emperor, proved to be the power behind the throne while serving as regent from 1861 to 1908. She supported the failed Boxer Rebellion of 1900, which attempted to purge the nation of foreign colonies and influence.

Other Asian countries recognize similar heroines. In Vietnam, the Trung sisters, Trung Trac and Trung Nhi, grew up in a military family and learned martial arts and military tactics, which they used to lead a rebellion in 40 CE against the Chinese, who had occupied their country for nearly two and a half centuries. For three years, until they died in battle, they led an army of mostly female warriors that drove the Chinese from their area. Their memory continues to live as national heroines.

Strong female figures are also recognized in the Middle East and Africa. The Egyptian Queen Cleopatra is well known as the ruler of the country from 51–30 BCE and as the seductress of both Julius Caesar and Marc Antony. Her political machinations resulted in a civil war that rocked the Roman Empire. The Ashanti of modern Ghana are known as great warriors and have produced world champion boxers, but a woman proved most heroic. Yaa Asantewa is less well known, but as a political activist she led her Ashanti followers in a war against British colonizers in 1900. Though the insurrection proved unsuccessful, the Ashanti maintained their autonomy in present-day Ghana and retained possession of their symbolic golden stool, which had been coveted by the British.

In America during the Revolutionary War against the British, Deborah Sampson took the alias of her brother and masqueraded as a man in order to serve in the colonial army. She joined the infantry and was severely wounded in battle. Other women typically followed their husbands' treks while in the army, performing domestic chores such as cooking, cleaning, and laundering clothes; but when husbands were wounded in action, they quickly took their place to 'man' the artillery (American Battlefield Trust 2020). In South America, Anita Garibaldi, the Brazilian wife of the Italian freedom fighter Giuseppe Garibaldi, fought alongside her husband in wars for independence. In Italy she died during the war of liberation from the Austrian Empire. Brazilians consider her to be a national idol.

Men have long considered the military to be the sole province of males. The small sample of women presented here puts the lie to such assertions. Likewise, sport as a surrogate war was thought to be beyond the capabilities of women well into the twenty-first century. Pierre de Coubertin, founder of the modern Olympic Games, campaigned to deny women the right to participate despite adequate evidence of their ability to do so.

The ascribed roles, customs, and expectations relative to one's gender has depended upon one's social class. Peasant women and those of the working class had little social capital and less social status to safeguard. They often quarreled, swore, and fought like their male counterparts. By the early eighteenth century, women, like men, defended their honor in public boxing matches. In 1722, one such woman, Elizabeth Stokes, claimed to be the female champion of London. In 1727, Elizabeth Wilkinson fought Hannah Highfield at Hockley in the Hole for a prize of three guineas. The following year, Elizabeth Stokes returned to action, coming out of retirement to answer a public challenge printed in the *Daily Post* by Ann Field, a donkey tender. Stokes admitted that she had not fought since gaining 'a complete victory' in nine minutes over 'the famous boxing woman of Billingsgate' six years previously, but said,

> as the famous Stoke Newington ass woman dares me to fight her for 10 pounds, I do assure her I will not fail meeting her for the said sum, and doubt not that the blows which I shall present her with will be more difficult for her to digest than any she ever gave her asses.
>
> (Stokes, quoted in Guttmann 1991: 75)

By mid-century James Figg's Amphitheater featured both male and female bouts (Gems 2014a: 214).

Despite a subsequent Parliamentary ban on boxing, the fights continued throughout the century. Details of a 1794 bout stated that

Great intensity between them was maintained for about two hours, where-upon the elder fell into great difficulty through the closure of her left eye from the extent of swelling above and below it which rendered her blind through having the sight of the other considerably obscured by a flux of blood which had then continued greatly for over forty minutes … not more than a place even as large as a penny-piece remained upon their bodies which was free of the most evident signs of the harshness of the struggle. Their bosoms were much enlarged but yet they each continued to rain blows upon this most feeling of tissue without regard to the pitiful cries issuing forth at each suc-cess which was evidently to the delight of the spectators since many a shout was raised causing each female to mightily increase her effort.

(Hargreaves 2001: n.p.)

The Times described a similar battle in 1807 in which Mary Mahoney, a market worker, contested with Betty Dyson, a fish ped-dler. Both 'Amazons' were 'hideously disfigured by hard blows' in a bout that lasted more than 40 minutes (Guttman 1991: 76). In 1822, a stake of 18 British pounds was put up when Martha Flaharty confronted Peg Carey. The arranged violence started at 5:30 in the morning so that co-workers might witness the warfare before they had to start their labors. Flaharty steeled her nerves with a pint of gin beforehand and salvaged the win despite being badly injured (Gems 2014). Such brutal spectacles and the violence, courage, toughness, and stoicism displayed in the pain given and received challenged the contemporary perceptions of a 'weaker sex.'

By that time even upper-class women had begun to question the nature of the patriarchal cultures in which they lived. Mary Wollstonecraft's (1792) *A Vindication of the Rights of Woman* argued for the social and political equality of women and the need for women's education. She had founded a school for girls to address that necessity. In France, her contemporary Olympe de Gouges, a playwright and political activist, joined the revolutionary movement that toppled the royal administration. Her pamphlet entitled *Declaration of the Rights of Woman and of the Female Citizen* denounced slavery and advocated for women's rights. She called for free speech and property rights as well as the care of single mothers and women's right to divorce. Her demand for the inclusion of women in the National Assembly went unheeded, and her unabashed attack on patriarchy drew the wrath of male leaders, who had her guillotined in 1793.

In the newly independent American states, Abigail Adams, wife of future president John Adams, beseeched her husband as he and other patriots fashioned a new republic. 'In your new code of Laws, I pray you remember the Ladies. ... Do not put such unlimited power in the hands of the Husbands. Remember all Men would be tyrants if they could' (Gems, Borish, and Pfister 2017: 52). But like their European counterparts, the men reserved power for propertied males. Poor white men, black men and slaves, indigenous people, and women were denied voting rights. Such designations afforded power and greater levels of masculinity to some rather than others.

Sport provided one means to publicly display one's masculinity and personal honor. In wartime, men were expected to demonstrate courage and stoicism to withstand the dangers of battle and the harsh elements of nature. In peacetime, sport sufficed as a substitute. The early English colonists solidified their hold on territories by continually pushing the Native Americans westward. In the northern colonies of New England, the Puritan influences limited sport; but hunting and physical strength and endurance proved essential qualities for subsistence and the public demonstration of one's physical prowess. Muster days for military purposes allowed men to demonstrate their shooting skills, wrestling abilities, and foot speed in races. Others gathered at taverns where cockfights, bear baitings, and bowling provided entertainment and opportunities to gamble. In the southern colonies, plantation owners enjoyed greater leisure and contested with their peers in billiards, bowling, cards, and horse racing. As early as 1674 a horse race that dishonored a wealthy 'gentleman' resulted in a court case when a tailor, James Bullocke, defeated Mathew Slader, a member of the gentry and a man of greater means. The county judge fined the tailor 100 pounds of tobacco, because it was 'contrary to Law for a Laborer to make a race being a sport for Gentlemen' (Gorn and Goldstein 1993: 22). The differentiation between the gentry and the common folk would become more clearly defined as the aristocrats engaged in conspicuous consumption.

The gentry asserted their masculinity by trying to better their fellow planters in competitive events and the size of their stakes. In 1693, John Baker contended with John Haynie for a wager of 4,000 pounds of tobacco and 40 shillings at a time when the average annual yield of the crop amounted to 1,500 pounds. The men raced with quarter horses, a distinctly American breed that ran a quarter mile on a straight path. Contracts had to be arranged for 'fair riding,' which meant that riders could not whip, jostle, knee, or unseat their opponents, and horses had to stay in their own lane. Thoroughbreds were not imported into the American colonies until 1730.

William Byrd III, one of the early importers of thoroughbreds and an inveterate gambler, assumed that his prescience would garner great rewards; but he lost a large sum in the horse's first race to another imported thoroughbred. He eventually gambled away his estate at cards and dice and had to sell 400 slaves and parcels of his immense estate. When such measures still could not cover his debts, and with his social status, honor, and masculinity in ruin, Byrd committed suicide in 1777 (Breen 1977).

Plantation owners might salvage their personal honor by using their slaves as jockeys rather than have their own horsemanship questioned. They also matched male slaves as boxers against the slaves of their colleagues for wagers and their own amusement. Slaves, both male and female, also proved more adept at swimming than white people, few of whom learned to swim. In coastal communities, male slaves proved their own courage and masculinity by fighting sharks, alligators, and manta rays with knives (Dawson 2006).

For the lower-class white males without property, their honor and sense of masculinity rested in their physical prowess. In the frontier settlements, men engaged in rough-and-tumble wrestling, a no-holds-barred confrontation that might even include dismembering an opponent's genitals. Such violent affairs might be arranged or result from a perceived insult or simply an announcement of an all comers challenge. An English traveler described one such fight that he witnessed in 1806 in Virginia when two men, one from Kentucky and the other from Virginia, argued over a horse race. The Virginian lunged at his foe and knocked him to the ground, then 'kept his knees in his enemy's body; fixing his claws in his hair, and his thumbs on his eyes, gave them an instantaneous start from their sockets. The sufferer roared aloud, but uttered no complaint.' The Kentucky man then bit off the nose of his opponent, who ripped open the lip of his rival, so that it hung below his chin. 'The crowd cheered the victorious Virginian, the Kentuckian returned to town to have his face repaired, and new rounds of drinking, gambling, and racing resumed' (Gorn and Goldstein 1993: 25–26).

In Ohio, a traveler came across a man whose nose had been bitten off. When he tried to offer consolation, he was reprimanded. 'Don't pity me, pity that fellow over there,' pointing with one hand to another who had lost an eye, and showing the eye which he held triumphantly in the other' (Altherr 1997: 141).

Such violence proved commonplace on the frontier. William Stuart traveled through western Pennsylvania in circa 1806–1807 and noted that

> every evening a gang assembled at the numerous taverns to drink. When they had become half drunk, they were noisy and quarrelsome, gouging out the eyes was one of their barbarous practices, and nearly one third of the German population had but one eye. I saw one day a horse with one eye, carrying on his back the husband, wife and child, each with only one eye.
>
> (1854: 27–28)

In order to obtain such trophies, men let their fingernails grow long and sharpened them to knifepoints. Public boasting of victories became part of the masculinity ritual. 'The danger and violence of daily life in the backwoods contributed mightily to sanguinary oral traditions that exalted the strong and deprecated the weak' (Gorn 1985: 32).

Even among the upper class, one's masculinity was directly tied to one's personal and family honor. Dishonor required public vengeance (Wyatt-Brown 1982). Among the upper classes, questions of honor were settled by dueling. In the early American republic, politicians that publicly insulted one another often settled such breaches of honor by duels. The most historic involved that of Alexander Hamilton, one of the leading founding fathers, and Vice President Aaron Burr. Burr killed Hamilton on the morning of 11 July 1804 in New Jersey, on the same spot that Hamilton's son had earlier been killed in a duel (Holland 2003).

THE GROWTH OF FEMINISM IN GREAT BRITAIN

The Victorian era in Great Britain witnessed the Industrial Revolution and the expansion of the British Empire and was recognized as the greatest power in the world; but apart from the reigning monarch, it largely remained a man's world. Women had few rights. They could not hold property, nor divorce until 1839. That year the Custody of Infants Act recognized the importance of maternal influence on the young and allowed for children under the age of 7 (raised to 16 in 1873) to remain with a single mother. The father paid alimony and retained legal control. In 1857, women gained the ability to divorce via a civil court; but it was an expensive proposition. Husbands retained all property rights until 1882. Women were largely relegated to the domestic sphere as wives and mothers.

Florence Nightingale challenged that ascribed role. In 1854 she traveled to the Crimea, where the British were engaged in a war with Russia, with the intention to nurse wounded soldiers. Her efforts won acclaim, and nursing gained respectability as a viable profession for women, largely because it reinforced the nurturing roles of motherhood and did not threaten the hegemonic gender order. Many women who intended to become medical doctors were forced to travel to the United States for study, due to opposition in England.

The early feminist movement in Great Britain emerged over the suffrage issue and education for females. Millicent Fawcett, an activist for women's rights, began agitating for such opportunities by 1875. She led the National Union of Women's Suffrage Societies from 1897 to 1919. Emmeline Pankhurst also campaigned for women's suffrage. In 1903, she founded the Women's Social and Political Union (WSPU), which assumed a more radical approach, supporting militant violence, arson, and hunger strikes to gain attention to the cause. Pankhurst and her daughters endured numerous arrests, but continued their crusade. A member of the WSPU, Emily Davison, attended the Epsom Derby in 1913, and as the horses charged along the rail, she stepped out onto the track and collided with the horse of King George V. She died two days later, and the WSPU ordained her to be a martyr for their cause; women only obtained limited suffrage (for propertied women over age 30) in 1918. The voting age was lowered to 21 in 1928.

Sport played little part in the quest for female emancipation in Great Britain. There is evidence of female cricket matches in the eighteenth century as well as archery clubs in the 1780s and women's soccer games in Scotland a decade later. Most telling, however, was a tennis match in 1768 in which a French woman, Madame Bunel, defeated an English gentleman, considered to be England's best male player, on two occasions. She did so in front of large crowds that included dignitaries, some of whom lost large wagers. This was surely a blow to male pride and masculinity, but it did not engender widespread social change. In a similar confrontation in 1804, Alicia Thornton challenged her brother-in-law to a horse race of four miles for a bet of 500 guineas. Thornton rode side-saddle, the customary position for women of the era, as straddling a horse denoted masculinity. Thornton led at the three-mile mark before her horse pulled up lame as thousands, many of them gamblers, witnessed the event. The brother-in-law refused a rematch, and a replacement male rider forfeited 3,000 pounds rather than face the equestrienne, who believed herself a better rider than any man. To prove her contention, Thornton then challenged one of England's top jockeys at two miles for a cup worth 700 guineas in a match that she won by a neck. Her feats won wide acclaim for a brief period, but caused no campaign for women's rights (Radford 2017).

As early as 1824, exercises were included in the curriculum of the Seminary for the Education of Young Ladies in Dublin. Male educators in England published two books on calisthenics for girls and women in 1827. A captain in the British Army, Phokion Heinrich Clias, traveled to France in 1841, where he taught courses in physical training for females; but his focus remained their grace and beauty, which only reinforced gender norms of the era. By the 1830s in France, however, Antoine Bureaud-Riofrey, a doctor, recommended ten hours of exercise daily for 7-year-old girls and 5 hours for those aged 14. Such exercises were to include walking, dancing, weight training with batons and dumbbells, work on the horizontal bar, and swimming, even though aquatic sports were unpopular at the time (Gems, Borish, and Pfister 2017).

Ann Glanville assumed control of her husband's boat after his illness and gained national celebrity both as an individual rower and head of an all-female crew. In 1833, at a regatta in France, the crew easily beat an all-male French team to become national heroines. Glanville's individual strength, publicly displayed in regattas, often enabled her to defeat men, and she was acclaimed as the female world champion, rowing into her seventh decade. Though feted by social superiors, her working-class origins limited her advancement, and her 14 children firmly established her domestic role (Porter 1905).

Throughout the nineteenth century, women accomplished other grand feats with limited recognition. In 1809, Maria Paradis, a poor maidservant, joined a male expedition and became the first woman to climb Mont Blanc, the highest peak in Europe. Because she was assisted by men, her achievement was lightly regarded. In 1838, Henriette d'Angeville, a French aristocrat, managed to conquer the same mountain under her own power, and did so wearing knicker-bockers, an affront to the gender dress code that restricted the wearing of pants to men. Lucy Walker became the first woman to ascend the Matterhorn in 1871, soon followed by the American Meta Brevoort; but neither won acceptance in the Alpine Club, which had been established in 1857. Once a woman conquered a peak, men no longer considered it a challenge, and women were not invited to join the club until 1974 (Pfister and Gems 2019).

Working-class women continued to play soccer in their limited leisure time, and some women of the upper classes enjoyed golf, with the first women's golf club formed at St. Andrews in Scotland in 1867. Membership rose to 500 by 1886. Others played tennis, with Maud Watson winning the first women's championship at Wimbledon in 1884. Lady Margaret Scott captured the first women's amateur golf championship in 1893.

Lottie Dod, also an accomplished mountaineer, proved to be the most versatile and talented sportswoman of the era. In 1887, at the age of 15, she won the Wimbledon singles title, the first of her five national championships in tennis. With her brother, she took up winter sports in 1896 and, thereafter, climbing mountains, tobogganing, curling, and passing the men's figure skating test at St. Moritz. She represented and captained the women's national field hockey team in 1899 and 1900. In 1904, Dod captured the British Women's National Golf Championship, and then won a silver medal in archery at the 1908 Olympics. Such a sustained record of extraordinary excellence gained notice, but did not threaten the entrenched gender hierarchy. During World War I, Dod assumed a more acceptable domestic role as a Red Cross nurse.

Lottie Dod was also an avid cyclist, the means by which she traveled through Italy. Cycling proved the one sport that offered the most freedom for women, enabling them to travel beyond the limited environment of the home and to experience the joys of nature. It also fostered a revolution in female fashion, as cyclists gradually eschewed the long skirts that got caught in bicycle spokes and caused accidents and injuries. In 1893, 16-year-old Tessie Reynolds cycled round trip between Brighton and London; but the fact that she did so wearing knickerbockers drew greater attention and was rebuked, as trousers infringed upon the propriety of the era as menswear. That same year, Reynolds won the first cycle race for women, and cycling wear assumed a liberating function (Fishpool 2018).

THE RISE OF FEMINISM IN THE UNITED STATES

The education of females held greater promise in the early nineteenth century. Women such as Almira Phelps and Catherine Beecher published books on the subject as early as the 1830s. Beecher even founded the Hartford Female Seminary in 1823. Phelps advocated gymnastics for women, and Beecher's curriculum included calisthenics for girls. Physical education was meant to improve what both perceived as the declining health status of American women (Gems, Borish, and Pfister 2017).

German women formed their own Turner gymnastic club when they were banned from the male associations. The German Revolution of 1848 spurred further female clubs. The Frankfurt club vowed that 'all physical constraints limiting free movement and impairing health should be rejected and cast off, outside the Turnen grounds as well. … The female gymnasts stood up for equality with men and for a future world revolution' (Gems, Borish and Pfister 2017: 89). Such liberating sentiments failed to survive in the collapse of the revolution thereafter.

American women expressed similar concerns. As early as 1848, they held a national convention in Seneca Falls, New York, to promote women's rights, including suffrage. The conference drew 300 participants, who also favored the abolition of slavery and temperance. Abolition came to resolution in the American Civil war; temperance was temporarily achieved in 1919. Two of the convention leaders, Elizabeth Cady Stanton and Susan B. Anthony, founded the National Women's Suffrage Association in 1869; but full suffrage did not come until 1920. Some women at the conference also endorsed the wearing of bloomers, a challenge to the proper female dress of the era, and withstood the criticism of the male media.

The education of females assumed greater speed with the founding of Elmira College in New York in 1855. When male colleges refused to admit his daughters, Matthew Vassar founded an eponymous college for women in 1861. By 1868, the women of Vassar had established their own baseball teams, a clear incursion into the sphere of masculinity.

Croquet became a popular sport in the 1860s, because it allowed young men and women to transgress the strict courtship norms of the Victorian age. Prospective male suitors were expected to be properly introduced to the family by a trusted acquaintance. Upon acceptance, he might visit the family home for conversation; but outside the home, a couple was expected to be chaperoned for such activities as skating or sleighing in the winter. Croquet could be played on family lawns in public view, which loosened the bonds of direct supervision.

In 1879, female archers met in Chicago for the first national women's championship. As a relatively sedentary sport, in which the women competed in long, bustle dresses, it posed no danger to the gender order. That changed slightly in 1874 when Mary Ewing Outerbridge introduced the game of tennis to a New York Club after she had learned to play in Bermuda. The first tournament for men only began in 1880. A women's national tournament did not appear until 1887. Movement was limited, as women still played in long dresses into the twentieth century; they lacked the speed or power of the men's game, generally hitting the ball underhand. That changed with the appearance of May Sutton, who wore short sleeves and shorter, ankle-length skirts. She not only covered the court faster than others, but also hit strong overhead shots. She won the American women's singles and doubles championships at age 17 in 1904, and then conquered Wimbledon a year later; although the British deemed her attire unladylike.

Throughout the latter nineteenth century, intrepid women challenged the notion of female frailty. In 1858, Julia Holmes became the first woman to climb Pike's Peak, one of the highest in the Rocky Mountains. An ardent suffragist, she served as secretary of the National Woman Suffrage Association. Her feat was surpassed by later female mountaineers. Annie Smith Peck, a college professor and ardent feminist, also proved to be a premier mountaineer. She first climbed the Matterhorn in 1895 at age 45, then she scaled the mountains of Mexico before heading to South America. There, at the age of 58, she conquered Mount Huascarán in Peru, then thought to be the world's highest peak. She often feuded with male guides, who refused to acknowledge her leadership abilities. Upon topping Mount Coropuna in Peru at age 61, she unfurled a banner that read 'Votes for Women.' Her public lectures drew attention to her feats and her independence as well as to the suffrage movement. Her rival, Fanny Bullock Workman, had immense wealth that enabled her and her husband to travel the world in search of adventure. They cycled across Europe, Algeria, and India, and their travel books were popular; but mountaineering in the Himalayas proved to be their main attraction. Fanny, an ardent feminist, excelled as a mountaineer – better than her husband. She felt that she could prove the equal of any man or woman. When Annie Smith Peck claimed the altitude record, Fanny Bullock Workman paid a surveying team to measure Mount Huascaran, which proved her scaling of Pinnacle Peak in 1906, at age 47, as the women's top altitude mark. In 1912 she was photographed atop the 21,000 foot Siachen Glacier holding a newspaper with the headline 'Votes for Women.' She became the first woman to speak at the Sorbonne in Paris and the first female admitted to the Royal Geographical Society in England (Gems 2017).

Both Peck and Workman were among the 'new women' of the late nineteenth century, independent and expressing and reveling in their physical vitality as they dismantled the restrictions of the Victorian era that bound them to the domestic sphere. The young, vivacious college women of the time took readily to sports and outdoor activities, adopting male sports such as baseball, basketball, and volleyball. The sport that garnered the most attention, however, was cycling. As early as the 1880s, professional female cyclists took to the big wheels to compete with men. French Canadian Louise Armaindo traveled to Chicago, where she participated in six-day endurance events, in one of which she covered 843 miles to defeat her male opponents. That same year, she covered 247 miles in 12 hours, well beyond the capabilities of most men. During the 1897–1898 cycling season, Swedish immigrant Tillie Anderson earned as much as $5,000 per year, far more than most men, destroying the perception of a 'weaker sex' (*Sporting and Theatrical Journal* 1884; Hall 2018). While the sporting press extolled the abilities of such athletic stars, the mainstream media and middle-class authorities disparaged females who challenged men. Like the professional riders, middle-class females adopted pants or knickerbockers to ride their bicycles. In 1895, the Chicago school board admonished a female teacher who cycled to school in her knickerbockers. When the town of Pullman forbade women's cycling on the community streets unless they wore skirts, one enterprising woman invented a cycling clip that gathered and held the skirt in a fashion similar to pants, thus evading any punishment. In New York, the authorities arrested another female cyclist for wearing slacks (Gems 1997). Male medical doctors weighed in, asserting that female cyclists would damage their reproductive organs through such activity. Preachers claimed that cycling was an immoral activity, pronouncing that it induced masturbation. Such confrontations continued throughout the decade, but women were not deterred. Feminist and suffrage leader Susan B. Anthony declared that bicycling

> has done more to emancipate women than anything else in the world. It gives women a feeling of freedom and self-reliance. I stand and rejoice every time I see a woman ride by on a wheel ... the picture of free, untrammeled womanhood.
>
> (Gems, Borish, and Pfister 2017: 208)

Vaudeville emerged in the 1880s and enjoyed popularity for the next half-century. Early female performers showed impressive strength and flexibility in trapeze acts, but the female weightlifters amazed audiences with their power. Josephine Blatt, whose stage name was Minerva, was hailed as the world's strongest woman in the *National Police Gazette*, the bible of the sporting classes. She reportedly lifted 700 pounds overhead and 100 pounds with one hand, and she also caught cannonballs during her acts, which took her throughout North and South America as well as Europe (Todd 1990). Miriam Kate Williams, known as Vulcana, was born in Wales but toured Great Britain, Europe, and Australia performing similar feats of strength. Katie Brumbach started as a circus performer who wrestled male challengers from the audience and never lost. She assumed the name Sandwina after defeating Eugen Sandow in a weightlifting contest in which she hoisted 300 pounds over her head. Sandow was considered to be the world's most perfectly developed man at the turn of the twentieth century, the epitome of masculinity. At his 1893 appearance in Chicago, two of the richest socialites in the city paid $300 each just to feel his muscles. That amounted to a full year's wages for working-class men (Chapman 1994). Such public displays of female strength, beyond the capabilities of the vast majority of men, greatly damaged the belief in male superiority.

While such displays questioned traditional gender roles and societal norms, female boxers made a direct assault on the customary expectations. Working-class women took readily to boxing soon after the Civil War, duly reported in the newspapers that provided lurid details as well as noting the physical characteristics and comeliness of the fighters. Such reportage both reinforced and challenged the norms of hegemonic masculinity. Harry Hill's Saloon in New York became a boxing center hosting male and female matches to the delight of the bachelor subculture that frequented the establishment. The bachelor subculture consisted of (not always) unmarried men who congregated in saloons, brothels, pool halls, baseball parks, horse tracks, and any location that afforded the opportunity for gambling and camaraderie. Their lifestyle reinforced and extolled the norms and practices of hegemonic masculinity (Gems 2014a; Chudacoff 1999).

Boxing served as a particular attraction for the bachelor subculture, and women's boxing provided a lascivious interest as well. Female fighters might be attired in 'unmentionables made of silk' (Park 2012: 740–741), 'beating each other almost to the point of nudity' (Gems 1997: 15). Richard Kyle Fox, editor of the *National Police Gazette*, provided cash prizes and championship designations to boxers and supplied lurid illustrations of the women, that attracted a larger male readership.

In 1887, a black female fighter even challenged the white heavyweight champion of the world, John L. Sullivan, to a bout, claiming to have already defeated several male opponents. Sullivan, however, shunned such provocations from all black people, male or female, as below the dignity of his station. Hattie Stewart and Hattie Leslie, both of whom got their start as vaudeville performers, were to decide the female championship. The *National Police Gazette* described the former as 'an excellent specimen of physical development, and stripped looked a perfect Amazon,' while Leslie was 'tall, powerful, and possessed great quickness' (Gems 2014a: 218). Leslie died of typhoid in 1892 before the match took place, but she left a legacy as one who had abandoned traditional domesticity and challenged the gender order.

One of Leslie's opponents, Gussie Freeman, worked in a Brooklyn rope factory, where she used her size and strength to batter males who harassed her female co-workers. She used those qualities to answer Leslie's 1891 challenge while on her New York tour. In a bloody spectacle that lasted four rounds until the police interrupted the fray, Freeman proved her mettle and began touring, before eventually opening a bar in her hometown, where she served as her own bouncer, thrashing men who proved a nuisance. Throughout her life, she defied gender norms to live and to represent herself as she pleased (Pfister and Gems 2018).

In the American West, frontier women had to assume roles similar to their husbands' and exhibit a hardiness and toughness required by the climate and environment. While boxing bar girls provided entertainment for male patrons, many more women plowed fields, rode horses, and even competed in rodeos by the end of the nineteenth century. This first wave of feminism signaled a long and gradual transition in the gender order over the next century.

As women transgressed upon the ascribed male turf, men turned to football. The American version evolved from soccer to rugby to the gridiron game favored in North America. Like war, it involved moving through enemy territory to capture an objective. It required power, strategy, leadership, and individual toughness, and it was very violent. With the onset of industrialization and the growth of sedentary occupations, middle-class men feared the loss of their masculinity. Philosophers, sociologists, and politicians indicated that their manly vigor might be saved through football, and college men took readily to the game despite its dangers. A college president reasoned that 'I would rather see our youth playing football with the danger of a broken collar-bone occasionally than to see them dedicated to croquet' (Gems 2000: 56). Another claimed that 'an able bodied young man who cannot fight physically can hardly have a true sense of honor, and is generally a milksop, a lady-boy, or a sneak. He lacks virility, his masculinity does not hold true' (Bruce 1910: 544). On a single day in the 1909 season, four players died in separate incidents, a figure that reached 30 at its conclusion. Despite the annual death toll, the game not only survived, but superseded all others to become the national sport.

At the turn of the century, women continued to assail the notion of male superiority. In the first modern Olympic Games in 1896, two women wished to run in the marathon race, but were denied. They did so anyway, unofficially, to prove female capabilities. In the 1900 Games, the events were spread across the summer and held concurrently with the Paris World's Fair, which provided opportunities for women in several sports. Women's Olympic swimming first appeared in 1912; but thereafter the International Olympic Committee (IOC) assumed greater control and limited women's events. Alice Milliat, a feminist and president of the French Association of Women's Sports, organized international competitions for women as early as 1921, which continued until 1934. The IOC finally relented and offered some track and field events for women in 1928, but the Olympic marathon did not become a reality until 1984. Long before that, Roberta Gibb (in 1966) and Kathrine Switzer (in 1967) had surreptitiously entered and finished the Boston Marathon.

The performances of such courageous women were public displays of intransigence during the second wave of feminism in the 1960s. In 1972 the US Congress passed Title IX, a national law that provided equal opportunity for all in any program that received federal funding. As that included schools, female athletes quickly seized the opportunity to litigate for better equipment, facilities, and opportunities. In 1971, only 294,015 girls played high school sports. That figure reached 3,000,000 by 2013. At the college level, there were only 16,000 female athletes in 1972, but more than 200,000 by 2014 (Gems, Borish, and Pfister 2017). By the 1980–1981 school year, the AIAW, the sports governing body organized by and for women, offered 39 championships. The NCAA, which governed male sports, then reasserted its hegemonic control by offering competing events for women and effectively running the AIAW out of business (Gems, Borish, and Pfister 2017). That power struggle continues as women's teams and female athletes campaign for full inclusion, equal rights, and equal pay at the professional level.

HISTORIOGRAPHY OF GENDER STUDIES

Simone de Beauvoir's publication of *The Second Sex* in 1949 (see de Beauvoir 1997), a study of the historical domination of men, is often attributed as the start of the second wave of feminism in Europe. It was followed by Betty Friedan's *Feminine Mystique*, published in the United States in 1963, in which she argued that the prescribed role of domesticity robbed women of reaching their full potential. An Australian, Germaine Greer, analyzed the sexual repression of women in *The Female Eunuch* in 1970. Numerous feminist scholars addressed particular issues thereafter. Gloria Steinem, editor of *Ms. Magazine*, became an ardent activist for a host of women's issues. Andrea Dworkin conducted anti-pornography and anti-prostitution campaigns as she addressed sexual violence issues. Interdisciplinary issues of race, gender, and social class domination were raised by bell hooks (Gloria Jean Watkins) in her *Ain't I a Woman? Black Women and Feminism* in 1981. She showed how the stereotyping of black women placed them into the lowest of social and economic categories.

The multitude and divergence of women's issues eventually wrought fractures in the feminist movement among the liberal feminists of the 1960s, who campaigned for greater social equality through political and social reforms. They were succeeded by the radical feminists of the 1970s, who wanted the elimination of patriarchy that dominated and oppressed women. Cultural feminists of the same period emphasized the natural differences of male and female traits, with the latter being superior. An example in the moral sense would be that men often settle disputes through violent confrontations, whereas women settle their arguments via negotiation. By the 1990s, a third wave appeared. The younger generation of feminists felt that their predecessors had focused on the concerns of white, middle-class women, thereby alienating women of color and those of a different gender identity. The third wave aimed to address the multiplicity of gender identities and sexuality in an approach termed intersectionality. They had a particular interest in the media portrayal of girls and women in popular culture, which fostered the 'girl power' movement that promoted female independence, confidence, and strength (see Leslie Heywood and Shari L. Dworkin (2003) *Built to Win: The Female Athlete as Cultural Icon*). In 2006, the

Me Too movement eventually produced an international rebuke to sexual harassment, sexual assault, and the sex trafficking trade.

GENDER STUDIES IN SPORT

Canadian scholar M. Ann Hall introduced the concept of gender studies in *Sport and Gender: A Feminist Perspective on the Sociology of Sport* in 1978. Sport studies have since expanded to include 'inter-relational concepts such as power, representation, narrativity and language with a more recent transdisciplinary and transnational perspective' (Bandy 2010: 129). By 1984, Nancy Struna called for the concept of gender to be a primary variable in sport history research. A year later, Roberta Park (1985) published a transatlantic study of women's sport in the Victorian era. Mangan and Park (1986) soon followed with an important anthology entitled *From 'Fair Sex' to Feminism: Sport and the Socialization of Women in the Industrial and Post-Industrial Eras*. Jennifer Hargreaves (1985, 1986a) led the way in England with articles on women's sport history; and Canadian Patricia Vertinsky responded with *The Eternally Wounded Woman* in 1990. Struna's (1996) *People of Prowess* carefully details colonial women's lives and their physicality. Susan Cahn's (1994) *Coming on Strong: Gender and Sexuality in Women's Sport* analyzes the lesbian experience as well as race and social class issues that inspired a wealth of similar studies. Susan Birrell and Cheryl Cole's (1994) anthology, *Women, Sport and Culture*, provides a good summary of theoretical debates and applications up to that time. Catriona Parratt's (2001) *More Than Mere Amusement* analyzes the leisure lives of working-class women in England over the course of two centuries.

American scholars Judith Butler, a third-wave feminist, and Judith Lorber pushed theoretical perceptions of the subject that influenced sport historians. Butler's *Gender Trouble: Feminism and the Subversion of Identity* (1990) and *Bodies That Matter: On the Discursive Limits of Sex* (1993) further illuminated the social construction of gender as something that is performed and introduced queer and literary theory to sport studies. Queer theory moved beyond categorizations of gay, lesbian, bisexual, and transsexual to include fluid identities (see Jayne Caudwell's (2006) *Sport, Sexualities and Queer Theory*). Lorber's (1994) *Paradoxes of Gender* saw gender as a product of socialization and subject to interpretation. Gender was something that one did rather than what one was.

Women's sport studies blossomed around the world. In Germany, Gertud Pfister and Christine Peyton's (1989) anthology *Frauen-sport in Europa* introduced a broader international perspective. Pfister, a sport historian and sport sociologist, was greatly influenced by Lorber, but produced her own extensive volume of works. Pfister and Ilse Hartmann-Tews edited an updated work in 2003 entitled *Sport and Women: Social Issues in International Perspective*. Other early works covered England (McCrone's (1988) *Playing the Game: Sport and the Physical Emancipation of English Women, 1870–1940*); Argentina (Morelli's (1990) *Mujeres Deportistas*); Australia (Daly's (1994) *Feminae Ludens*); France (Arnaud and Terret's (1996) *Histoire du sport feminine*); China (Hong's (1997) *Footbinding, Feminism, and Freedom: The Liberation of Women's Bodies in Modern China*); Canada (Hall's (2002) *The Girl and the Game: A History of Women's Sport in Canada*); Italy (Gori's (2004) *Female Bodies, Sport, Italian Fascism: Submissive Women and Strong Mothers*).

Among a wealth of more contemporary works, see Gertrud Pfister and Mari Kristin Sisjord's (2013) edited volume, *Gender and Sport: Changes and Challenges*; Jean Williams's (2014) *A Contemporary History of Women's Sport*; Jaime Schultz's (2014) *Qualifying Times: Points of Change in U.S. Women's Sport*; and Rafaelle Nicholson's (2019) *Ladies and Lords: A History of Women's Cricket in Britain*. There is still a need for more research on women's sport, particularly relative to women of color and female athletes from a greater variety of cultures.

The increasing interest in gender research in the late twentieth century included men's studies. Among the early works, J. A. Mangan and James Walvin (1987) edited an impressive anthology, *Masculinity and Morality: Middle-class Masculinity in Britain and America, 1800–1940*, that featured several top sport historians of the era. Elliot Gorn's (1986) *The Manly Art: Bare-Knuckle Prize Fighting in America* was an interdisciplinary examination that covered masculinity, labor, and social history. It spawned a number of other analyses of boxing: Loic Wacquant's (2004) *Body and Soul: Notebooks of an Apprentice Boxer*, a sociological autoethnography that considered the racial and social class elements of the sport, as did Kasia Boddy's (2008) *Boxing: A*

Cultural History and Gerald Gems's (2014a) *Boxing: A Concise History of the Sweet Science*, that also covered the religious aspects of the sport.

Sport historians and sport sociologists introduced a variety of theoretical approaches. Mike Messner and Don Sabo's (1990) *Sport, Men, and the Gender Order* applied feminist theory to the study of masculinity. Bruce Kidd's (1987) 'Sports and Masculinity,' in *Queens Quarterly*, and Steven Riess's (1991) 'Sport and the Redefinition of American Middle-Class Masculinity,' in the *International Journal of the History of Sport*, provided new insights into men's studies. Australian scholar Raewyn Connell's (1995) *Masculinities* introduced the concept of hegemonic masculinity, which places in subordinate roles not only women but also those men who do not measure up to dominant norms or standards of gender. Brian Pronger's (1990) *The Arena of Masculinity* is an early excursion into homosexuality research.

Men's studies continued to move forward with analyses of identity formation, continued subordination of women, and media research. Mary Louise Adams's (2011) *Artistic Impressions: Figure Skating, Masculinity and the Limits of Sport* provides an excellent study of the historical gender transition in a particular sport. In 2015, Simon Creak published *Embodied Nation: Sport, Masculinity, and the Making of Modern Laos*, an innovative work on the relationship of sexuality and nationalism. Gender studies have now reached a point where university students can major in this subject.

BODY CULTURE

Body culture has a long history, but it gained traction in the modern world in the late nineteenth century in the German back-to-nature movement – that promoted hiking, nudism, communion with the environment, weightlifting, and gymnastics – which spread to other European countries and the United States. Bodybuilding and fitness became popular, as detailed in David Chapman's (1994) *Sandow the Magnificent* and Robert Ernst's (2004) *Weakness Is a Crime*.

Anthropologists and sociologists took a greater interest in the body by the 1920s, and two decades later, French philosopher Maurice Merleau-Ponty introduced phenomenology. Later, French scholars debated whether the body was 'a source of understanding, love, and identity or disgust, shame, and alienation' (Eichberg 2010: 164).

Pierre Bourdieu's (1977, 1984) concept of habitus also applied as the body became a means of public display through sport. Body culture assumed greater relevance in sport studies by the 1980s, and within feminist theory the body assumed a form of objectification, resistance, and power relations. It became central to health studies, where it might harbor disease or present an image of health. Sport or exercise became a means to fitness or even nationalism, as in John Bale's (2004) *Running Cultures* or Susan Brownell's (1995) *Training the Body for China*. Erik Jensen's (2010) *Body by Weimar: Athletes, Gender and German Modernity* argues for a transition in gender roles during the post-World War I era in Germany. J. A. Mangan edited two anthologies (1999, 2000) that examined the fascist ideology and its attempt to create the Aryan Superman. Henning Eichberg (2004) showed the political nature of the body in *The People of Democracy: Understanding Self-Determination on the Basis of Body and Movement*. Jennifer Hargreaves and Patricia Vertinsky (2006) compiled an assortment of essays that show the breadth of the genre, including a chapter on Muslim women, in *Physical Culture, Power, and the Body*. That topic is covered more extensively in Tansin Benn, Gertrud Pfister, and Haifaa Jawad's (2011) *Muslim Women and Sport*, which covers six countries ranging from patriarchal to egalitarian societies.

This selected assortment of sport history studies is by no means complete, but only a representative indication of the breadth of gender research within the field. There is still much work to be done and knowledge to be discovered, gained, and shared, which awaits the next generation of sport scholars.

FURTHER READING

Margot Badran (2009) *Feminism in Islam: Secular and Religious Convergences.* Oxford: Oxford University Press.

Susan J. Bandy, ed. (2004) *Nordic Narratives of Sport and Physical Culture. Transdisciplinary Perspectives.* Aarhus: Aarhus University Press.

Susan J. Bandy (2010) 'Gender,' in Pope, S. W. and Nauright, J., eds., *Routledge Companion to Sports History.* New York: Routledge, 129–147.

Gail Bederman (1995) *Manliness and Civilization: A Cultural History of Gender and Race in the United States.* Chicago: University of Chicago Press.

Howard P. Chudacoff (1999) *The Age of the Bachelor.* Princeton, NJ: Princeton University Press.

Claudia Guedes (2020) *Mulheres a Cesta* [documentary film on the hardships and accomplishments of the first women's national basketball team in Brazil] at https://www.youtube.co/watch?v=oJ-YTxlobVk and with subtitles at https://www.youtube.com/watch?v=PeLhfrBQ6xc&feature=youtu.be

Jennifer Hargreaves and Eric Anderson, eds. (2014) *Routledge Handbook of Sport, Gender and Sexuality*. London: Routledge.

bell hooks (1981) *Ain't I a Woman? Black Women and Feminism*. Boston: South End Press.

Michael S. Kimmel (1996) *Manhood in America: A Cultural History*. New York: Free Press.

Rory Magrath, Jamie Cleland, and Eric Anderson, eds. (2020) *Palgrave Handbook of Masculinity and Sport*. Cham: Palgrave Macmillan.

J. A. Mangan (2011) *'Manufactured' Masculinity: Making Imperial Manliness, Morality and Militarism*. Abingdon: Routledge.

E. Anthony Rotundo (1993) *American Manhood: Transformations in Masculinity from the Revolution to the Modern Era*. New York: Basic Books.

Jaime Schultz, Jean O'Reilly, and Susan Cahn, eds. (2018) *Women and Sports in the United States: A Documentary Reader*. Chicago: University of Chicago Press.

RACE

In the United States, race has been a contentious issue since the arrival of African slaves in 1619. Even after emancipation in the American Civil War, black people were mistreated, segregated, and even lynched. In 2016, Colin Kaepernick, a black professional football player, took a public stand against the police brutality that accounts for multiple black deaths annually in the United States. He was admonished by President Donald Trump and banished from the National Football League (NFL). In 2020, the continuing deaths of black people at the hands of police erupted in a wholesale national protest with the slogan 'Black Lives Matter.' Athletes assumed leadership roles in the movement. Sport became a public demonstration of the campaign for social justice.

THE CONCEPT OF RACE

Race can be defined as a categorization of people based on shared physical and social characteristics. Although there is no biological basis for the concept of race, there has been a long history of racial classification. As early as 1684, French physician Francois Bernier, who had traveled throughout Europe, northern Africa, the Middle East, and India, published a work that classified humans into four groups.

By the eighteenth century, scientists attached behavioral and psychological traits to racial groups. They debated the process of racial formation – that is, monogenesis versus polygenesis (whether humans emanated from a single source or multiple sources). In 1779, German scholar Johann Friedrich Blumenbach determined that there were five different races, based on his studies of craniometry (skull size), geography, nutrition, and social customs. Such studies continued into the nineteenth century as racial anthropometry; anthropologists who measured the skulls and presumably brain sizes asserted that those with larger skulls were more intelligent. Louis Agassiz, a Swiss scientist and university professor, favored the polygenesis viewpoint, arguing the religious doctrine of creationism by a deity. In his version of scientific racism, prominent throughout the nineteenth century, he proclaimed as many as 12 separate races. Such reasoning was contradicted by Charles Darwin in his publication of *The Origin of Species* in 1859. Darwin favored monogenesis; but his theory of natural selection and the monogenetic descent of man was not fully accepted until the 1930s.

Colonialism and the slave trade brought non-British people to England and North America, where they were deemed to be inferior to white people. The British class system also considered social elites to be mentally and physically above those of the lower classes. The scientists of the nineteenth century tried to use differences in skin color, facial types, skull size, and hair by physiognomy, the study of facial features, to impart mental intelligence and moral characteristics. Such studies, conducted by white scientists in Europe and the United States, assumed white superiority. In the latter location, slavery was justified by the belief that black Africans were less than fully human.

The issue of slavery resulted in a civil war in the United States. Despite the resultant emancipation of slaves and the granting of citizenship, black people remained relegated to less than equal social status and were forced to live in segregated areas. In both the British Empire and the American colonies by 1900, the subjugated peoples of North America, the Caribbean, Africa, Asia, and Australia were deemed to be inferior and in need of acculturation; this was despite their centuries of highly developed cultures.

Strict segregation became the law of the land in the southern United States. A court case reached the Supreme Court in 1896 after Homer Plessy sued when the train conductor removed him from the segregated car reserved for white people. Plessy had only one great-grandparent who was black, making him seven-eighths white; yet just one drop of black blood designated a person as black.

The Supreme Court denied Plessy's claim, which allowed states to enact segregation laws as long as black people were considered to be 'separate but equal.' Such laws would permeate the southern states until they were overturned in 1954. Despite the federal ruling, many white residents and their southern politicians continued for decades to resist integration efforts.

During the Progressive Era (c. 1890–1920) in the United States, eugenics (the scientific selection of favorable human inherited characteristics with the aim of shaping future populations), became fashionable, as it claimed that undesirable traits, including low intelligence, could be eliminated. Sociologist Edward Ellsworth Ross penned *The Old World in the New* in 1914; followed by Madison Grant's *The Passing of the Great Race* in 1916, which warned of the dangers of racial mixing and the decline of the white race. The eugenics movement became especially popular in the United States, England, and Germany. Sir Julian Huxley, an English biologist in the early twentieth century and a eugenics advocate, theorized that the percentage of black versus white blood in a person would determine their intelligence and morality, and that such racial inequality would justify the segregation of the races. In later life, he came to favor the designation of ethnic groups rather than races.

Between 1860 and 1920, more than 28 million people migrated to the United States (Wills 2005: 45). In 1907, the US Congress authorized the Dillingham Commission to study the immigrants. After three years of research, it concluded that there were 45 separate races, some more desirable than others, and this resulted in immigration quotas. Anthropologist Franz Boas and the sociologists of the University of Chicago determined that race was a social construct, and they began to focus on the concept of ethnicity rather than race as a cultural signifier. Still, whiteness signified privilege in Anglo societies, and not all white-skinned groups were initially considered to be white.

The Irish, Italians, Slavs, and Jews as well as all Asians were not considered to be white and had to accept and adopt the norms of whiteness before winning gradual and belated acceptance in the American polity. In 1874, an African American doctor described the Irish immigrants as

> remarkable for open, projecting mouths, prominent teeth, and exposed gums, their advancing cheekbones and their depressed noses carry barbarism on their very front. ... Degradation and hardship exhibit themselves in the whole physical condition of the people ... giving such an example of human degradation as to make it revolting. They are only five feet two inches, upon an average, bow-legged, bandy-shanked, abortively featured, the apparitions of Irish ugliness and Irish want.
>
> (Quoted in Roediger 1998: 56–57)

Italians faced even greater denigration. Social commentators marked them as lower than the Irish, 'beaten men from beaten races, the worst failures in the struggle for existence' (Gems 2013: 58). In the South, they were considered to be black, consigned to segregated areas and segregated schools. They suffered the second-highest number of lynchings, surpassed only by black Americans. In the North, Italians were paid less than white people for the same job. Jobs in the blast furnaces of the American steel plants were reserved for Slavs, considered to be the only ones who could withstand the heat. Jews, despite the accumulation of wealth, were banned from white business, social, and golf clubs, and they faced quotas at the most prestigious universities. The Chinese were excluded from immigration to the United States in 1882, and the Japanese and other Asians were banned in 1924.

In England, Indians, Pakistanis, Africans, and Asians faced the same assimilation and acculturation process. With the global migration of peoples in search of better lives, racial tensions simmered through the late nineteenth and early twentieth centuries and finally erupted after World War I. In both the United Kingdom and the United States, race riots flared throughout as nonwhite people sought jobs and decent housing. During World War II, the anti-Semitism and racial bigotry of Nazi Germany became evident as Hitler tried to exterminate Jews and Roma. Racial tensions flared again in the 1950s and throughout the remainder of the century as the civil rights movement generated a quest for social justice and equality for minority groups. Such political, social and nationalistic battles were often played out in sport.

SPORT AND RACE

On the plantations of the American South, black slaves were forced to fight with their counterparts from other plantations for the amusement of their white masters, who might bet sizable sums on the outcome. Some became quite proficient in the activity. Bill Richmond, a former slave, won his liberation when the British forces invaded the colonies during the American Revolutionary War. He returned to England with the British after the war, and there his boxing skills earned him a championship match, which he lost to Tom Cribb in 1804. Richmond served as the trainer for another black American, Tom Molyneaux, who also traveled to England in search of fame and fortune. Molyneaux disposed of all his British opponents but lost to Cribb in 1810. Molyneaux claimed the championship when Cribb retired, but the latter was forced out of his leisure lest the British title fall to a foreigner. Cribb duly defended the championship before 20,000 spectators in 1811. The interracial bouts, however, were more about nationalism than race (Gems 2014a).

Baseball quickly became the national sport in the United States after the Civil War, but when black players joined in the growth of the game, they were banned from its highest echelons. In the late nineteenth century, black jockeys surpassed their white competitors in America, winning the biggest races, but doing so for their white employers who pocketed the winnings. Black cyclist Major Taylor set records and became a world champion, but his skill brought the animosity of white foes that colluded against him and caused him to seek his fortune in other lands. When black football players emerged as stars, southern teams refused to play interracial contests, demanding that the black athletes were ignominiously left behind, a public humiliation that continued for over 50 years.

By the end of the nineteenth century, race would become a dominant factor in boxing matches, as sport allowed for the direct confrontation between racial opponents and a test of the Darwinian survival of the fittest. Boxing champion John L. Sullivan imposed a color ban, unwilling to chance a loss to a nonwhite man for the symbolic role of the world's toughest man. Peter Jackson, a black boxer from the West Indies, fought a 61 round draw with James J. Corbett in 1891. When Corbett beat Sullivan for the championship the next year, he refused a rematch with Jackson.

When Jim Jeffries retired from the ring as undefeated champion in 1905, the title eventually fell to Canadian Tommy Burns, who embarked on an international tour to capitalize on his newfound fame. Jack Johnson, considered the black champion, trailed Burns to Australia, where the latter agreed to a match for a lucrative sum in 1908. Johnson's easy victory resulted in a search for the 'great white hope,' any white fighter who could return the crown to its rightful place among the white race. The flamboyant Johnson reveled in his fame, wearing expensive clothes, racing his sports car, openly flaunting his white paramours, and eventually marrying, on three occasions, different white women. When the ongoing campaign failed to find a Caucasian who could defeat Johnson, white people clamored for Jim Jeffries to end his retirement and return to the ring. The arranged bout took place in 1910 for a purse that exceeded $100,000. Johnson toyed with and bloodied Jeffries, knocking him through the ropes and thoroughly refuting the Social Darwinian belief in black inferiority. As black people throughout America rejoiced, white people resorted to violent race riots and lynchings. Unable to defeat Johnson in the ring, white politicians charged him with morality crimes to imprison him, causing him to flee the country. As a proud, defiant, free black man, Jack Johnson resisted, challenged and disproved the concept of racial supremacy. White people retained political power, however, and black heavyweight fighters would have to wait two decades for another chance at the heavyweight title. Black fighters in Britain were prohibited from championship bouts until 1948 (Carrington 2002).

At the 1912 Olympic Games, Native American Jim Thorpe won the pentathlon and decathlon, and was hailed as the greatest athlete in the world. Scientists measured his body in attempts to discern any physical advantage. He also led the nation in scoring on the football field; but when he admitted to playing baseball for money during 1909 and 1910, a violation of the amateur code, he was stripped of his medals and dishonored. Ironically, given that the indigenous people were the original inhabitants of the land, Thorpe was not even a citizen. Native Americans were not granted citizenship until 1924.

By the 1930s, the United States was in need of a hero. The world-wide economic depression had devastated the American economy, and Nazi Germany had pretensions to global conquest. The rivalry played out in athletic wars before the real conflagration ensued. Joe Louis, the son of black sharecroppers, emerged as an unde-feated contender and the glory of the black populace. His victories became joyous and festive occasions. Black novelist Richard Wright recounted the meaning of a Louis win: 'Joe was the concentrated essence of black triumph over white ... and what could be sweeter than long-nourished hate vicariously gratified?' (quoted in Roberts 2014: 189). Poet Maya Angelou listened to Louis's fights on the radio. She said,

> if Joe got tagged, or if he stumbled or was in trouble it seemed apocalyp-tic. My race groaned. It was our people falling. It was another lynching, yet another black man hanging on a tree. One more woman ambushed and raped. A Black boy whipped and maimed. ... It was a white woman slapping her maid for being forgetful.
>
> (Angelou, quoted in Roberts 2014: 189)

Actor Ossie Davis stated that 'Joe was our avenging angel. ... He was spiritually necessary to our sense of who we were, to our man-hood' (quoted in Roberts 2010: 101). Louis inspired a young Nelson Mandela to take up boxing in South Africa.

The legacy of Jack Johnson forced Louis to comport himself in a humble, religious manner, never gloating over a fallen foe, never to be seen with a white woman, and being deferential to white people. Despite his demeanor, white writers characterized him in a negative light. One described his victory over the Italian fascist champion. 'Something sly and sinister, and perhaps not quite human came out of the African jungle last night to strike down and utterly demol-ish a huge hulk that had been Primo Carnera, the giant' (quoted in Gems 2014a: 107). Paul Gallico, one of the premier sportswriters in America for the *New York Times* wrote that Joe Louis was

> a magnificent animal. ... He eats. He sleeps. He fights. ... Is he all instinct, all animal? Or have a hundred million years left a fold upon his brain? I see in this colored man something so cold, so hard, so cruel that

I wonder as to his bravery. Courage in the animal is desperation. Courage in the human is something incalculable and divine.

(Quoted in Carrington 2002: 17)

When Joe Louis faced Max Schmeling, the German champion, in 1936 it was more than a boxing match, as the two fighters represented oppositional political systems. The international radio broadcast was provided in English, Spanish, and German, and 60 million Americans tuned in; although many southerners and German Americans favored Schmeling. In a surprise, the German won in a 12th-round knock-out, Louis's first loss. Singer Lena Horne listened to the bout and admitted that she 'was near hysteria toward the end ... and some of the men were crying' (Demas 2004: 263). Poet Langston Hughes also noted 'grown men weeping like children and women sitting on the curbs with their heads in their hands' (Demas 2004: 263).

Soon thereafter a bevy of black American athletes, led by Jesse Owens, redeemed racial and national pride in the 1936 Olympics, held in Berlin. Hitler intended it to be a showcase for his Third Reich and a display of his doctrine of Aryan supremacy; but the American men won 14 gold medals in the track and field events to only 5 for the Germans. German Jew Gretel Bergmann was removed from the women's team due to the Nazis' anti-Semitism, despite the fact that her high jump record would have won the gold medal.

By 1938, Joe Louis had gained the heavyweight championship and a rematch with Max Schmeling. Sixty-six thousand spectators filed the stadium and 60 million American listeners tuned in on the radio for a short-lived international broadcast as Louis redeemed himself with a first-round knockout of Schmeling. His victory restored black pride in a still segregated America. In Harlem, a predominantly black section of New York City,

they rejoiced with all their might. ... There was never anything like it. ... Take a dozen Harlem Christmases, a score of New Year's eves, a bushel of July 4ths (US independence day) and maybe – yes maybe – you get a faint glimpse of the idea.

(Roberts 2010: 170–171)

Baseball grew exponentially after the American Civil War and soon became the national game in the nineteenth century. Black people, however, were banned from the Major League professional teams. They formed their own professional leagues in the 1920s. The American military forces remained segregated during World War II; but in its aftermath, Branch Rickey, the general manager of the Brooklyn Dodgers, attempted his 'great experiment' by signing a black player, Jackie Robinson, to a contract in 1947. Robinson endured racist slurs, confrontations, and injurious intentions of opponents; but his stellar play attracted fans and admirers and produced a championship. Robinson's feats and gradual acceptance broke the color barrier seven years before the US Supreme Court officially struck down the practice of segregation. Robinson's success fostered the integration of the National Basketball Association (NBA) in 1950.

The rise of Muhammad Ali coincided with the civil rights movement of the mid-twentieth century. The brash Ali became the outspoken leader of the 'athletic revolution,' in which athletes assumed a greater role in the quest for social and racial equality. Ali refused to serve in the army during the Vietnam War, and was banned from boxing for nearly four years and threatened with imprisonment. Ali prevailed in the courts, insuring the basic rights of freedom of speech and freedom of religion for all Americans, and in the ring as he regained his championship in dramatic fashion. While Ali waged his legal battles, Tommie Smith and John Carlos, American sprinters at the 1968 Olympic Games, used their awards podium as an international stage to bring attention to the plight of black Americans with their iconic gloved salute. They were subsequently banned from the team, sent home, and ostracized, even receiving death threats for their action. In the following years, other athletes in several sports bravely protested the inequalities inherent in the administration and practice of sports as well as in American society.

Their campaign gradually achieved results. In 1999, Marge Schott, owner of the Cincinnati Reds baseball team, was forced to sell her controlling interest after a long series of racist and anti-Semitic remarks. In 2017, Donald Stirling, owner of the Los Angeles Clippers basketball team, was also forced to sell his team due to a history of racist remarks and behavior. Since the arrival of Michael Jordan in the NBA in 1984, and with his rise to international stardom, basketball players in general have become among the most outspoken relative to social justice issues. Football player Colin Kaepernick kneeled during the pregame playing of the national anthem in 2016 to protest police brutality and social inequality, and he was soon joined by other players. This resulted in a conservative backlash, and Kaepernick was blacklisted by owners. Moreover, despite NFL policies to the contrary and the large number of black players, relatively few African Americans gain head coaching jobs. At the college level, black women make up less than 10 percent of the athletes, despite African Americans representing about 13 percent of the population (Wiggins 2018).

Other social justice advocates in both Canada and the United States have been protesting the use of Native American or minority group images as mascots for professional and school teams since the 1970s, but with limited success. Such images are considered to be forms of ethnic or racial stereotyping. The NCAA issued a policy to penalize teams that continued to use offensive mascots after 2005, revoking any opportunities to host post-season playoff events.

Canadian sport historians have been particularly proactive in addressing social justice for First Nations people. The *Journal of Sport History* published a special issue in 2008 on indigenous sport and a special edition in 2019 that included the role of sport in uncovering social injustices, as well as resistance, activism, and reconciliation relative to the indigenous peoples of various countries.

The United Kingdom has experienced similar issues relative to racism and sport. Its colonial legacy introduced western forms of sport to indigenous peoples throughout its empire, and transnational migration flows brought people of color to the United Kingdom. Cricket assumed greater importance in the West Indies with the first Inter-Colonial Tournament in 1891–1892. The first black individuals on the West Indies team appeared in 1900. Learie Constantine, a black cricket star from Trinidad, traveled to England, where he played professionally, starting in 1928. But he found that there was a long history of opposition to nonwhite players, particularly in Yorkshire. (Carrington and McDonald 2001). In 1945, Constantine was refused a room at the Imperial Hotel in London, and it was not until the 1976 Race Relations Act that such discrimination was legally rectified.

C. L. R. James, another Trinidadian cricketer, published *Beyond a Boundary* in 1963, considered to be the best book written about the sport. James discusses the values of the game, and its racial and political dynamics that brought about his own radicalism as it built a sense of nationalism throughout the islands. Cricket became a means to test oneself and nationalist sentiments against the colonial ruler. The combined West Indies team won its first test match against England in 1950 amid political tensions as the colonial territories quested for independence.

As migration from the colonies rose in the post-World War II years, racial tensions grew in England. Segregation of nonwhite people increased, and riots ensued throughout the 1950s. Cricket became a means to promote decolonization and test racial stereotypes.

The first cricket match in India took place as early as 1721. Native Indians formed their own club in Bombay in 1848. The first test match for India did not occur until 1932, and it's first win was two decades later. India achieved independence in 1947 and won the cricket World Cup in 1983 and 2011. Such victories represented racial statements of equality, beating the former master at his own game. Jubilation reigned throughout the country as people danced in the streets. Former colonies would replicate India's World Cup wins in successive years: Australia in 1987, 1999, 2003, 2007, 2015; Pakistan in 1992; and Sri Lanka in 1996.

Such wins fueled national pride but did not quell racism, as race riots persisted, largely in opposition to Pakistani and Caribbean immigrants in the early decades of the twenty-first century. Racism worsened noticeably on the soccer pitches of Europe as fans taunted black European and African players during matches and viciously attacked them on social media.

South Africa gained its independence in 1961, but the British had left a legacy of racism with segregated sports and separate administrations between white people and people of color. 'Sport was not a medium of cross-racial contact. It could not be in circumstances where the colonial census tagged Africans Coloureds, Indians, and Whites as "races" and defined racial political identities through the force of law' (Vahed 2004: 130). A 1968–1969 cricket tour of South Africa by the English team was cancelled when South Africa refused to allow Basil D'Oliveira, of half Indian descent, to compete with the touring team. South Africa's apartheid policies resulted in the country's expulsion from the Olympic Games from 1970 to 1992

An international sporting ban after 1988 pushed South African politicians to abandon their apartheid policies, and the country resumed international athletic competition in 1992.

Australian sporting practices assumed white superiority in the late nineteenth century, as white people refused to compete with indigenous athletes. Australian rules football has had a long history of abuse by fans and players who taunt nonwhite opponents with racial slurs, and teams have been accused of positioning players according to racial stereotypes (Hallinan 1991; Adair 2014). Indigenous soccer, rugby, and cricket players have endured racist remarks for decades. Anthony Mundine, an Aboriginal rugby player, quit the sport and turned to boxing, where he enjoyed greater success. His sporting celebrity provided him with a public forum to condemn racism (Gems 2014a).

WHITENESS STUDIES

Whiteness studies appeared in the 1980s and assumed greater significance a decade later as an interdisciplinary inquiry into white hegemony and privilege based upon skin color. Whiteness affords greater social status and power, which amounts to a systematic form of racism. Whiteness studies have been particularly prominent in the United States and the United Kingdom. Race has always and continues to be a major social and cultural factor in both countries. Although it has no biological validity, its social construction and acceptance has resulted in perceptions of racial superiority.

Theodore W. Allen, author of *The Invention of the White Race* (1998), initiated his research relative to whiteness and its relationship to social class as early as the 1960s. David Roediger's (1991) *The Wages of Whiteness* is considered to be a seminal text in whiteness studies, as he ties the social construction of race to identity and working-class labor. As previously stated, migrant groups such as the Irish, Italians, Slavs, and Jews were not accorded equal social standing with the established Anglo hierarchy and had to gain acceptance over time. They did so, often in violent confrontations with free blacks over jobs, urban territories, and political power.

Black writers had long understood the values of whiteness. By the late nineteenth century, the black scholar W. E. B. Du Bois had begun his investigations into the separate lives of black people and white people. In *The Souls of Black Folk* (1903), he expresses the double consciousness of black people forced to live in two worlds, one black and the other white. Toni Morrison, black writer and winner of both the Pulitzer Prize and the Nobel Prize in Literature, added to the canon of whiteness studies in 1992 with the publication of *Playing in the Dark: Whiteness and the Literary Imagination*, in which she analyzes how institutionalized slavery served to fashion a perception of white racial superiority. Nell Irvin Painter's (2010) *The History of White People* traces the concept of whiteness from the ancient Greeks to modern times. Even among the Greeks and Romans, slavery denoted an inferior social class. Scientific racism eventually resulted in the designation of ethnicities with varying levels of acceptance, which could be a transitional state. Additionally, she analyzes the concept of beauty, which is also socially constructed. Nancy Isenberg's (2016) *White Trash: The 400-Year Untold History of Class in America* notes that whiteness has various levels of acceptability and privilege. Not all whites are created equal, and the impoverished underclass has limited chances for social mobility, not unlike the racial discrimination faced by black Americans.

For a contemporary analysis of whiteness in England, including its meanings for the far right white supremacy movement, BBC Radio 4 (n.d.) offers 'Whiteness.' Professor Joseph Pugliese has written several books that address whiteness in Australia. His Deathscapes project aims at achieving social justice relative to the history of violence perpetrated against indigenous peoples (Deathscapes n.d.).

A BRIEF HISTORIOGRAPHY OF SPORT AND RACISM

There are hundreds of books relative to sport and racism that address the myriad factors relative to the social construction, practice, and repercussions that are pertinent to the subject, and many more are still to be written. Among the general works, see John Bale and Mike Cronin's (2003) *Sport and Postcolonialism* on the aftermath of imperial ventures and how the independent states adopt or adapt sport as a means of resistance, assertion, or recognition of national identity

Patrick Miller and David Wiggins's (2004) *Sport and the Color Line: Black Athletes and Race Relations in Twentieth-Century America* is an anthology that provides insights on segregation practices and the quest for social justice. Patrick Ismond's (2003) *Black and Asian Athletes in British Sport and Society: A Sporting Choice?* offers theoretical perspectives as well as analyses of ethnicity, identity, and sexism. *Routledge Handbook of Sport, Race and Ethnicity*, edited by John Nauright and David Wiggins (2019), is a comprehensive, interdisciplinary collection of international case studies on the titled topics. *Race and Sport in Canada: Intersecting Inequalities*, edited by Simon Darnell, Yuka Nakamura, and Janelle Joseph (2012), shows the continuing effects of racist practices on sport in that country. *Asian American Athletes in Sport and Society*, edited by C. Richard King (2015), is a collection of essays on an important but under-researched topic. Chris Hallinan and Barry Judd's (2016) *Indigenous People, Race Relations and Australian Sport* addresses another little researched subject relative to the meanings of sport from an indigenous viewpoint.

FURTHER READING

Theodore W. Allen (1998) *The Invention of the White Race: Racial Oppression and Social Control*. London: Verso.

Karen Brodkin (1998) *How Jews Became White Folks and What that Says About Race in America*. New Brunswick, NJ: Rutgers University Press.

Ben Carrington and Ian McDonald (2001) *Race, Sport and British Society*. London: Routledge.

W. E. B. DuBois (1903) *The Souls of Black Folk*. Chicago: A. C. McClurg & Co.

Gerald R. Gems (2014) 'Historians Take on Ethnicity, Race, and Sport,' in Riess, Steven A., ed., *A Companion to American Sport History*. DeKalb, IL: John Wiley & Sons, 404–433.

Stephen Jay Gould (1981) *The Mismeasure of Man*. New York: W. W. Norton.

Jennifer Guglielmo and Salvatore Salerno, eds. (2003) *Are Italians White? How Race Is Made in America*. New York: Routledge.

Matthew Pratt Guterl (2001) *The Color of Race in America, 1900–1940*. Cambridge, MA: Harvard University Press.

Noel Ignatiev (1995) *How the Irish Became White*. New York: Routledge.

Matthew Frye Jacobson (1998) *Whiteness of a Different Color: European Immigrants and the Alchemy of Race*. Cambridge, MA: Harvard University Press.

C. L. R. James (1963) *Beyond a Boundary*. London: Stanley Paul.

Samuel O. Regalado (2013) *Nikkei Baseball: Japanese American Players from Immigration and Internment to the Major Leagues*. Urbana: University of Illinois Press.

David R. Roediger (1991) *The Wages of Whiteness: Race and the Making of the American Working Class*. New York: Verso.

Maureen Smith, ed. (2019) 'Special Edition: Indigenous Resurgence, Regeneration, and Decolonization through Sport History,' *Journal of Sport History* 46:2, 143–324.

Colin Tatz (1995) *Obstacle Race: Aborigines in Sport*. Sydney: University of New South Wales Press.

Wray Vamplew, ed. (2008) 'Forum: Indigenous Sport,' *Journal of Sport History* 35:2, 191–283.

5

SPORT AND NATIONALISM

At the turn of the twentieth century, the United States began to challenge the global supremacy of Great Britain. The 1908 Olympic Games, hosted by London, provided an opportunity for the public display of nationalism. At the opening ceremony, the American flagbearer allegedly failed to dip the national flag to acknowledge the British monarch. Disputes ensued throughout the Games over the nature and violation of rules as well as the British emphasis on amateurism versus the Americans' intent on winning. In the battle for cultural superiority, the Americans claimed victory by winning 15 of the 25 track and field events, while the British maintained their triumph in amassing the most points in all events (Mathews 1980; Mallon and Buchanan 1999).

EUROPEAN NATIONALISM

Nationalism permeated early modern Europe as England and other European states resisted their capture and occupation by Napoleon's French legions. In 1811, Friedrich Ludwig Jahn, a German nationalist and gymnastics teacher, established a Turnplatz, an open-air exercise facility, near Berlin for the purpose of training young men to resist the French. In addition to gymnastics and fitness activities, hiking and nationalistic songs instilled national pride and a martial spirit. Nationalistic Turner clubs continued in the postwar period, but during the failed German Revolution of 1848, the Turners faced imprisonment or execution. Many fled to the United States, where they established nationalistic Turner clubs to maintain their German culture (Pfister 1996; Hofmann 2001).

Similar European clubs followed the example of the German Turners. The Czech Sokols, founded in Prague in 1862, followed the Turner fitness regimen but assumed a more militaristic approach during the Austrian-Prussian War of 1866. Early Sokols members also traveled to America, where they established a club in 1865. The Polish Falcons followed a similar path with the creation of their first club in 1863; but with the failure of a Polish uprising that year, they too migrated to the United States, although the first Falcon club in America did not appear until 1887 in Chicago.

BRITISH NATIONALISM

In England, the public schools attempted to instill a particular British ethos in their students, largely upper-middle-class male youth in quest of social mobility. Sport played a prominent role in the curriculum, intended to impart a sense of fair play, discipline, and physical hardiness and to foster leadership skills necessary for the administration of the far-flung British Empire. In the elementary schools, military drill was meant to instill 'the spirit of nationalism, patriotism, imperialism and Christianity' (Mangan and Ndee 2003, 88).

British sports, such as cricket and soccer, were exported to the colonies with the intent to acculturate indigenous inhabitants and teach the proper English values. The endeavor met with mixed results, as natives both adopted and adapted the sport forms for their own purposes (Mangan 1986; Guttmann 1994). Lacrosse had been played by indigenous tribes in America for centuries before the European settlers arrived. In 1856, the white residents of Montreal formed their own lacrosse club, and by 1860 it was considered to be the national game. In 1866, William George Beers fashioned a set of rules, which became standardized. The game had migrated to Scotland by 1890, where girls' school teams were formed, and by the turn of the century both males and females played the game. The

1904 Olympic Games included a lacrosse tournament, and this had a Native American team of American Indians of the Mohawk tribe; but by that time, the game had been thoroughly coopted and transformed by the Anglo hierarchy. By 1936, it found official organization in Australia (Claydon 2019).

Ice hockey has a long, but questionable, history. Stick and ball games played outdoors on the ice had occurred in Europe for centuries, and this arrived in Canada by the early nineteenth century. Citizens of Montreal, however, are acknowledged as the first to play indoor hockey, in 1875. The Canadian version of the rules, printed in 1877, became the dominant and official regulations. Leagues formed in Canada by 1880, and professional teams took the ice by the turn of the century. Thus, an unorganized winter activity in Europe became a modern sport in one of its dominions. Canada officially named lacrosse as its national summer sport and ice hockey as its official winter sport (Martel 2019).

The game of cricket accompanied British settlers of North America; but it was eventually superseded by baseball, played in Canada by the early nineteenth century. Baseball surpassed cricket in most areas of the United States by the mid-nineteenth century, as Americans favored the faster pace of baseball and the fact that it could be played in smaller spaces than needed in cricket (Gems, Borish, and Pfister 2017). While most of the world favors soccer-style football, the North American version is decidedly different, having evolved from soccer to rugby to the gridiron version. Even the latter varies, as the Canadian rules provide for a larger field, more players, slightly different scoring, and a greater emphasis on offensive play. Both styles of American football no longer have any resemblance to the game of soccer, indicative of the break from the mother country (Greenham 2019).

The equestrian sport of polo had been played in India for centuries before the English established their dominance there. The necessity for equestrian skills proved helpful for the training of military cavalry units. British Army officers founded a club in 1862, and the sport was introduced to England in 1869. With the English usurpation of power in India, British traders, soldiers, sailors, and religious missionaries brought soccer to the territory. While the British intended that sport instill particular values in their Indian subordinates, they did not intend to mingle with them. Sporting practices were largely segregated. When the Indian Mohun Bagan team defeated the East Yorkshire Regiment for the 1911 Challenge Shield, it represented a measure of revenge and a resurgence of nationalistic pride for the Indians.

> It fills every Indian with joy and pride to know that rice-eating, malaria-ridden, barefoot Bengalis have got the better of beef-eating, Herculean, booted John Bull in the peculiarly English sport. Never before was there witnessed such universal demonstration of joy, men and women alike sharing it and demonstrating it by showering of flowers, embraces, shouts, whoops, screams and even dances. ... A subject race, humiliated by hauteur, ridiculed by so-called racial superiors and derided by a discriminating ruling class, had at last, delivered a fitting reply.
>
> (Dimeo 2001: 69)

English traders introduced cricket to India early in the eighteenth century, but the first integrated match did not occur until 1877. It would take more than a century for Indian cricketers to win the World Cup; but their consistent rankings among the world's best teams have bolstered a sense of national pride and erased the long history of denigration and perceptions of inferiority.

C. L. R. James (1963), in *Beyond a Boundary*, gives meaning to the role of cricket in the former British colonies in the Caribbean. More recently, Clem Seecharan (2006), in *Muscular Learning: Cricket and Education in the Making of the British West Indies at the End of the 19th Century*, contends that the sport, along with education, provides 'instruments of belonging and deliverance' in the quest for greater social and economic status. Anand Rampersad argues that cricket players in the West Indies 'produced a creolized product to symbolically avenge the wrongs of colonialism. The cricket ball and bat became symbolic whips used to extract a sense of retribution for the animosities meted out during slavery and later on in indentureship' (2014: 239). The victories of the West Indies over the English team in the 1980s marked the former colonies as equal contenders for global honors. Such conquests are shared by the spectators and fans, whose jubilation is found in their own brand of music, dance and literature.

England gained suzerainty over South Africa during the Napoleonic Wars and ruled the territory throughout the nineteenth century.

consolidating territory through warfare with native black tribes and tenuous relations with the earlier white Dutch settlers known as Boers. The tension between the two white factions resulted in the South African War of 1899–1902, won by the British. The Union of South Africa in 1910 formalized the denial of suffrage rights to most people of color and enforced segregation practices. Although British sports such as cricket had been introduced in the nineteenth century, segregation of athletic facilities became the norm. Black cricket matches lasted less than a day, as their leisure time was limited. Black people found the physicality of rugby more suitable to their lives of labor. When the apartheid system finally came to an end in 1994, rugby served as a unifying force under newly elected President Nelson Mandela. Both black people and white people reveled in national pride as 'their' team won the rugby World Cup in 1995 (Booth and Nauright 2014).

British ships sailed to Australia in 1788 in order to initiate a penal colony there. Over the next century, white settlers confiscated the lands of the Aboriginals, often through indiscriminate violence. As in South Africa, indigenous people were segregated from the white population. Assimilation efforts did not occur until the mid-twentieth century, and such programs had little appeal to those who wished to retain their indigenous culture. Further integration transpired in the 1960s, but Aboriginals did not get full suffrage rights until 1967.

The white settlers imported British sports throughout the nineteenth century. Soccer, horse racing, cricket, rugby, and field hockey proved popular. Cricket was taught to the Aboriginals with the intent of teaching the white British values inherent in the sport. As early as 1868, an all-Aboriginal cricket team traveled to England. The white settlers developed their own divergent sport practices with the evolution of Australian Rules football in 1869. While the indigenous peoples learned to play the 'white' games, they had little chance to test themselves against white people until the twentieth century. Two Aboriginal women played on the Australian cricket team that traveled to England during 1934–1935. By the end of the century, Aboriginal athletes had earned considerable distinction in sport; but sport also provided a means for resistance to white dictates and injustice (Tatz 1995; Phillips and Osmond 2018; Osmond 2019).

Aboriginal Evonne Goolagong emerged as a global tennis star, winning seven Grand Slam titles in the 1960s and 1970s, bringing greater recognition to the native population. Indigenous track star Cathy Freeman was chosen to light the Olympic flame at the 2000 Games held in Sydney. Upon winning the women's 400 meter run, she paraded around the track with both the Australian national flag and the flag of the Aboriginal people, calling attention to her ancestral roots. Anthony Mundine, a top player in rugby league but continually overlooked in national team selections, turned to boxing. As a world middleweight champion he used his celebrity and the boxing ring as his pulpit to decry racism in Australia and to campaign for Aboriginal rights (Gems 2014a).

The New Zealand colony developed in similar fashion to Australia. Christian missionaries arrived early in the nineteenth century, and white settlers migrated from England and Scotland. Formal colonization was established in 1841, and the native Maori, a Polynesian people, experienced the loss of their lands by confiscation and violence. A gold rush in the 1870s further increased white settlement. New Zealand was the first country where women gained suffrage (in 1893), and this included Maori women. But the Maori still experienced a level of racial segregation, thought this did not reach the extent of the Australian standards.

The Maori took readily to the white sports by the twentieth century. As early as 1883, Maori boxer Herbert Slade traveled to the United States in an unsuccessful bid to win the heavyweight championship from John L. Sullivan. A Maori rugby team toured England in 1888, during which time they performed the traditional haka dance, a pre-combat ritual. The white rugby union team, the All Blacks, adopted the haka dance as well in 1905. Maori players particularly liked and excelled at rugby and rugby league, testing their skills and physicality on tours to Australia and England from 1908 to 1910 Maori men and women have adopted rugby, the national sport of New Zealand. The Maori All Blacks men's team requires proof of Maori ancestry. The Maori are also represented on the men's and women's national teams. The women's national team, the Black Ferns, won the international championship in 2013 and 2018. The All Blacks national men's team won the rugby World Cup in 1987 2011, and 2015, and this team is among the premier international

squads. Its performance of the pregame haka dance has been criti-
cized as a cultural appropriation of Maori culture. It is evident, however, that sport has also been a unifying factor in New Zealand by
bringing disparate ethnicities together in a common interest.

Kenya, in eastern Africa, had been part of the British colonial
empire. Soccer reigned as the national sport until the famed long-
distance runners assumed global dominance by the onset of the
twenty-first century. Both male and female Kenyan runners have
attained preeminence on the track and in marathon events, eliciting
their conscription by other countries (Bale and Sang 1996).

England is considered the birthplace of modern soccer. The game
was played in schools by the mid-nineteenth century and adopted by
the working class by the 1870s. English merchants, missionaries, soldiers, sailors, and expatriates spread the game throughout the world,
and it found particular acceptance in South America, Africa, and Asia.
By 1900, the game had reached such proportions that it became
an Olympic event. FIFA (the Fédération Internationale de Football
Association), the world governing body for soccer, was founded in
1904, the inaugural year of the world championship.

JAPANESE NATIONALISM

Japan had isolated itself from the rest of the world for centuries before
the US Navy forced entry to the islands in 1853 and secured a treaty
that opened its markets to trade. During the Meiji period (1868–
1912) the Japanese government studied western culture, becoming
a modern state through industrialization, education, and adoption
of western sport forms. With the abolition of the samurai class of
professional warriors in 1876, sport became a means of maintaining
national values of discipline, self-sacrifice, and honor. The Japanese
imported American and European experts to introduce western science and technology to the country. In 1871, an American teacher,
Horace Wilson, brought the game of baseball as well. Japanese students sent to the United States also learned the game and brought
it back to their homeland, where it quickly spread throughout the
islands.

When the US Congress began banning Asian immigration in 1882,
sport became a means to assert racial and national pride. In 1891,

the then Yokohama Cricket Club (now the Yokohama Country and Athletic Club), which enrolled only Anglos as members, refused a baseball challenge from Ichiko, a Japanese prep school. When Ichiko lost a baseball game to an American Christian missionary school in 1893, it embarked on a Spartan training regimen to overcome the taint on national honor.

National honor was redeemed in the Sino-Japanese War of 1894–1895, in which the thorough Japanese victory secured Taiwan and, eventually, Korea as colonies. An American teacher at Ichiko finally managed to arrange a match with the Yokohama club in 1896. To the utter dismay of the Anglos, the Japanese schoolboys dominated in a 29-4 win, and the players were feted as national heroes. The student body president proclaimed that 'this great victory is more than a victory for our school, it is a victory for the Japanese people' (Gems 2006: 28). The Americans recruited top players from US Navy ships for a rematch, but they too fell to the students by a score of 32-9. Japanese newspapers heralded the win in front-page headlines. Within a month, another US Navy team attempted to defeat the Japanese students. Sure of victory, American government representatives and a naval band accompanied the team. Ten thousand spectators showed up to witness a 22-6 triumph by the Japanese team. The 1896 annual report of the Ichiko Baseball Club expressed both the pain and the jubilation of the Japanese.

> The Americans are proud of baseball as their national game just as we are proud of judo and kendo. Now, however, in a place far removed from their native land, they have fought against a 'little people' whom they ridicule as childish, only to find themselves swept away like falling leaves. No words can describe their disgraceful conduct. The aggressive character of our national spirit is a well-established fact, demonstrated first in the Sino-Japanese War and now by our great victories in baseball.
>
> (Roden 2001: 298)

The Americans requested yet another rematch to be held on 4 July, their national Independence Day. This time, they sent an all-star team from the US Navy, that included a former professional player and managed to win a close 14-12 victory. It proved to be only a temporary restoration of American pride, as Ichiko won 9 of 11 contests with American teams over the next eight years. The baseball wars would continue over the next four decades as Japanese teams traveled to the United States and American college and professional teams went to Japan to demonstrate their athletic, racial, and national superiority (Gems 2006).

The Japanese waged another war with Russia in 1904–1905 over the Korean peninsula. The Japanese victory garnered not only Korea and part of Sakhalin Island, but political leadership in Asia. In the post-World War I years, they assumed control of former German island colonies in the Pacific, providing a location for military bases and strategic airfields. In 1931, Japan invaded Manchukuo on the Chinese mainland, further extending its empire.

The athletic battles for nationalistic pride and political influence increased with the initiation of the Far East Olympics in 1913 by the Young Men's Christian Association (YMCA) in Manila, then under the colonial administration of Americans. With coming of World War I, the YMCA saw sport as a positive alternative to war. Japan had won the 1917 version of the Far East Games, and Elwood Brown, a former basketball coach in the United States and YMCA director in the Philippines, who organized the athletic festival, stated that

> the Western world may be grinding its best youth into mincemeat, but the Eastern world is making its lads into fine, strong citizens. On the battlefield Western civilization may be scattering its good will and brotherhood to the four winds; but on the athletic field the East is welding a great amulet which will encircle the Far East in a band of international fellowship.
>
> (Quoted in Gems 2006: 39)

Brown grossly misinterpreted Japanese intentions.

Japan first entered the Olympic Games in 1912, as sport offered a means to challenge the Social Darwinian notions of racial superiority. At the 1932 Olympics, held in Los Angeles, the local Japanese residents shunned in their adopted country and provided financial and emotional aid to the Japanese athletes, who finished fifth in the overall medal count. The Japanese swimmers proved to be the best in the world (Yamamoto 2016). At the 1936, Games the Japanese men won six gold medals in swimming and track and field. In the marathon race, they scored a gold medal and a bronze medal, won by Korean athletes who competed for their colonial ruler. Tokyo was granted the hosting rights for the 1940 Olympics, a sign of the international prestige that the country had amassed in the early decades of the twentieth century before the explosion of World War II forced the cancellation of the Games.

AMERICAN NATIONALISM

English settlers began arriving on the eastern shores of America in the late sixteenth century, eventually forming 13 original colonies. The colonists continually moved westward, confiscating the territories of the indigenous tribes. Shortly after the successful American Revolutionary War, the new US frontier stretched midway across the continent. After the Mexican–American War of 1848, it extended from the Atlantic to the Pacific coasts of the continent. By 1879, the conquest of the native Indian tribes was nearly complete, and that year, the federal government established the Carlisle Indian Industrial School, the first of many designed to assimilate the disparate tribes into white society. Sports became an integral means of acculturation. The students learned competition, the basis for the capitalist economic system. Team sports taught leadership skills and cooperation, the necessary characteristics for the democratic political system. Sports also required a referee to enforce the rules, which taught obedience to authority.

Students learned such lessons well, but not always with the intent of their administrators. The Carlisle football teams challenged the best teams of the white colleges. The Indian teams took great pride in defeating the army team, a symbolic victory over their ancestors' oppressors. Against the elite upper-class schools, such as Harvard, Penn, and the University of Chicago, they employed trick plays to 'outsmart' them. 'Football served the native American players as a means to both resist and adapt to the dominant culture that was imposed on them' (Gems 2000: 121).

With the surge of immigration to the United States after 1880, municipal governments employed the same strategy to acculturate the wide variety of ethnic groups that populated American cities. Sports became, and remain, a distinct part of the curriculum in American schools. Physical education teachers and coaches became prominent members of the teaching staff as a multitude of school teams competed for local, regional, and national honors.

The American government applied the same strategy in its new colonies gained after the short Spanish–American War of 1898. Cuban students in the United States had learned to play baseball, the American national game, and returned to form their own clubs on the island in the 1860s. Competition with American teams ensued thereafter, well before the island came under American rule. The Cuban independence movement started in 1895 as the local populace sought relief from its Spanish governors. It erupted in war when an American battleship mysteriously exploded in Havana Harbor in 1898, providing an excuse for the United States to attack Spain's global empire in retaliation. The quick American victory brought American governors to the island rather than the hoped-for independence. American Protestant missionaries flooded the island in an attempt to convert Catholic souls. The YMCA introduced other American sports, and games with American colleges and professional teams became contests of national pride. Although Cuba gained nominal independence in 1902, the United States continued its intervention thereafter. American professional baseball teams traveled to Cuba for their pre-season training, but refused to hire nonwhite Cubans for its teams. Cubans formed their own professional league in 1917 in retaliation. Cuban boxers faced no such restrictions; they traveled to the United States, winning championships, in the succeeding decades as sport offered a means to assert nationalistic pride (Gems 2006).

Puerto Rico had already gained its autonomy from Spain in 1897 before the Spanish–American War erupted. Despite this status, Spain ceded Puerto Rico to the United States after the war. Puerto Ricans became wards of the Americans without citizenship, until 1917, and without full suffrage rights. American schools taught the English language and gave moral training designed to divorce the Puerto Ricans from Catholicism. Cubans had brought baseball to Puerto Rico before the landing of American troops. American teachers and the YMCA brought a greater number of competitive activities. Nevertheless, Puerto Ricans clung to their native culture. The banned cockfights continued, and ball games became sites of cultural contention. By 1930, Puerto Rico entered the Central American Games as a separate nation, and it managed to do the same at the 1948 Olympics. Like Cuba, its boxers became symbols of national pride. After Jackie Robinson desegregated Major League Baseball in the United States, dark-skinned Puerto Ricans became stars in America. Puerto Rican pride is manifested in their separate national flag, distinct national anthem, and the declaration of Spanish as its national language. International athletic competitions allow Puerto Ricans to showcase their distinct national identity (Sotomayor 2016).

Like the Cubans, Filipinos also revolted against their Spanish supervisors. By 1898, the revolutionary army under Emilio Aguinaldo had already surrounded the Spanish garrison in Manila before the American army arrived. The Americans failed to recognize Aguinaldo as the new president and installed their own administration, which resulted in a guerrilla war that lasted until 1913. The Philippines would not gain independence until after the end of World War II in 1946.

The long American occupation of the archipelago resulted in an Americanization program that surpassed any of its other colonial ventures. Similar to the other colonies, Protestant missionaries hurried to the islands, where they constructed churches and schools to attract the Catholic population to their cause, though without great success. The American school system achieved much better results. Before American teachers began arriving in 1901, soldiers had introduced the Filipinos to baseball and boxing. With the introduction of a formal curriculum, physical education and sports became prominent features. A grade of 75% in Physical Education was required for promotion to the next grade, and bonus points could be applied to deficiencies in other areas. English, rather than Spanish or the polyglot tribal tongues, became the language of instruction. School sports teams taught the same values of competition, democracy, and respect for authority promulgated in the American Indian schools. The conspicuous display of the American flag and baseball leagues were meant to instill American patriotism. Boys and girls in each class formed competitive teams for intramural play, and school teams competed with others for local, provincial, and national honors. 'The director of education boasted that no country in the world, certainly no state in the American Union, has such a carefully worked out plan to make athletics national in scope and to determine who are the athletic champions' (Gems 2006: 59–60). Some ambitious teams even challenged the American military units. Occasional Filipino victories blemished the Americans' belief in racial superiority.

Despite the YMCA's segregation practices, interracial contests occurred outside of their auspices. Francisco Guilledo, born to a peasant family in 1901, assumed the alias of Pancho Villa – the Mexican bandit who terrorized the Southwest United States during World War I – during his professional boxing career. He met the US Army champion Mike Ballerino in the ring 13 times and never lost (11-0-2). He traveled to the United States in 1922 and a year later became world flyweight champion and a national hero. Thereafter, a host of Filipino boxers made the long voyage to America to challenge white boxers (Gems 2016).

The Americans also channeled Filipino nationalism into surrogate sporting wars. They invited the Japanese to the country in 1912 for a series of baseball games against Filipino foes, whom the Japanese considered to be American lackeys. The Japanese had just defeated the Russians in a war and viewed themselves as the rightful power in the Pacific. A thousand fans congregated to see the game in Cebu, where an American reported that

> the rivalry was spirited. Once or twice it bordered on bitterness. In short, the game was for blood. Having defeated a white foe in war, no doubt the Japs could not brook defeat by their neighboring islanders. When Cebu triumphed 3-1, bedlam broke loose, Japan was whipped, and the Cebu men became heroes.
>
> (Gems 2006: 56)

The international athletic contests for national supremacy assumed greater and more visible importance with the establishment of the Far East Games. Elwood Brown transformed the Manila Carnival, previously a business exposition, into an international athletic festival in 1913 with invitations to Japan, China, Malaysia, Thailand, and Hong Kong. Eighteen thousand spectators witnessed the baseball rematch with Japan. More than 150,000 watched the track and field, basketball, swimming and diving, football, tennis, volleyball, and girls' basketball games, in which the Filipinos emerged as victors.

> An American journalist reported that [up] to the time of the American occupation the Filipino had done absolutely nothing in athletics. The

race, in an athletic standpoint, was in very poor condition. They were, perhaps, the weakest of all Orientals. Today, they are at the head.

(Gems 2016: 96–97)

The regional contest continued until 1934 when the association crumbled amidst Chinese and Japanese turmoil over Manchuria. While in operation, however, the contests enabled the Americans to redirect Filipino nationalism.

Elsewhere in the Pacific, American missionaries brought baseball to Hawaii as early as 1849. In 1893, white American settlers conducted a coup that forced Queen Liliuokalani out of office, creating a brief independent republic. With the outbreak of the Spanish–American War in 1898 and the United States in need of a Pacific fueling station, it annexed the islands despite the claims of the indigenous population. The islands became a social experiment with their polyglot population of native Hawaiians and imported Portuguese, Japanese, Chinese, Filipino, Korean, and Puerto Rican workers. As well, when some of the black American soldiers sided with the Filipino guerrillas in the Spanish–American War, their units were shipped back to Hawaii. Sport provided a common interest for all. Ethnic and integrated teams played in the islands' baseball leagues, while the indigenous Hawaiians maintained traditional sports, such as surfing, that attracted white people and other ethnic groups. As early as 1912, Hawaiian swimmers, though not yet citizens, became members of the American Olympic team. Hawaiian Duke Kahanamoku, one of the swimming stars, spread surfing to the United States and Australia. Hawaii continued to serve as a cultural crossroads throughout the twentieth century, finally granted statehood in 1959.

The United States continued to employ sports as a political tool, teaching American values by promoting baseball throughout the Caribbean, Mexico, and Central America. In the territories of Guam and American Samoa, American football assumed precedence, and by the 1960s it has surpassed baseball as the national sport.

SPORT AS A NATIONAL SIGNIFIER

In Ireland, sport served similar functions in the national resistance to British rule. The founding of the Gaelic Athletic Association in

1884 – with its attention to native sports, such as hurling, Gaelic football, camogie, and traditional pastimes – reinforced Irish culture and Irish nationalism. Irish immigrants to the United States formed their own associated clubs to funnel money to the to the Irish independence movement. On Easter week of 1916, the rebels launched an armed insurrection that culminated in a guerrilla war between 1919 and 1921, that eventually won Irish independence (Cronin, Murphy, and Rouse 2009; Bradley 2020).

In Scotland, the Highland Games celebrated the ethnic culture as early as the eleventh century in some accounts. Resurrected in the nineteenth century, the Games included traditional dances and the playing of the bagpipes. With the migration of Scots, the national celebration spread to countries in Europe, North and South America, Australasia, and Indonesia. Events like the caber toss mark the Scottish heritage, while stone throws and hammer throws have been modified for acceptance in international track and field competitions (Bowness and Zipp 2020).

Zionism, a nationalist movement to establish a Jewish state, gained traction in late nineteenth-century Europe, and Jews who had been dispersed throughout the world began migrating to Palestine in the eastern Mediterranean in the 1880s. Palestine had been the historic homeland of the Jews, shared with Arab peoples. After World War I, tensions between the ethnic groups flared into violence. In the aftermath of World War II, the Jewish–Arab disputes erupted into warfare that ensued from 1947 to 1949, during which time Israel declared its independence as a national state in 1948. Israel was intended as a home for Jews around the world who had historically suffered from anti-Semitic pogroms and the horrors of the Nazi extermination campaign. The resettlement of Jews in Israel displaced native Arabs, resulting in continued warfare and violence with Palestinians and the Arab League, consisting of Arab nations bordering Israel.

The Maccabiah Games were first contested in Tel Aviv in 1932 with the intent of drawing Jewish athletes to Palestine in a celebration of Jewish culture. A second version of the athletic festival continued in 1935. Such events were intended to promote a Jewish consciousness, and many Jewish athletes boycotted the 1936 Olympic Games hosted by Nazi Germany. With the independent status of Israel obtained, the Maccabiah Games resumed in 1950 and have been staged quadrennially after 1953. The Games draw a large, international assortment of Jewish athletes in a nationalistic spectacle that supports Jewish identity and migration to bolster statehood (Kaplan 2015).

National sports in other countries continue to define cultural differences. Kabbadi is the national sport of Bangladesh, but is also popular throughout India, where a professional league exists. Seven players per team take turns trying to invade the opponents' territory, tagging as many as possible and returning to their own side without being tackled. Each tag earns a point, as does a tackle for the opposing side.

Martial arts, many of them developed in Asia, serve as the national sports in several countries. Muay Thai is the national sport in Thailand. Similar to boxing, it allows the use of elbows, knees, and legs to strike the opponent. Taekwondo, the national sport of South Korea, is characterized by kicks delivered above the opponent's waist. It is contested as an Olympic sport. Other countries adopted particular styles of wrestling. In Turkey, wrestlers oil their bodies before grappling with an opponent. The object is to put an opponent on his back. Such wrestling tournaments have been conducted in the country since the fourteenth century. Japanese sumo wrestlers have also competed for centuries. They attempt to throw an opponent to the ground or push him out of a ring. Sumo wrestling is a professional sport in Japan, and it has attracted many foreigners as competitors who vie for rankings in a series of tournaments to become a grand champion. Although soccer is the national sport in Brazil, capoeira – a stylized, artistic martial art developed by slaves as a form of self-defense – is endemic to the country. It has evolved into an acrobatic dance form with music, similar to breakdancing. Its popularity has reached international proportions.

Buzkashi is the traditional national game of Afghanistan, but it is also played in other central Asian countries. Rules as to the number of players and timed periods differ by country, but the general object is for a horseman to carry and deliver a goat carcass to a goal while being impeded by opponents, who may employ the use of their whips to hinder the progress of the rider in possession of the carcass. A dropped carcass may be retrieved by any rider, and the contest continues. Buzkashi is a professional sport in Kazakhstan, and wealthy sponsors supply the trained horses, not unlike thoroughbred owners who hire jockeys for western-style horse races.

Sepak takraw, the national sport of Malaysia, has been played in that country for centuries, but has now spread throughout Southeast Asia. It is similar to volleyball, but a rattan ball must be propelled over a net without the use of the hands or arms. Other parts of the body are permissible. Three players may be on the court, and scoring is the same as in volleyball. Sepak takraw is included in the Asian Games.

Pelota is a game that has been played in the Basque region of Spain since the thirteenth century. There are several variations in which the ball can be propelled against a wall by hand or by racket. Like tennis, it can be played as singles or doubles. The game has spread beyond the Basque boundaries to European countries and throughout Latin America. Professional players compete in the version known as jai alai in Spain, France, and the United States. The speed of the propelled ball can cause injury, even death, and jai alai is tied to gambling in the United States.

Some sports still serve as symbols of nationalism, and nations still employ sports to promote nationalistic spirit and national pride. In the age of global media, however, all manner of sports can be accessed on the internet and popularized throughout the world. National sports can quickly become international.

FURTHER READING

Alan Bairner (2001) *Sport, Nationalism and Globalisation*. New York: SUNY.

David Black and John Nauright (1998) *Rugby and the South African Nation*. Manchester: Manchester University Press.

Doug Booth (1998) *The Race Game: Sport and Politics in South Africa*. London: Frank Cass.

Paul Dimeo and James Mills, eds. (2001) *Soccer in South Asia: Empire, Nation, Diaspora*. London: Frank Cass.

Mark Dyreson, J. A. Mangan, and Roberta J. Park, eds. (2013) *Mapping an Empire of American Sport: Expansion, Assimilation, Adaptation and Resistance*. New York: Routledge.

Janice Forsyth and Audrey R. Giles, eds. (2013) *Aboriginal Peoples and Sport in Canada: Historical Foundations and Contemporary Issues*. Vancouver: University of British Columbia Press.

Gerald R. Gems (2016) *Sport and the American Occupation of the Philippines: Bats, Balls, and Bayonets*. Lanham, MD: Lexington Books.

Allen Guttmann (1994) *Games and Empires: Modern Sports and Cultural Imperialism*. New York: Columbia University Press.

Eric Hobsbawm (1987) *The Age of Empire: 1875–1914*. London: George Weidenfeld and Nicolson.

Grant Jarvie and Graham Walker, eds. (1994) *Scottish Sport in the Making of the Nation: Ninety Minute Patriots?* Leicester: Leicester University Press.

Richard Holt (1989) *Sport and the British: A Modern History*. Oxford: Clarendon Press.

Dominic Malcolm, Jon Gemmell, and Nahlin Mehta, eds. (2010) *The Changing Face of Cricket: From Imperial to Global Game*. London: Routledge.

J. A. Mangan (1981) *Athleticism in the Victorian and Edwardian Public School: The Emergence and Consolidation of an Educational Ideology*. Cambridge: Cambridge University Press.

J. A. Mangan, ed. (1996) *Tribal Identities: Sport, Nationalism, Identity*. London: Frank Cass.

Don Morrow and Kevin Wamsley (2017) *Sport in Canada: A History*. Don Mills, Ontario: Oxford University Press.

Timothy H. Parsons (2020) *The British Imperial Century, 1815–1914*. Lanham, MD: Rowman & Littlefield.

Greg Ryan and Geoff Watson (2018) *Sport and the New Zealanders: A History*. Auckland: Auckland University Press.

6

SPORT AND RELIGION

Sport organizers have often viewed it as a means to foster amicable relations between countries. Religious rivalries have often been contested on athletic fields; but that is not the case in the Middle East. The Jewish soccer team Beitar Jerusalem was established in 1936, but has refused to employ any Arab Muslim players. Its fanatical supporters yell anti-Arab chants at games and threaten violence against their opponents. Arab countries have banned Israeli teams since 1974 and refused entry to Israeli athletes. Their refusal to compete with Israel has forced the latter to contest its FIFA matches in Europe since 1992. For both sides, sport has become a political weapon.

SPORT AND RELIGION IN THE ANCIENT WORLD

In ancient Egypt, the ruling pharaohs were considered to be gods on earth, intermediaries with the afterlife, revered by their subjects. Despite such ascendant status, even the pharaohs had to demonstrate their physical abilities to rule by running around their palaces or temples as a measure of physical fitness. Some pharaohs also showed their strength by shooting an arrow for distance. The Egyptian goddess of sport, Sekhet, oversaw the recreational sports of the common people (Guttmann 2004).

In ancient Greece, the city-states were often at war; but Greeks were more united in their religious ideology, which revolved around 12 major gods who were worshiped in temples and honored in regular festivals that included athletic events. The oldest of the spectacles can be traced back to 776 BCE with the start of the Olympic Games, held quadrennially in veneration of Zeus. The Pythian Games in honor of Apollo, the god of youth and beauty, originated in 582 BCE and were staged at Delphi. That same year, the Isthmian Games were established at Corinth to pay homage to Poseidon, god of the sea. The Nemean Games, which also glorified Apollo, started in 573 BCE. Women, who were largely banned from the Olympic Games but ran races at the other festivals and minor competitions, had their own events to honor Hera, the wife of Zeus (Gems 2014b).

In Meso-America, the Mayan Empire exended from southern Mexico through Central America into present-day Guatemala. Its creation myth, known as Popol Vuh, involved a ball game. Their temple complexes included an arena for a ball game, similar to modern soccer in that players could not use their hands to score goals. The game was also associated with human sacrifices to the gods. In the southwestern region of North America and northern Mexico, long-distance running, sometimes accompanied by kicking a ball or stick, was associated with fertility rites. The Hopi, Navajo, and Zuni tribes continue the running traditions of their ancestors. The Tarahumara of north central Mexico were especially noted for their ability to run long distances in a single event or across several days (Oxendine 1988).

EUROPEAN RELIGIOUS INFLUENCES

When King Henry VIII of England divorced Catherine of Aragon in 1534, he violated the doctrine of the Catholic Church that forbade such action. When he was expelled from the Catholic Church, he declared himself head of the Church of England (Anglican Church). Henry loved to hunt and to play tennis, but he placed some restrictions on sports during his reign. Peasants and commoners were forbidden to play tennis, bowling, skittles, or shovelboard, and football was banned in 1540. Such prohibitions were meant to limit gambling and in the case of football, which might produce severe injuries and death, to insure fitness for military purposes (Trueman 2015).

With the growth of Protestantism during the sixteenth century, factionalism ensued over doctrinal differences. One group, the Puritans, sought a complete break with the Catholic Church and its rituals and ceremonies. They adopted the Calvinist belief that man was sinful by nature and humans were predestined to heaven or hell. Sport, if it had no useful purpose, was forbidden. Philip Stubbes, a Puritan, wrote that 'any exercise which withdraws us from godliness, either upon the Sabbath or any other day, is wicked, and to be forbidden'; he especially disdained football as 'a friendly kind of fight [rather] than play or recreation, a bloody and murdering practice [rather] than a fellowly sport or pastime' (Gems, Borish and Pfister 2017: 12).

Sabbatarianism became a prominent issue, and Puritans complained to King James I regarding the sporting practices of others on Sundays. The king ruled in the *Declaration of Sports* (also known as the *Book of Sports*) in 1618 that sport had beneficial qualities, such as preparation for war, and served as a substitute to drinking in taverns. He allowed sporting activities to be conducted on Sunday afternoons after morning church services. Some Puritans left the country and settled in Holland. In 1620, they set sail for America, where they established the Massachusetts Bay Colony. There they attempted to enforce their religious beliefs as a model for the rest of the world. Puritans who remained in England would eventually foment a civil war in 1642.

On Christmas Day of 1621, Governour William Bradford of Plymouth in Massachusetts reprimanded the young men whom he found 'in ye streets at play, openly; some pitching ye ball and some at stooleball, and such like sports' (quoted in Higgs 1995: 2). The Puritans tried to enforce their views on useless sport, such as bowling, which was popular at taverns. The game was played with nine pins, and when the law stipulated the ban on the game of nine pins, some wily bowler simply added or subtracted a pin, a technicality that circumvented the ruling. Nor could the Puritans enforce their beliefs throughout the vast stretches of America. As more settlers traveled to the new world, new colonies brought Quakers to Pennsylvania, Catholics to Maryland, and assorted other religious groups to new communities. Even in Massachusetts, Puritan beliefs dissipated over time.

By the mid-nineteenth century, sport became a means to achieve a 'muscular Christianity,' a religious masculine ideal depicted in the novels of Charles Kingsley and in Thomas Hughes's *Tom Brown's Schooldays* (1857). The authors idealized the education of public school boys, who learned to be religious, moral, and athletic gentlemen and whose patriotic spirit would benefit the British Empire (Putney 2001).

In the United States, abolitionist preacher Thomas Wentworth Higginson took up the call of the British authors relative to espousing a muscular Christianity. Higginson reached a national audience with his essay 'Saints and Their Bodies,' in which he advocated gymnastics, sports, and outdoor exercises for men to obtain spiritual as well as physical health (Higginson 1858).

In England the game of cricket assumed religious characteristics by the nineteenth century. 'Lord's, the appropriately named home of the premier Marylebone Cricket Club, became sacred ground trod with reverence by those who weighed and pondered and worshipped' (Baker 2010: 221). W. G. Grace, the greatest of cricket players, assumed the proportions of a deity. The British would go on to spread their secular religion throughout their colonial empire.

THE YMCA AS A RELIGIOUS FORCE

The Industrial Revolution had transformed England by the mid-nineteenth century; but it had not improved the health of workers mired in unhealthy labor and living conditions. In 1844, one of them, George Williams, invited friends to Bible study and prayers as a spiritual antidote. The group became known as the Young Men's Christian Association (YMCA). It soon expanded its meetings to include public lectures, classes, and reading rooms to attract others. The YMCA reached the United States by 1851 when a building was opened as a refuge for sailors. Throughout the next decade, the American YMCA provided housing for young men, and in 1869 the New York YMCA offered a gymnasium to attract athletes. Canadian YMCAs soon followed and the North Americans staged track meets, tennis tournaments, baseball, football, and ice hockey games (Baker 2010).

A Young Women's Christian Association (YWCA) was established in England in 1855, and a women's prayer group in the United States evolved into a YWCA in 1866. By 1870, African American women hosted their own club. The YWCAs, however, initially disdained physicality; but the 'new women' of the latter decades, took readily to sport, and by the 1890s, gyms became a prominent feature (Putney 2001).

Thomas Hughes toured America in the 1870s espousing muscular Christianity and even founding a utopian colony in Tennessee in 1880 (Putney 2001). The merger of sport and religion had reached an accommodation never foreseen by the American Puritan forefathers.

American companies employed the YMCA to inculcate Christian virtues in their workforces 'to keep them from evil. To win them to become Christian gentlemen, industrious workmen, good citizens, loyal to their homes and the church' (Smith, Grant, and Starkey 1898: 29). Dwight Moody, one of America's most prominent evangelists, toured the country and Europe promoting the cause. Billy Sunday, a former professional baseball player, toured the United States for decades, drawing large crowds through histrionic displays in theaters. For some, however, the gym moreso than the message proved most attractive. Ed Morris, a professional baseball player, wrote to the *Sporting and Theatrical Journal*, the bible of the bachelor subculture, that he had not 'become religious, his object in joining the Association being to get the use of its gym' (*Sporting and Theatrical Journal* 1887: 7).

The gambling on sport and the increasing violence of the American version of football would temper the belief in sport as a bastion of morality by the end of the nineteenth century; but the YMCA maintained its role as a champion of muscular Christianity. During the American Civil War, YMCA volunteers had administered to the physical and spiritual needs of soldiers on both sides of the conflict, including service as surgeons and nurses. In the Spanish-American War, the YMCA provided entertainment, and in World War I it constructed huts where soldiers could seek solace, make use of its library, watch films, listen to music, and particiapte in its recreational programs. The YMCA provided sports equipment for cricket, tennis, boxing, and hockey. It even established a soccer league in France for British troops. Its services extended to prisoners of war (Hanna 2015).

The YMCA's close association with the American military fostered its growth as an international entity. YMCA instructors invented the games of basketball and volleyball in the 1890s, and they introduced both to the Philippines. The YMCA accompanied the first contingent of troops in the Spanish-American War of 1898, supplying sports equipment and competitions in baseball and boxing by 1901. By 1907, it had constructed separate dormitories for white people and Filipinos, adhering to the segregation practices in the United States. It also applied for a tax exemption as a religious organization.

Despite the American constitutional separation of church and state, the YMCA became a virtual arm of the American administration in the islands thereafter, introducing American sport forms to the local populace. YMCA employees served the colonial government as director of public education, members of the playground committee, and in the preparation of the recreation manual. YMCA Director Elwood Brown created the Philipines Amateur Athletic Federation (PAAF) in 1911 with Governor General W. Cameron Forbes, a former football coach, as the president. They intended to change the physical and moral character of the indigenous peoples. YMCA Secretary General J. M. Groves claimed sport to be a 'substitute for the false ideal of a gentleman as a perfumed dandy, afraid of soiling his fingers, an ideal grafted on an Oriental stock' (quoted in Gems 2016: 72).

The moral crusade included American soldiers and expatriates as well as the Filipinos who gambled on cockfights, frequented brothels and dance halls, and rejected church services. A multitude of Americam Protestant missionaries founded schools and introduced the American national game of baseball as a wholesome activity and a means to socially control youth.

The YMCA and the colonial administrators were greatly aided in their moral campaign by Episcopalian Bishop Charles Brent, who arrived in the Philippines in 1902. Brent subscribed to and practiced muscular Christianity, playing a number of sports with other white leaders. He was one of the founders of the Columbia Club in 1904, which provided bowling, billiards, an indoor swimming pool, and a gym, but no hard liquor. The Philippines Supreme Court granted the club a tax exemption, counting its athletic efforts as religious work.

Brent succeeded Governor General Forbes as president of the PAAF in 1914. He also established hospitals, settlement houses, and schools, but maintained segregation in the latter. Brent stated that 'it grieves me whenever I see one of my fellow citizens tied to a Filipina; it seems to be unnatural, and ordinarily, I cannot get away from a sense of degradation connected with it' (quoted in Gems 2016: 91).

The Catholic Church, which ruled religious matters in the Philippines for centuries, did not take kindly to the massive invasion of Protestant missionaries. It sent additional priests to the islands to reinforce its own interests and provided its own sport programs to compete with the Protestants. Those who joined the YMCA were threatened with excommunication. The Catholic efforts combined with the Americans' segregation practices eventually led to the diminished influence of the YMCA, particularly after the departure of Bishop Brent and Elwood Brown to serve the American military in World War I (Gems 2016).

The YMCA efforts to minister to soldiers in Europe during World War I met with mixed results. Working-class soldiers often rejected the middle-class piety that the YMCA workers tried to instill as over-bearing. They disliked having to pay for cigarettes at the YMCA huts when they could get them for free from the Knights of Columbus, a Catholic fraternal organization founded in 1882, intended to provide benefits to working-class immigrants in the United States. Sports activities had some success in social control, occupying soldiers' lei-sure time when they might have been at a local brothel. Some con-sidered the male YMCA workers as 'slackers,' too cowardly to serve in combat. One critic stated, 'that sissyfied son of a gun is using up gasolene over here to warn us fellows against the skirts, when he ought to be down in the trenches where he belongs or get the blazes out o' here' (Putney 2001: 191).

Elwood Brown organized the Inter-Allied Games, a military Olympics, in the wake of World War I. The YMCA spread its reli-gious message and its games, particularly basketball and volleyball, on an international scale. Basketball became the national sport of the Philippines, but it remained a Catholic country.

While the YMCA's overt religiosity became more muted over the course of the twentieth century, the linkage of evangelical Christianity with sport continued. In 1945, the Youth for Christ movement began, later growing into an international enterprise. The Fellowship of Christian Athletes was established in 1954, followed by Athletes in Action in 1966. Both are evangelical Christian groups that proselytize members of youth, college, and professional teams. In 1990, an American football coach founded Promise Keepers, which promotes conservative Christian values through its international membership.

CATHOLIC SPORT

In Europe, Catholics banded together in 1906 as the French formed a gymnastic federation. With the approval of Pope Pius X in 1908, it expanded its reach to include Catholicism in other countries. By 1911, it became an international union.

In Ireland, the founding of the Gaelic Athletic Association forged nationalist identity with the Catholic religion. When Catholic migrants to Scotland formed their own soccer clubs and vied with the Scottish Protestant teams, the games assumed religious fervor. In Glasgow, the Protestant Rangers, founded in 1872, and the Catholic Celtics, established in 1888, waged religious and political battles. Throughout most of the tewntieth century, Rangers refused to employ Catholics. Confrontations on the pitch often resulted in violence, even deaths, outside of the stadium (Baker 2010).

With the rise of the YMCA in the late nineteenth century, American Catholic leaders established their own agencies to counteract Protestant influences. By the turn of the century, the programs of the Knights of Columbus included opportunities for sports such as baseball. Some Catholic high schools traveled across the country to meet opponents. Over the next two decades, Catholic schools in the major American cities formed their own sports leagues and challenged the public schools, presumed to be Protestant entities, to local championship matches. Rejected as less than full members in Protestant America, sport became a religious crusade for recognition and inclusion.

During World War I, Catholics comprised between 35% and 40% of the US Army. They assumed that this level of military service would win them acceptance among the Protestant majority; but distrust remained. When a Catholic, Al Smith, ran for president in 1924 and again in 1928, he was roundly rejected.

Notre Dame University, a small Catholic college in the American Midwest, assumed the mantle of Catholic champion in the 1920s. Led by famed coach Knute Rockne, it amassed four national football championships in the 1920s and became the most famous college team in the United States. In 1924, the resurgent Ku Klux Klan – a racist white supremacist organization that ostracized black people, Catholics, and Jews – marched on South Bend, Indiana, home of Notre Dame. It threatened to blow up the institution but was foiled by students, led by their football stars.

The athletic confrontation between Catholics and Protestants was played out among school teams in Chicago when the Catholic high school football champion challenged the Public League champion in 1927 to determine true city title holder. In a titanic struggle, the small Catholic school faced one ten times its size, yet it prevailed before 50,000 spectators. The city championship became an annual affair, with 120,000 fans at the 1937 contest – more than have ever witnessed the professional Super Bowl – in a secular battle for religious supremacy (Gems 1996b).

The Catholic Youth Organization (CYO), founded by Bishop Bernard Sheil in Chicago in 1930, soon reached international proportions. Initially organized as a boxing tournament, the CYO soon expanded its offerings, and its basketball league became the largest in the world. Sheil accepted non-Catholics into the organization, but required a pledge to God, country, and Christianity; although Jewish boxing champions Benny Leonard and Barney Ross served the CYO as boxing instructors. Within a year, CYO fighters were engaged in international bouts, soon traveling the world, and three of its fighters made the 1936 Olympic team. Many others would go on to professional boxing careers, managed by Catholic officials. The CYO's immense sporting enterprise garnered greater acceptance of Catholicism as it forged working-class ethnic communities into a patriotic American whole (Gems 2014a).

JEWISH SPORT

B'nai B'rith, a Jewish fraternal organization, founded in New York in 1843, expanded to international proportions throughout the nineteenth century. Its campaign against anti-Semitism and promotion of the state of Israel gathered momentum thereafter. Similar to the CYO for Catholic youth, the B'nai B'rith Youth Organization offered sports programs for Jewish youth. The two programs cooperated in joint ventures during the twentieth century.

The Maccabiah Games, known as the Jewish Olympics (profiled in Chapter 5), were first held in 1932 in Tel Aviv. The winter version followed a year later in Poland, and the second, and last, Winter Games, took place in Czechoslovakia in 1936. Such sporting activities, known as 'muscular Judaism,' countered the racist stereotype of the feeble Jew who lacked physical prowess.

Boxing enabled Jews to destroy such persistent myths. The first great Jewish boxer, Daniel Mendoza, was born in England of Sephardic ancestry in 1764. A scientific fighter, Mendoza pioneered defensive techniques that allowed him to defeat much bigger men. Though measuring only 5'7" (170 centimeters) and weighing 160 pounds (73 kilograms), he managed to capture the English heavyweight championship, which he held in the bare-knuckle era from 1792 to 1795.

Jewish boxers would continue to win laurels throughout the nineteenth century; but Ted 'Kid' Lewis, the son of Russian Jewish immigrants, won esteem as world welterweight champ during World War I. His American contemporary Benny Leonard, lightweight champion, espoused his Judaism by wearing the Star of David in his boxing trunks. He also refused to fight on Jewish holidays. Leonard became a symbol of Jewish American assimilation, raising war bonds in World War I, acting as a CYO boxing instructor, and serving in the US Maritime Service during World War II (Gems 2014a).

Barney Ross turned to boxing to relieve his family's impoverished existence after the murder of his father. He traded his amateur trophies for cash at local pawn shops before turning professional. Like Benny Leonard, he refused to fight on Jewish High Holy Days and wore the Star of David on his trunks. He became world welterweight champion in 1934, and when World War II erupted, he joined the Marine Corps and became a combat hero. After the war, he engaged in gunrunning activities in support of the new Jewish state in Palestine, a symbol of muscular Judaism (Gems 2014a).

Much of the early historiography of Jewish sport has amounted to cheerleading for Jewish athletes who managed to demonstrate assimilation into American culture and win greater acceptance of Jews.

Jeffrey Gurock (2005) has documented the particular difficulties of Orthodox Jews and their participation in the sporting culture. Ari Sclar states that a 'closer examination to the conflicts that religious Jews have in integrating the values of Judaism and sports may help lead the study of Jewish athleticism toward more complex meaning systems that contain ideas about identity, religious, traditions, and values' (2014: 177).

MUSLIM SPORT

Arguably the best-known Muslim athlete throughout the twentieth century was Muhammad Ali. When Ali (then Casssius Clay) faced Sonny Liston for the heavyweight championship in 1964, Malcolm X told him that

> this fight is the truth, It's the Cross and the Crescent fighting in the prize ring – for the first time. It's a modern crusade – a Christian and a Muslim facing each other with television to beam it off Telstar for the whole world to see what happens.
>
> (Quoted in Higgs 1995: 16)

Ali would later face prison for adhering to his Black Muslim (also known as Nation of Islam) belief in nonviolence and his refusal to fight in the Vietnam War. Elijah Muhammad, leader of the Black Muslims, had been incarcerated for his refusal to join the military in World War II.

In the wake of Ali's ascendance as a religious and social icon, 'Kareem Abdul-Jabbar marched at the head of an impressive parade of African-American athletes from all sectors of American sport trumpeting the rituals and moral code of the Islamic faith' (Baker 2010: 225). Jabbar excelled in the NBA as a leading scorer, winning six championships and taking the Most Valuable Player award six times; but he assumed greater importance as a political and social activist. Mahmoud Abdul-Rauf also played in the NBA, but he suffered a suspension in 1996 after he failed to stand for the pregame national anthem as a protest against racism. Death threats followed and his home was set on fire, and he had to seek employment abroad.

Nawal El Moutawakel, a Moroccan track star, became the first Muslim woman to win an Olympic gold medal at the 1984 Olympics in the 400 meter hurdles race. Her accomplishment paved the way for future Islamic female athletes, and she became an IOC vice-president and Minister of Sports in her home country. Other female Muslim athletes have had a more difficult journey. Hassiba Boulmerka, an Algerian runner, won the gold medal in the 1,500 meter run at the 1992 Olympics, but received death threats from those who felt she exposed too much of her body in the process. Ruqsana Begum, a world Muay Thai champion, grew up in a more moderate environment in England, but had to overcome an arranged marriage to meet her goals.

Muslim male athletes don't face the same religious hurdles. Mo Farah, born in Somalia but raised in England, had great success on the track, winning both the 5,000 meter and the 10,000 meter runs at the 2012 and 2016 Olympics. Beloved by British fans, he uses his fame in philanthropical endeavors for his homeland.

Mo Salah, an Egyptian favorite in the English Premier League, is also beloved in his homeland, where his charitable works benefit the poor. A proficient scorer, he celebrates his Muslim faith by prostrating himself in a prayerful bow after each goal. Another Muslim soccer player, Zinedine Zidane, led France to the 1998 World Cup title, making him a national hero. He was named the FIFA Player of the Year three times, and in 2004 UEFA (Union of European Football Associations) acknowleged Zidane as the best European soccer player of the past 50 years. In 2016, he was named one of the 500 most influential Muslims in the world.

Imran Khan, one of the best cricket players in the world, starred as a bowler for Pakistan. As the team captain, he led Pakistan to a World Cup championship in 1992. His post-playing career proved to be even more impressive, as he formed his own political party, winning election to the office of prime minister in 2018. His philanthropy has benefited nations throughout Asia.

Religious strife has been a hallmark of Asia for centuries, and this has been played out in sport. In 1947, India achieved its independence from Great Britain, but the country was soon divided into separate autonomous nations. Muslims inhabited Pakistan, which consisted of East and West Pakistan on two sides of India, where Hindus and Sikhs remained in residence. In a 1971 war of liberation, East Pakistan won its independence to become the nation of Bangladesh.

Continual tension has persisted between the religious partisans, noticeable in the surrogate wars on the cricket field. India and Pakistan first met in a cricket match in 1952; but politics and open warfare between the countries resulted in cancellations of team tours between 1962 and 1977, and again at the turn of the twenty-first century. Matches were conducted at neutral sites, but sectarian violence has superseded the potential value of sport as a diplomatic opportunity and shared pleasure.

The Beitar Jerusalem soccer club, mentioned earlier, has exhibited serious racial and religious biases over the years. It had never hired an Arab or Muslim player for its team. When two non-Arab Muslim players were signed to the club in 2013, its clubhouse was set on fire by intransigent fans, and the players soon departed. The hostile fans of the club persist in racist chants and violent behavior, vowing, to the dishonor of the club, never to accept an Arab or Muslim.

SPORT AS A SECULAR RELIGION

Since the late twentieth century, scholars have noted the shared characteristics of sports and religion. As religiosity has waned in the postmodern world, some have even ascertained that sport has become a form of secular religion (Hoffman 1992, 2010; Prebish 1993; Higgs 1995). In 1912, French sociologist Emile Durkheim defined religion as the shared beliefs that are celebrated in scared rites in order to foster social cohesion. By 1990, Danish scholar Ove Korsgaard (1990) reflected that sport might serve as a symbolic victory of life over death. Players and fans alike might experience such an occurrence as games go into overtime. Both religion and sport promote idealistic philosophies that promote character development, ethical conduct, meritocracy, discipline, and self-sacrifice. Both have rules of conduct, enforced by clergy in the case of religious groups or league administrators, who serve as the high priests of sport (Gems 2020).

Both religion and sport engage in rituals, pageantry, festivals, and spectacles. Baptism is a religious ritual, as is a bar or bat mitzvah. Ball games are often started with the ritual of a national anthem, and the Olympic Games reward medal winners in a similar ceremony. Choirs raise spirits in a church, while sports fans do so with cheers and chants. Religious festivals are superseded in media attention by the Olympic Games. The World Cup spectacle and the pilgrimage of many to its site is not unlike the Muslim worship at Mecca. The sacred sites of religion have a counterpart in the sports halls of fame. There, the fans see the sporting artifacts, not unlike those at the religious shrines. While the religious travel to houses of worship, sports fans make trips to the stadiums that have been termed the 'cathedrals' of sport (Trumpbour 2007). Just as religion has it saints, sport has its heroes and secular gods, who seemingly surpass the feats of ordinary humans. Religious priests dispense the dogma of their particular faith, while sport scribes perform the same duty for avid fans. Both have true believers, devotees, and converts (Higgs 1995).

Both religion and sport can produce mystical as well as phenomenonological experiences in the kinesthetic beuty of human performance and the miraculous feats of athletes. The runner's high can result in a trance-like state, perhaps similar to the religious rapture of those who commune in some fundamentalist congregations. Such catharsis might be readily felt by a fan whose team or favored athlete suddenly turns a supposed defeat into an unimagined victory (Gems 2020).

Both sport and religion induce hope for the future and provide a sense of transcendence; but they also require an emotional commitment and a social bonding with fellow devout followers as part of a shared experience in what Benedict Anderson has termed an 'imagined community' (Gems 2020; Anderson 1993).

In looking back on her storied tennis career during the interwar years of the twentieth century, Helen Wills Moody captured the essence of that spirit where she found

> another world in which there is sunshine, the wonderful feeling of movement through space and air, speed, the thrill of muscles in action and the remoteness from everything except the game of the moment. There are, also, degrees of pleasure, surprise, suspense, disappointment, and many of the emotions that exist in life itself. The game may seem to suffice in completing a world of its own, a world in which its devoted follower may move as in a dream. And, if you have played your game well, you feel contented.
>
> (Quoted in Engelmann 1988: 440)

FURTHER READING

Eric Bain-Selbo (2009) *Game Day and God: Football, Faith, and Politics in the American South*. Macon, GA: Mercer University Press.

William J. Baker (2007) *Playing with God: Religion and Modern Sport*. Cambridge, MA: Harvard University Press.

Jeffrey S. Gurock (2005) *Judaism's Encounter with American Sports*. Bloomington: Indiana University Press.

Allen Guttmann (2004) *Sports: The First Five Millennia*. Amherst: University of Massachusetts Press.

Robert J. Higgs (1995) *God in the Stadium: Sport and Religion in America*. Lexington: University Press of Kentucky.

Shirl J. Hoffman (2010) *Good Game: Christianity and the Culture of Sports*. Waco, TX: Baylor University Press.

Richard Ian Kimball (2009) *Sports in Zion: Mormon Recreation, 1890–1940*. Urbana: University of Illinois Press.

Tara Magdalinski and Timothy J. L. Chandler, eds. (2002) *With God on Their Side: Sport in the Service of Religion*. London: Routledge.

Arne Naess-Holm (2008) *Batting for Peace: A Study of Cricket Diplomacy between India and Pakistan*. Saarbrucken: VDM Verlag.

Clifford Putney (2001) *Muscular Christianity: Manhood and Sports in Protestant America, 1880–1920*. Cambridge, MA: Harvard University Press.

7

SPORT AND LEISURE

Many leisure activities practiced in Europe were transferred to the American colonies. Gander pulling continued into the late nineteenth century. It crossed class and gender lines, as any male might enter the competition, which attracted crowds of male and female spectators who might gamble on the outcome. The objective of the contest was to pull the greased head off of a goose that hung by its feet from a post or a tree limb. Usually conducted on horseback, it might also be done on a waterway by standing in a rowed boat. The successful competitor won the goose as his dinner and public acclaim as a symbol of his masculinity.

Leisure is nonwork, free time which may be devoted to rest or recreation. The recreational activities available in modern societies are many, but that was not always the case. Leisure was limited in varying degrees for slaves, peasants, and the industrial working classes. In the ascribed and hereditary social order of European nobility, leisure activities served to define one's social class. The leisure activities of the gentry distinguished them from the common folk. With the onset of the Industrial Revolution, the emergent middle class of entrepreneurs and white-collar workers gained more leisure time than the laborers who generally worked six days per week for minimal wages. The latter had little time or money to pursue recreational activities.

Religion can also affect how one spends one's leisure time. Early Puritans favored work over play and admonished those who failed to subscribe to their sabbatarian principles. In the Hindu caste system of India, the established hierarchical social order limits opportunities for many. The untouchables on the lowest tier of society may have enforced leisure time due to lack of employment or menial work, but little income to pursue recreational activities.

LEISURE IN A STRATIFIED SOCIAL SYSTEM

Cuju, a form of football, was played in Asia for centuries and attracted spectators. The game crossed social class lines, as it was played by royalty as well as the common people in China. Both men and women played cuju, as well as archery and polo. The latter was a favorite of the Chinese emperors. Both royalty and commoners engaged in an early form of golf in which curved sticks were used to hit a ball into a hole. The Chinese later adopted figure skating and speed skating competitions as winter sports. Japanese practiced kendo (swordplay), archery, and other martial arts to develop mental as well as physical skills. Sumo wrestling remains a major spectator sport with regular tournaments, while judo, aikido, and karate have drawn practitioners for centuries.

In the feudal system of medieval Europe, social hierarchy greatly determined leisure activities. The monarchy and associated nobility held vast expanses of land, where they built country estates and lodges for leisure and entertainment purposes. There, they played games such as dice, cards, and chess. Some had private tennis courts, but hunting proved most popular. Royalty reserved private hunting grounds, and poaching of its deer could result in blinding or the death penalty. Hunts might continue over several days, followed by nights of feasting, dancing, and revelry.

For the knights who served the lords, leisure time afforded the opportunity to engage in tournaments that tested their martial skills and which might bring additional income and social stature. The tournaments originally consisted of mock warfare in which groups of allied knights attacked other groups in attempts to capture opponents, who then had to forfeit their expensive armor and horses and pay a ransom. William Marshal (c. 1147–1219), widely considered to be the greatest knight of his era, proved so successful at such ventures that he amassed wealth and celebrity, serving five kings and winning elevation to the regency (Asbridge 2015).

Such tournaments eventually evolved into elaborate chivalric festivals of martial display that included jousting, in which knights with lances tried to unhorse their opponents. A circuit of such tournaments existed throughout Europe, and some knights traveled extensively to demonstrate their martial prowess and to win favor and riches. In 1559, King Henry II of France competed in such a tournament in Paris. While jousting, his opponent's lance shattered, and splinters pierced his eye and brain, resulting in his death (Cavendish 2009).

Falconry was a sport reserved for nobility. It had long roots in the Middle East and Asia before making its appearance in Europe. It languished after the Renaissance era, but is still practiced in Mongolia. King Henry VIII of England particularly enjoyed tennis and had a court built at his Hampton residence in 1528. Lawn bowling also proved popular. Henry's daughter Queen Elizabeth I was especially fond of hunting. Among the peasantry, raucous football games in towns and villages occurred with some frequency. Injuries and occasional deaths ensued as rules were deficient and the game continued until one side reached the assigned goal, often the village boundary of the opponent. Regular village festivals included running races, wrestling and cudgel matches, shovelboard, and pitching the bar that required throwing or tossing a weighted object for distance. Urban dwellers were entertained by bloody animal fights in which a chained bull or bear would be attacked by a group of hostile dogs. Patrons bet on not only the winner of the battle but how many dogs might be killed before the winner was determined. Such 'sport' transferred to the American colonies, where there was a greater abundance of bears to be had. Cockfights, too, were a pleasure of the common man, who lacked the means to gamble on horse races (Holt 1989).

In Venice, Italy, during the sixteenth century, young men gathered on the city bridges, pummeling each other with sticks and fists until one side gained control. Such bouts of violence drew thousands of spectators. Eventually, agreed-upon rules resulted in singular boxing matches among local favorites (Davis 1998). In Siena, the Palio horse race originated in 1656 as a means for the winning district to claim honor, not unlike the sponsored neighborhood chariot races of ancient Rome.

Fox hunting assumed prominence as a social sport among the upper class in Britain during the seventeenth century; a legal ban was placed on the activity at the dawn of the twenty-first century. The activity required an expanse of land, a horse, and a pack of hunting dogs. Polished equestrian skills were needed to arrive upon the cornering of the fox. Fox hunting also took hold in Germany, and in the American colonies and Australia, where the practice continues.

Members of the lower classes also hunted throughout history, but as least as much for sustenance as for sport. Throughout the world, such hunting is regulated to safeguard the maintenance of animal stocks; although big game hunters in Africa and India have come under attack for their indiscretions as well as poaching activities.

The wealthy distinguished themselves by the types of sport in which they could and did engage. Upon his return from exile in the Netherlands in 1660, the Dutch gifted King Charles II of England with a yacht. The Dutch would also introduce such ships to their colony in North America. Cork, Ireland, established the first yacht club in 1720, and in England, races on the Thames River in London became more common at this time. In the United States in 1816, at a cost of $50,000, George Crowninshield, a Boston merchant, built a yacht which he dubbed *Cleopatra's Barge*. The next year he embarked for Europe to challenge European yachtsmen. In 1844, John Cox Stevens established the New York Yacht Club, with membership limited to the city's elite. Stevens defeated the British yachtsmen in the first America's Cup race in 1851; this is a nationalistic competition that continues in the twenty-first century (Gems, Borish, and Pfister 2017).

Gambling on sport permeated all classes; but exorbitant wagers remained the province of the upper class. In 1750, the Duke of Cumberland, son of King George II, bet the enormous sum of 10,000 British pounds and even offered 10 to 1 odds on a boxing match between the champion Jack Broughton and challenger Jack Slack. The duke put his money on Broughton, but lost when the boxer was blinded by a blow and lost the match (Gems 2014a).

Large amounts were also wagered on horse races. In the American colonies, the southern gentry placed great emphasis on the speed of their horses and bet accordingly. A resident of the Virginia colony remarked in 1724 that 'the common planters, leading easy lives, don't much admire labor or any manly exercise except horse-racing, nor diversion except cock-fighting' (Guttmann 2004: 120). Some lost immense sums; but that only reinforced their social capital, as they could afford to absorb such setbacks. Well into the twentieth century, the wealthy traveled to horse racing tracks in elaborate coaches drawn by fine horses and driven by uniformed liverymen. Bedecked in elaborate costumes, the women dressed to attract attention, what sociologist Thorstein Veblen in *The Theory of the Leisure Class* (1899), a critical assessment of how the upper class competed for recognition and social standing, termed 'ostentatious display' and 'conspicuous consumption.'

The slaves of the American plantation owners enjoyed limited leisure time in which they played music and danced, sometimes secretly caricaturing the owners. Fishing and gardening supplemented meager diets. Like the gentry, they gambled, but with lesser stakes, at cards, dice, and bowling. Slaves served as jockeys for their masters' horse races, in which case a loss might be blamed on the rider to lessen the tarnish of the owner's honor. Slaves engaged in running and jumping contests, but also wrestled and boxed, often pitted against opponents from other plantations for the amusement of their masters (Wiggins 1980).

Slaves, whose lives were mired in physicality, often proved more adept at swimming than the white people.

John Clinkscales contended that in the antebellum years one of his father's slaves ... named Essex was 'by odds the best swimmer on [his] father's place' and possibly even [in] the country, suggesting his reputation was perhaps earned in interplantation contests. In the seventeenth century Richard Ligon observed planter-organized contest in which Barbadian slaves had to catch a duck placed in a large pond. The captor was awarded the duck, presumably to eat or sell it. The proprietor of these Sunday 'recreations,' Colonel Drax, 'calling for some of his best swimming Negroes, commanded them to swim and take his Duck (sic); but forbad them to dive, for if they were not bar'd that play, they would rise up under the Duck (sic), and take her as she swome (sic), or meet her in her diving, and so the sport would have too quick an end.

(Dawson 2006: 1341)

In the coastal regions of the Carolinas, slaves dove for pearls. In the ocean and waterways they confronted sharks and even engaged in combat, often killing them with knives (Dawson 2006). Such displays of courage and physical prowess proved their masculinity, which the white populace had denied. Anthropologist Clifford Geertz (1972), in his seminal essay on Balinese cockfighting, indicates that sport can be read as a text. The whole village participated in the cock-fights, and when the rooster of the common folk defeated that of the chief, the commoners enjoyed a temporary exultation within the village, gaining a sense of social status and economic capital on the wagers won. Such inversions of the status hierarchy, though tempo-rary, relieved class divisions and maintained a level of harmony in the community. Similarly in the American colonies, enslaved peoples found the means to occasionally satisfy their psychic and emotional needs through their sporting practices.

INDUSTRIAL REVOLUTION

The Industrial Revolution began in the latter eighteenth century in England and spread to Europe and the United States thereafter. Spurred by new forms of energy (steam and electricity), transporta-tion and shipping networks fostered by railroads, and imperial colo-nies that supplied natural resources and markets for finished goods, a global capitalist economy emerged, situated in urban localities. Manufacturing and mechanized products produced goods faster and more cheaply than the individual craftsmen of earlier eras. Such his-torical remnants were forced to move on or accept wage labor in the multitude of factories that appeared in the cities.

The Industrial Revolution spawned a number of occupations, such as managers, clerks, accountants, and entrepreneurs, that joined the doctors, teachers, lawyers, civil servants, and others who composed an emergent middle class with more income and more leisure time. The additional leisure time was filled with entertainment and rec-reation options, such as theatrical and musical productions, circuses, amusement parks, the emergence of vaudeville by the late nineteenth century, and new forms of sport.

Croquet, skating, cycling, tennis, and golf offered opportuni-ties for public socialization that changed the traditional courtship rituals of the Victorian period. Chaperones were no longer required or might be evaded. The middle class enjoyed expendable income that might be spent on beach holidays or cycling excursions. By the mid-nineteenth century, men in America turned to baseball, which soon became the national game in the United States. Middle-class women started their own teams by the 1860s. Golf greatly expanded in the nineteenth century and was played by both men and women. The course in St. Andrews in Scotland, played as early as the fifteenth century, had always been available for public use. The first public course in the United States opened in New York City in 1895, as the game became more accessible to middle-class aspirants.

The convergence of capitalism, urbanization, and industrialization did not improve the conditions for the working class. They worked long hours, six days a week, in factories or sweat shops, for meager wages. Some families, including children, worked every day in home-based enterprises, assembling garments or other products. They subsisted in unhealthy conditions in small, fetid apartments, with little light and without fresh air. Most tenement dwellers had to use shared outhouses or resort to chamber pots, and running water was shared with other residents. Indoor toilets did not become commonplace until the twentieth century. Rats infested the premises, and noxious fumes from the factories permeated the urban air. Disease was rampant and life expectancy limited. The little leisure time available presented an opportunity to escape the premises.

Labor strikes in England and the United States began by the late eighteenth century and occurred with greater regularity thereafter as laborers sought better wages and working conditions. Leisure time also became an issue. Influenced by Marxism and socialism, tradesmen and factory employees formed labor unions to confront employers' dictates. By the late nineteenth century, workers campaigned for 'eight hours for what we will,' a limit to their work day (Rosenzweig 1983). For males, limited leisure was often spent in neighborhood saloons, which provided a variety of services for their clients. There they might engage in billiards or bowling, cash a check, mail a letter, find employment, get a shower, and have a cheap meal (Duis 1983; Powers 1998). Others might engage in ball games at local parks while families could enjoy picnics in the outdoors. After the turn of the twentieth century, nickelodeons in the neighborhoods offered silent movies for adults and children.

Employers even attempted to manage their workers' leisure time. In the United States in 1880, George Pullman constructed a company town south of Chicago, complete with extensive sports facilities so that 'the disturbing conditions of strikes and other troubles that periodically convulse the world of labor would not be found here' (Buder 1967: viii). Pullman sponsored teams and athletic festivals to occupy his employees' leisure time, and he mandated temperance. The only bar, in the town hotel, was off limits to employees. Pullman's operation provided a wealth of positive media attention, and other companies soon copied his industrial recreation program. When an economic depression in 1894 caused Pullman to discharge workers, reduce working hours, and cut the wages of others, while maintaining high rent for the workers' housing, the workers organized a massive strike that affected national railroad transport, and violence ensued, requiring the intervention of the federal military. Despite the repercussions, the workers maintained the athletic program in the aftermath, and industrial recreation programs continued to grow throughout the country.

Children played in the city streets or in the designed playgrounds, first opened in Germany in the mid-nineteenth century and soon adopted in England and later in the United States. The parks and playgrounds of the United States were intended, as a means of social control, to teach children the middle-class value systems via play (Cavallo 1981; Gems 1997). Trained instructors supervised games to teach competition, respect for authority, and cooperative team play that would benefit the capitalist democracy.

Economic depressions occurred in cycles during the late nineteenth century, interspersed with two world wars in the twentieth century. Such economic upheavals created forced leisure time for the unemployed. Sport and gambling filled the void for some. In Chicago, neighborhood softball leagues run by local gamblers during the Great Depression of the 1930s provided temporary relief for some players and their fans. Mario Bruno, an Italian immigrant and a team organizer, stated that he won $1,650 on a single game, when the local bank would not offer him even $100 for his paid-up home. Neighborhood teams might earn as much as $1,500 in prize money, equivalent to the annual family income in 1933. Such an underground economy kept money circulating throughout the impoverished urban neighborhoods (Gems 1997).

Robert Owen, a Scottish textile manufacturer and social reformer, campaigned for an eight-hour work day as early as 1817. Women and children were granted an eight-hour day in England in 1847. French workers received a twelve-hour day the next year. Workers typically labored for 10 to 16 hours per day, six days a week. The quest for leisure continued for workers throughout the nineteenth century, and came to fruition for railroad workers in the United States in 1916 when they were granted an eight-hour work day. Labor unions continued to win concessions for workers throughout the twentieth century. Minimum wage laws were enacted in New Zealand in 1894, Australia in 1896, the United Kingdom in 1909, and the United States starting in 1912; but such laws did not cover all industries or all workers. In 1919, Spain became the first country to award all workers an eight-hour day.

Gradually throughout the twentieth century, the eight-hour day, 40-hour week became standard and wages improved, providing more leisure time and more expendable income for workers' leisure. Bourdieu's concept of habitus applied to workers' leisure interests. The physicality of working-class jobs resonated in their leisure pursuits. In England and much of Europe, the working class was attracted to rugged team games, primarily soccer. In the United States, American football superseded baseball as the national sport by the 1960s, and basketball grew in greater proportions among some ethnic and racial groups (Gems and Pfister 2009).

With the growth of the middle and upper classes during the twentieth century, new sport forms emerged and old sport forms became more accessible. Faster modes of travel, such as cruise ships and jet planes, enabled adventurous athletes to pursue skiing, scuba and climbing venues previously available only to the wealthy with unlimited leisure time. Alternative and extreme sports attracted the avant-garde and thrill seekers. Active lifestyles revolved around sporting activities and could be pursued on a year-round basis.

LIFESTYLE SPORTS

Pedestrianism

Humans have engaged in pedestrianism since they became upright beings, but the sport of pedestrianism started to evolve in seventeenth century England when aristocrats wagered on the endurance capabilities of their footmen, who ran along the side of their carriages and cleared paths for their travel. Pedestrianism gained greater media attention when Captain Barclay (Robert Barclay Allardice) won large sums of money for his feats in the first decade of the nineteenth century. In 1809, he managed to cover 1,000 miles in 1,000 hours. Emma Sharp, a female pedestrian, duplicated the mark in 1864.

Norwegian Mensen Ernst worked as a footman for a European prince, but earned extra money by racing dogs, horses, or other men. From 1820, he traveled through Europe engaging in such productions. In 1828, he walked from Egypt to Germany, and four years later covered the distance from Paris to Moscow in 14 days to win 4,000 francs. It took him only 59 days to walk round trip from Constantinople to Calcutta. In 1843, he started from Prussia in northeast Germany to find the source of the Nile in Africa; but on the way he contracted dysentery, which cost him his life (Gems, Borish, and Pfister 2017).

Pedestrianism eventually adopted a go-as-you-please (walking or running) format, and by 1835 American sportsman John Cox Stevens offered a $1,000 purse to the winner of a 10-mile race, with a bonus of $300 if the victor covered the course in less than hour, considered to be an impossibility. The stakes drew an international field of competitors to the Union Race Track in New York. Henry Stannard, an American farmer, finished in 59 minutes and 48 seconds, to much acclaim. The *American Turf Register and Sporting Magazine* reported that

> Stannard … has been in good training for a month. He is a powerful, stalwart young man, and did not seem at all fatigued at the termination of the race. He is greatly indebted to Mr. Stevens, for his success; Mr. S. rode around the course with him the whole distance, and kept cheering him on, and cautioning him against over-exertion in the early part of the race;

at the end of the sixth mile, he made him stop and take a little brandy and water, after which his foot was on the mile mark just as the thirty-six minutes were expired; and as the trumpet sounded he jumped forward gracefully, and cheerfully exclaimed, 'Here I am to time;' and he was within the time every mile.

(Gems, Borish, and Pfister 2017: 107)

The media attention drew crowds and international competitors for such races in succeeding decades. Edward Payson Weston won particular adulation in 1867, walking from Portland, Maine, to Chicago (1,136 miles) in 26 days for a prize of $10,000. In 1909, Weston, at the age of 70, walked across the American continent from New York to San Francisco in 100 days. Weston would be superseded by Daniel O'Leary, an Irish immigrant to the United States, who traveled to Europe and Australia to demonstrate his feats of endurance, once covering 500 miles in less than six days (Reisler 2015).

Cycling

A faster means of locomotion, cycling surpassed pedestrianism in the late nineteenth century. The middle and upper classes who could afford the cost of bicycles took heartily to the pastime as a means of socialization, and cycling clubs permeated urban locations in Europe and America. Cycling proved a boon to the tourism business, and weekend century runs of 100 miles became commonplace. Those of greater means and prolonged leisure were attracted to extended cycling trips through Europe and Asia (Gems 2017).

Cycling became a commercialized competitive event in the latter decades of the nineteenth century, with male and female riders contesting for prize money in urban hippodromes. (See Chapter 3 for gender aspects of cycling and Chapter 4 for racial aspects of cycling.) Like the pedestrian races, cycling races became a phenomenon in urban centers around the world, including some mixed-gender races. The cyclists tested their endurance in six-day races for total distance. In 1903, the Tour de France became the first of several international road races.

Auto racing displaced cycling in the twentieth century in the United States, though Europeans, Asians, and Africans continued to use cycles as a common means of transport and daily commuting. The popularity of cycling enjoyed a resurgence in the 1970s as means to health and fitness. A decade later, mountain biking attracted cyclists to off-road locations, and Californians engaged in BMX (bicycle moto-cross), an activity that requires stunts and speed, on constructed dirt tracks. Many health clubs adopted stationary cycles as part of their regimen of fitness routines for health-conscious members spending their leisure time engaged in cardiovascular workouts.

Running

In early hunting societies, running was essential for chasing game. It was the feature of many of the early Greek Olympic events, and a staple of village festivals thereafter. Fell running in Scotland presaged the cross-country running of the nineteenth century. The Olympic marathon in 1896 renewed interest in long-distance races. A Greek, Spyridon Louis, won the event, becoming a national hero; but few know that two women also ran the distance unofficially. When a woman named Melpomene tried to register for the race, she was denied by the organizers. She ran on her own before the Games and finished in four and a half hours. After Louis's victory, a female admirer ran the same route in his honor: Stamatia Rovithi, a 35-year-old mother of seven children, finished in five and a half hours, but admitted that she had stopped to do some window shopping on the way (Gems, Borish, and Pfister 2017).

The interest in the Olympic marathon event spawned imita-tors. The famous Boston Marathon soon followed in 1897 and was run annually until disrupted by the COVID-19 virus epidemic in 2020. By the 1920s, long-distance races gained media attention in the United States. In 1927, an endurance race from New York to California was won by a Native American, Quanowahu of the Hopi tribe (Cooper 1998). American promoters imported Tarahumaras from northern Mexico, famed for their feats of endurance, through-out the next decade (Dyreson 2004).

Interest in jogging for health grew in the 1960s and became a full-blown fitness fad by the next decade. Medical professionals rec-ommended it for its cardiovascular benefits, and runners joined races of ever longer distances – from 5,000 meters, 10,000 meters, half marathons, marathons, to ultradistance races beyond 100 miles – as a recreational pastime. In 1974, Californians brought together running and swimming to initiate combined races, and by 1978 cycling was part of the daunting Iron Man competition in Hawaii, that included a 2.4-mile swim, a 112-mile cycle, and a full marathon. More recent endurance challenges include mud runs, which started at the turn of the twentieth century and soon transformed into military-style obstacle courses that have attracted millions of practitioners seeking a sense of adventure. The appeal of such endeavors entices those who wish to challenge themselves without the necessity of extended travel or great expense, promoting a lifestyle that transcends race, social class, gender and age, as all can seek the health benefits of exercise (Gems, Borish and Pfister 2017).

French youth further diversified sporting options with the establishment of parkour in the 1980s. The activity consists of a blend of running, jumping, and daring gymnastic stunts to overcome urban obstacles. Scottish cyclist Danny MacAskill has transformed the activity into a lucrative alternative career, and his performance can be viewed on numerous YouTube videos.

Roller skating/rollerblading

Joseph Merlin, a Belgian inventor, introduced roller skates as early as 1760. More refined models followed. By the mid-nineteenth century, indoor skating rinks were built in the United States and skating spread to England and Australia. The public activity eschewed the need for chaperones in the Victorian era, changing traditional courtship patterns, until supplanted by the bicycle (Oliver 2007).

Speed and endurance races ensued by the late nineteenth century In 1935, the sport of roller derby first appeared in Chicago. This involves teams skating around a short track with the intent of lapping opponents to score points, while opponents attempt to hinder or block such efforts. Roller derby became a popular contact sport for both males and females. More popular televised sports doomed roller derby, but it made a resurgence after the turn of the twenty-first century with teams and leagues throughout America.

The reconfiguration of roller skate wheels into a single line of wheels resulted in the evolution of rollerblading in the 1980s. Youth used the skates to play street hockey, while adults found rollerblading suitable for cardiovascular health and fitness. Competitive speed skating on oval tracks occurred indoors, and endurance races were staged outdoors (Oliver 2007).

Skateboarding

Skateboarding was born in southern California during the 1950s as a youth-oriented sport. While originally associated with surfing, it developed its own identity associated with particular musical genres such as punk rock, grunge, and hip-hop, that matched it rebellious attitude. By the 1970s, skateboard parks emerged, and later on public venues were established to attract youth and socially control their free-wheeling urban adventures. By the 1980s, skateboarding had grown to international proportions, and more daring practitioners attempted more difficult tricks and stunts with aerial maneuvers. The growth and popularity of the activity drew corporate interest, and sponsorship, media, movies, and merchandising became prevalent, with international championships by the end of the decade. ESPN, the American all sports television conglomerate, initiated the X Games in 1995 as an Olympic-style event for alternative sports, including skateboarding (Beal 2007).

Climbing sports

Human beings have had to climb natural obstacles since the dawn of time, but such activity only assumed the characteristics of modern sport in the late eighteenth century after Michel-Gabriel Paccard and Jacques Balmat climbed Europe's highest peak, Mont Blanc, in 1786 (see Chapter 3). By the mid-nineteenth century, mountaineering attracted middle-class adherents. Lawyer Alfred Wills climbed the Wetterhorn in the Swiss Alps in 1854 and then wrote a book about his adventure, which brought him a measure of social capital. The Alpine Club of Great Britain was founded shortly thereafter, in 1857, and similar groups were soon established in Austria, Italy, and France. A race to climb the Matterhorn ensued, won by Englishman Edward Whymper's climbing party in 1865, though at the cost of five lives lost, an indication of the dangers posed at high altitudes. Whymper's team had used ropes, and better crampons and ice picks would be developed to assist later climbers (Atwater 2020).

Mountaineers continued to travel the world, intent on conquering the highest mountains on each continent, until only the highest peak remained: Mount Everest in the Himalayas. In 1924, George Mallory and Andrew Irvine made an ill-fated attempt to reach the summit, assisted by indigenous Sherpa porters and oxygen cylinders. Both Englishmen died in the attempt, and it is unknown if they reached the summit. The conquest was fully documented when accomplished by Edmund Hillary and Tenzing Norgay in 1953. Groups in organized expeditions continue to attempt that feat despite the immense costs of travel, transportation, supplies, equipment, guides, and licenses, that usually require sponsorship. The time allotted to the endeavor requires an extensive amount of leisure as well as financial capital (Atwater 2020).

Buildering

Urban climbing enthusiasts found ways to challenge their skills by other means. In the early nineteenth century, Friedrich Ludwig Jahn, 'father' of the German Turner movement, provided climbing opportunities on an outdoor gymnastic facility in Berlin. By the turn of the twentieth century, Geoffrey Winthrop Young, an English mountaineer, published books on scaling buildings and rooftops in England, as climbers engaged in an early form of parkour (Gems and Pfister 2019a).

By the latter twentieth century, the French climber Alain Robert, known as Spiderman, epitomized the urban builderer. Born in 1962 he began climbing as a teenager, often free soloing without the use of ropes or other safety gear. Robert has climbed many of the world's tallest buildings as well as monuments including the Burj Khalifa (828 meters) in Dubai in 2011 (van Hilvoorde 2007).

Rock climbing

Rock climbing is more popular and more accessible for those of limited means. The activity can be practiced in natural outdoor venues or indoors on artificial climbing walls. Rock climbing gained popularity in Europe and America in the early twentieth century. Climbers used ropes, not to climb but to arrest falls, a technique pioneered in Germany in 1910 and transferred to the United States in the 1930s. Such activitie enabled the climbers to test their strength, agility, flexibility, and psychological makeup in self-challenges (Wassong 2007). In the United States, climbers ascended rock formations in Yosemite National Park in California and throughout the American West in search of an existentialist 'flow' experience during the 1960s. John Gill, one of the climbers who became a college math professor, also began assigning numerical difficulty ratings to the climbing routes (Gems and Pfister 2019a).

In winter or at high altitudes, ice climbing may be required to ascend waterfalls or ice-covered rock formations. Climbers use ice axes and crampons to navigate such locations. The most daring climbers engage in free soloing, which has resulted in many deaths. Free solo climbers push the physical and psychological limits in quests to conquer natural and personal boundaries. Alex Honnold, perhaps the best-known and most publicized of the free solo climbers, reached the top of El Capitan in the Yosemite National Park in California in less than four hours in 2017. 'Honnold squeezed his body into narrow chimneys, tiptoed across ledges the width of matchboxes, and in some places, dangled in the open air by his fingertips (Atwater 2020: 440).

During the 1960s climbers constructed artificial indoor walls in Sheffield, England, where practitioners could compete not only for the heights attained but also for speed. Indoor climbing walls soon became commonplace in Europe and North America. Such competitive ventures evolved into varieties of sport climbing. Lead climbing involves someone who is harnessed and roped, belayed by another on the ground and able to utilize bolts in the climbing face for safety. On indoor artificial walls, an automatic belaying system and fixed bolts assure a safer environment. Indoor venues also allow for speed climbing in which opponents scale a 15-meter wall on the same adjacent routes. The first to the top is the winner, and competitors can also compete by timed climbs. Both male and female climbers are internationally ranked. Bouldering can also be practiced on natural or artificial surfaces, usually not more than 6 meters in height. Boulderers eschew any harness; instead, they place padded mats below the climbing routes to cushion falls. Climbing routes are rated according to difficulty, which can challenge all levels of ability. All climbers engage in an individual challenge that requires strength, endurance, and flexibility. By 1985, climbers sought to test themselves against others in international competition. A rope climbing event had been part of the Olympic Games from 1896 to 1932, and rock climbing became an Olympic event in 2020.

WINTER SPORTS

Ice skating

Ice skating has been practiced across millenniums in northern Europe and later in China. The Dutch popularized the recreation in Europe, skating on frozen canals in the winter. Indoor rinks using artificial ice began appearing in the nineteenth century. Impromptu and, later, organized races evolved into the sport of speed skating. Figure skating had taken hold in the eighteenth century; but a formal association, the International Skating Union, that formalized the rules was not established until 1892 in the Netherlands.

American magazine *Harper's Weekly* enlightened spectators in 1893 as to the rules, which required

> forward and backward skating. ... The first principle of perfect skating is grace. ... In order to be successful in the spins and whirls, a strong stomach is necessary; otherwise dizziness is sure to follow. When you take into consideration that a skater will make fifteen revolutions on one foot and as many as thirty on two feet, at a very high rate of speed, it is a wonder that they are not seasick
>
> (Quoted in Gems 1996a: 213)

The Elfstedentocht, a 120-mile (200-kilometer) tour of 11 cities in the northern Netherlands, serves as both a speed skating and endurance contest as well as a recreational activity for thousands of participants when the winter weather conditions permit.

Ice skating served a revolutionary purpose in the western societies of Europe and North America. It provided an acceptable public recreation that allowed young men and women to engage in joint exercise without the requirement of a chaperone, gradually transforming courting patterns and societal norms in the Victorian era.

Skiing

Snow skiing has been a means of transport in cold climates for thousands of years, but only became a commercialized recreational activity with the establishment of ski resorts in the early twentieth century. Due to the expense of equipment, travel, and fees, it is largely a sport of the middle and upper classes. It is a nomadic endeavor, as ardent skiers journey around the world in search of adequate snow and climate conditions.

The inaugural Winter Olympics in 1924 included cross-country skiing for men at Chamonix, France. A women's event was added in 1952. Alpine skiing was introduced to the Olympic Games in 1936, with downhill and slalom events for both men and women.

Snowboarding is an alternative form of skiing that grew out of the counterculture movement after the 1960s. Young snowboarders adopted punk and hip-hop styles of dress and slang as an alternative to the established ski culture. Early snowboarders didn't 'ask what you do, they ask where you work – knowing that what you do is snowboard, just like them, and any job you might have is simply a means for it' (Thorpe 2007: 291–292). It is mostly practiced by young male enthusiasts, although female snowboarders have increased in number. Snowboarders engage in jumps and other aerial tricks, similar to the skateboarding culture; but both have become increasingly mainstream. Competitive snowboarding events started in 1981. Snowboarding became the featured event at the 1997 X Games, televised by ESPN. It became an Olympic event in 1998.

Ski jumping

Ski jumping originated as a result of a popular form of transport over the hilly terrain in Norway. By the early nineteenth century, Norwegians began competing by ski jumping for distance; and by mid-century, organized events occurred. Norwegians also brought ski jumping to America at that time. The first American tournament ensued in 1891 (Goksoyr 2007).

AQUATIC SPORTS

Swimming and diving

Archaeological evidence indicates that swimming has been a human activity for millennia (Shuster 2020). Egyptians swam in the Nile

River, and Homer's *Iliad* provided evidence of swimming during th Trojan War in the twelfth century BCE. Ancient Greeks engaged i swimming for both work and pleasure. The Etruscans, predecesso of the Romans in Italy, left artifacts depicting swimming and divin, while the Romans were famous for their public baths, that include swimming and plunge pools. Swimming became part of militar training (Olivova 1984; Miller 2004).

The first instructional book, *The Swimmer*, by Nicholau Wynmann, appeared in 1538. Everard Digby, an English academi published *De Arte Natandi*, a Latin text that covered the biomechan ics of swimming, complete with illustrations. It was translated int English in 1595.

Beach excursions became popular among the upper class i England, with transport capabilities provided by coaches; but th first indoor swimming pool was not built until 1828. A Nation: Swimming Society organized competitive races by 1837. Captai Matthew Webb earned international fame as the first to swim acro: the English Channel in 1875. The Amateur Swimming Association founded in England in 1880, and the Amateur Athletic Union, estab lished in the United States in 1888, organized swimming competi tions. A swimming championship for women took place in Scotlan in 1892 (Tranter 1998). Swimming was included in the first moder Olympic Games in 1896. Diving was added in 1904.

With the increasing leisure afforded by the workers' rights cam paigns of the late nineteenth century, swimming became a rec reational activity that crossed all class lines. For the working clas: swimming became a means to better hygiene, as most did not hav access to proper bathing facilities. Public beaches and public swim ming pools provided more than just recreation (Love 2008; Wilts 2009). By the late twentieth century, swimming had become one c the preferred activities in the health and fitness movement.

Scuba diving

Herodotus wrote of ancient Greek underwater diving by the us of reeds to breathe. Sponge, pearl, and shellfish divers simply hel their breath (known as freediving). Modern freedivers compet individually or in teams to set records for depths without the us of compressed air tanks. In the sixteenth century, diving bells were invented to allow for longer duration under water. In 1865, French engineers devised a means to deliver compressed air to divers via a hose from the surface. Air tanks fitted to the divers became available in the early twentieth century but were not perfected until World War II, through the work of Jacques Cousteau and Emile Gagnan. Goggles, fins, and snorkels began to appear in the 1930s (MarineBio, n.d.). Snorkeling and scuba diving became a larger part of recreational tourism by the end of the century.

Waterskiing

Ralph Samuelson, a Minnesota teenager, became the progenitor of waterskiing in 1922 through the process of trial and error using a towline pulled by a motorboat. He would also be the first to try ski jumping from an elevated platform. By 1933, waterskiing exhibitions were included in the Chicago World's Fair. The American Water Ski Association, established in 1939, held its first championship that year. The sport became a popular recreation throughout the United States and Europe (Bellis 2020).

Surfing

The indigenous peoples of Polynesia adopted surfing long before it became a rebellious, hedonistic, and nomadic lifestyle of American youth in the mid-twentieth century. As early as 1823 an American missionary to Hawaii declared that 'surfing was a daily amusement at all times. ... Hundreds at a time have been have been occupied in this way for hours together' (Gems 2006: 67). Hawaiians introduced the sport to California after the turn of the century and Duke Kahanamoku, an Olympic swimming champion, brought surfing to Australia, where locals adopted it as their own. By mid-century, surfers had become part of the counterculture with their own music, clothing, slang, and anti-authoritarian lifestyle. 'Surfing signified self-expression, escape, and freedom' (Booth 2007: 320).

As surfers chased the big waves around the world, the sport became more competitive, commercialized, and professionalized. International surfing competitions became televised, creating celebrated stars who joined the ranks of millionaire athletes who promoted their own merchandise; but for the vast majority of surfers, the sport remains a passion and a way of life.

Windsurfing

Windsurfing developed in the mid-twentieth century when surfers adapted a sail to their boards, and it spread from the United States and Europe to Japan and Australia. Like surfing, its practitioners assume a lifestyle geared toward independence and counterculture values.

Windsurfing allows for gymnastic jumps or loops in the air, which requires a sustained commitment to practice. Windsurfing for both men and women became an Olympic event in 1984; but traditional windsurfers eschew competition. Committed windsurfers travel to ideal destinations as sport tourists, and the pursuit of such pleasures requires an expendable income beyond the means of most in the working class (Wheaton 2007).

Parasailing

A gliding parachute capable of ascent first appeared in 1962. By 1974, such sailing chutes were towed by boats, and passengers might be harnessed to the sail, initiating a commercialized recreational endeavor. In the 1980s, the activity assumed a competitive characteristic as parasailers towed by vehicles attempted to land on targets. Parasailing companies abound at waterside vacation spots around the world.

Canoeing and kayaking

Archaeologists have unearthed the remnants of canoes that were used thousands of years ago. These continue to serve the same purpose of transporting an individual across a body of water, although modern canoeists generally employ such craft for recreational purposes. The sport was popularized by Scottish lawyer John MacGregor, who traveled in parts of Europe, the Middle East, Egypt, and North America by canoe. He founded the Royal Canoe Club in England in 1866 and the American Canoe Association in the United States in 1880 (Gullion 2007).

Boat racing had preceded the canoeing organizations, as ferrymen raced each other from ship to shore in order to procure more loads and earn additional revenue. Such work activities evolved into professional races. College students engaged in amateur boat clubs and challenged rivals. The famous Oxford–Cambridge race series started in 1828, and American universities copied their English counterparts. Harvard University traveled to England to contend with Oxford in 1869. Rowing races were among the most popular professional sports in the United States by the 1870s. Competitive canoe races began in the 1870s in England and became an Olympic event in 1936 (Gullion 2007; Gems, Borish and Pfister 2017).

Kayaks were enclosed, narrower versions of the canoe, first used by the indigenous peoples of the northern arctic areas. Kayak paddles differ from canoeing oars in that they are double bladed, and paddling techniques differ with those of the canoeists. Kayaks gained popularity as recreational watercraft in the 1970s. Kayakers compete in sprint races, slalom, wildwater races (a combination of sprint and obstacle racing), and marathons. Whitewater kayaking and rafting are adventure sports that descend fast-flowing rivers that may include rapids and waterfalls with increasing levels of danger. The International Canoe Federation regulates both canoeing and kayaking racing (Gullion 2007).

Paddleboarding

Hawaiians used paddleboarding as a means of transport between islands long before it became a leisure activity. Paddleboarding emanated from surfing and gained popularity as a recreational activity in the twenty-first century. It can be done on any body of water and provides a good form of cardiovascular exercise and endurance training.

AERIAL SPORTS

Hang-gliding

Otto Lilienthal pioneered hang-gliding in Germany during the 1890s until his death, caused by a crash. Hang-gliding later developed during the 1970s as a means to obtain motorless flight by harnessing a pilot to either a fixed or flexible wing. Paragliding, in which participants use parachutes to glide, commenced in 1978, and world championship competitions followed in Austria in 1989. Hang-gliders compete in aerobatics, speed, and cross-country events (Vassort 2007).

Skydiving

The first verified attempt at skydiving occurred in 1797 when Andre Jacques Gernerin jumped from a hot-air balloon over Paris. The extensive military use of aircraft in World War I necessitated a quest for suitable parachutes. By World War II, paratroopers became standard in national armies. Recreational skydivers took up the practice thereafter. Some engage in group formations while in flight, whereas others practice skysurfing on a board while in flight (Laurendeau 2007). Safer yet similar experiences can now be obtained at indoor wind tunnels, that don't require parachutes or previous training.

Bungee jumping

Bungee jumping has its roots in the coming of age and fertility rituals of males on Pentecost Island in Vanuatu in the South Pacific, where young men tied vines to their ankles and jumped from 30-meter heights. New Zealander H. J. Hackett commercialized the activity by establishing bungee jumping locations in his native country and charging fees to death-defying adventurers and thrill-seeking tourists, who are attached to elastic cords to arrest their fall. The success of such ventures spawned similar enterprises around the world (McConnell 2007).

BASE jumping

Other pioneers adopted the challenge to buildings, towers, and cliffs jumping from heights and deploying a parachute. Most early BASE jumpers were skydivers looking for a new challenge. They pushed physical and psychological limits, resulting in injuries and deaths. Most have a higher socioeconomic status, as travel to such sites requires a level of discretionary income (Cooper and Laurendeau 2007).

BASE jumpers pushed their limits even further in the 1990s with the adoption of wingsuits, which provide greater pilot control and longer flight time. Launching from extreme heights, including some of the highest mountains in the world, they contend for world records in flight time and distance covered. The evolution of individual human flight has been further extended by the use of jet-powered rockets attached to the body for propulsion. Due to its inherent danger, BASE jumping is illegal in some locations.

STRENGTH SPORTS

Bodybuilding

The ancient Greeks clearly had an interest in beautiful bodies, portrayed in their sculptures, as did the artists of Renaissance Europe. That interest renewed in Europe at the end of the nineteenth century as Eugen Sandow was declared the most perfectly developed man and exhibited his well-defined body throughout the world in exhibitions. His American counterpart, Bernarr Macfadden, initiated contests to find the most perfectly developed men and woman after the turn of the century (see Chapter 3; Chapman 1994; Ernst 2004). Such beauty contests continued throughout the twentieth century.

By mid-century, weight training assumed a new role in producing strength for athletes (Shurley, Todd, and Todd 2019). Thereafter, strength training became part of the health and fitness regimen of self-conscious practitioners. Bodybuilders engaged in weight training, but focused on the development of muscle definition or sculpting. They displayed their physiques in public exhibitions for titles such as Mr. Universe or Mr. Olympia. In the quest for such accolades, many turned to doping to produce the desired results. The greatest repository of knowledge relative to weight training and bodybuilding is at the H. J. Lutcher Stark Center at the University of Texas at Austin, which publishes *Iron Game History: The Journal of Physical Culture.*

CrossFit

In 1996, Greg Glassman and Lauren Janai conceptualized a multidimensional fitness routine that became known as CrossFit. By 2000, they had opened a gym in California to promote their high-intensity workout, that included aerobics, calisthenics, and weightlifting. It proved to have widespread appeal to both men and women, and they sold thousands of franchises worldwide. The CrossFit Games, instituted in 2007, consisted of competitive events for youth, men and women, coed teams, and masters athletes. The televised competition drew international contestants who battled for the title of world's fittest man or world's fittest woman.

HISTORIOGRAPHY

The concept of leisure has changed over time and did not gain much attention from historians until the later decades of twentieth century (see Keith Thomas 1964; Peter Bailey 1978; Hugh Cunningham 1980; Stephen Jones 1986; and Peter Burke 1995). In the United States, Dulles (1940) provided an early study of recreation. Piess (1986) and Nasaw (1993) analyzed early studies of popular amusements.

Relative to the continuing emergence of adventure and extreme sports, Robert Rinehart cautions that such studies should assume 'a fresh, contextualized, dynamic and fluid' approach in 'exciting new ways of "seeing" sport forms as they develop, as they are lived, as they fade away or morph into amalgams of themselves' (Rinehart 2007: 297). He states that 'the demands of, relative merits of, and rewards for participants' commitments have, with several notable exceptions, also not been adequately explored (Rinehart 2007: 302). There is still much work to be done in this respect relative to the race, gender, and class aspects of such sports, as women and people of color have been relative newcomers to such activities and have not been wholly welcomed (see Rinehart and Sydnor 2003; Kusz 2007 and Fletcher 2008).

FURTHER READING

Douglas Booth and Holly Thorpe, eds. (2007) *Berkshire Encyclopedia of Extreme Sports*. Great Barrington, MA: Berkshire Publishing.

Clifford Geertz (1972) 'Deep Play: Notes on the Balinese Cockfight,' *Daedalus* 101:27, 1–37.

Gerald R. Gems and Gertrud Pfister (2009) *Understanding American Sports*. New York: Routledge.

National Geographic (n.d.) 'NG Live! Free Soloing with Alex Hammond' [video], https://video.nationalgeographic.com/video/00000144-0a3d-d3cb-a96c-7b3da3db0000

Roy Rosenzweig (1983) *Eight Hours for What We Will: Workers and Leisure in an Industrial City, 1870–1920*. Cambridge: Cambridge University Press.

E. P. Thompson (1963) *The Making of the English Working Class*. New York: Vantage Books.

8

MEGAEVENTS

Megaevents need not be international in nature. The largest audience for a sports event occurs annually in Indiana at the Indianapolis 500 auto race. The speedway, built in 1909, seats 257,325 patrons, but can be expanded to 400,000 with improvised seating in its infield. The track is 2.5 miles (4 kilometers) long. The 500-mile race requires drivers to complete 200 laps.

OLYMPIC GAMES

The ancient Olympic Games of the Greeks are well documented as early as 776 BCE (see Chapters 1, 3, 4, and 6). Archaeological, literary, and artistic evidence revealed the history of the festival, the events, and the athletic heroes inscribed on stelae and statuary. We know the religious nature of the contests, as well as the homage paid to other deities in similar rituals. The Olympics also served as a form of political diplomacy. A truce was enacted a month before and during the games to allow athletes and patrons to travel to the festival without fear of violence. At the gathering, diplomats from warring city-states might further negotiate a settlement of their differences (Miller 2004).

The original Games consisted of only two events: a sprint and a long-distance run. Horse races, chariot races, and a pentathlon that included running, jumping, wrestling, discus throwing and javelin throwing were added later, as was boxing and the pankration (Miah and Garcia 2012). The latter was a brutal encounter in which no holds were barred except for biting, gouging, and blows to the genitals. The fighting continued until one contestant submitted. Although ancient Greek athletes did not quantify scores, some astounding feats are recorded on statues. For example, Theagenes of Thasos was undefeated in boxing over a 22-year career (Ancient Olympics n.d.). Women were not permitted at the Games, even as spectators; but they had their own athletic competitions in the Heraean Games, starting in the sixth century BCE.

The resurrection of the modern Games in 1896 are generally attributed to Baron Pierre de Coubertin, a French aristocrat. He traveled to England and the United States to study the role of athletics in the school systems and assumed a leading role in sport conferences, that culminated in the revival of the Olympics (MacAloon 1981; Young 1996). The importance of Demetrios Vikelas, head of the Olympic Commission and first president of the IOC, is understudied and requires further attention (Georgiadis 2003).

The early modern Games faced inherent problems. The 1896 Games in Athens lacked financing, but was saved by Greek philanthropist George Averoff and private donations. The 1900 and 1904 Games were largely lost within the larger context of world fairs; the latter festival included the racist Anthropology Days, a pseudoscientific experiment to compare athletic abilities across racial groups to ascertain white supremacy (Brownell 2008b). The dwindling status of the Olympics required an interim version in 1906 to revive interest; but the 1908 Games in London featured acrimonious dissension between the hosts and the American contingent, that invoked sport as a means to assert its own nationalistic desire to supplant Great Britain as world leader. Rather than adherence to the ancient Greek truce, World Wars I and II forced the cancellation of the Games. In 1972, a terrorist attack disrupted the Munich Games and resulted in the deaths of 14 people. The 1980 and 1984 editions resulted in boycotts over political and ideological differences. The 2020 Games had to be postponed due to a worldwide pandemic caused by the COVID-19 coronavirus, an event which has yet to be sufficiently assessed by sport historians.

See the special issue of the *Journal of Sport History* on the relationship of Britain with the Olympic Games (Vamplew 2012).

ROMAN GAMES

The Romans generally eschewed Greek influence, offering their own version of athletic festivals to meet their own social needs. Like the Greeks, Romans honored their gods with ritual spectacles that included chariot races. Public games were conducted at some festivals, and Roman generals celebrated their victories in public triumphs, a heroic procession that ended with athletic contests. By 336 BCE, such games evolved into annual Ludi Romani (Roman Games) or Ludi Magni (Great Games), that included circuses (the site of chariot races), animals, and theatrical performances. Circus games consisted of chariot races, a demonstration of acrobatic horsemanship, boxing, and wrestling matches. Armed men hunted the animals in the arena and engaged them in mortal combat. Gladiatorial bouts between human foes became a popular amusement by the fourth century BCE (Olivova 1984; Nossov 2009; Futrell 2009).

Such bloody spectacles served as a means of social control. Politicians seeking to court or maintain favor with the populace sponsored regular games. Emperor Julius Caesar maintained his own gladiatorial school with 5,000 trainees. Emperor Augustus conducted numerous gladiatorial spectacles during his reign, employing 10,000 combatants (Nossov 2009: 17).

The Romans constructed elaborate facilities for their games. The Colosseum remains a primary tourist attraction. The Circus Maximus accommodated at least 200,000 fans for chariot races, and they cheered wildly for their favorite teams of individual heroes.

> Pliny the Elder tells of a fan who took swallows with him to the games, their feet dyed the colour of his winning team, to bring rapid news of victory to his home. Another fan, despairing over the defeat of his (team's

colour, flung himself on the funeral pyre and was consumed in flames
with the dead charioteer.

(Olivova 1984: 176)

Another commentator described

this mass of people, unemployed and therefore with too much time on
their hands. For them the Circus Maximus is temple, home, social club
and centre of all their hopes. You can see them beyond the city, arguing
about the races ... and declaring that the country will come to ruin unless
their favourite wins in the next races. And on the day they all rush to the
circus even before daybreak, to secure a place.

(Olivova 1984: 177)

The comparisons with modern fans might offer fruitful enterprise
for sport historians.

CORRELATED OLYMPIC GAMES

PARALYMPICS

World War II created horrendous casualty figures. In the postwar
period, Great Britain wished to recognize its impaired veterans. At the
opening of the 1948 Olympic Games in London, the organizers initiated the completion with an archery event for veterans in wheelchairs.
That impetus resulted in the Paralympic movement. In 1960, the
first Paralympic Games, in Rome, featured 400 athletes competing in
wheelchairs. By 1976, competitors had expanded to those with other
disabilities, including amputees and the blind. That Olympiad included
winter events, which continued thereafter (Paralympic Games, n.d.).

The International Paralympic Committee was established in 1989.
The Paralympics have since subdivided by the type and level of
impairment. Athletes with physical, visual, and intellectual impair-
ments are accommodated in ten categories relative to corporeal
conditions and levels of restriction linked to functionality. Both individual and team sports are included in the summer and winter events.
(See Chatziefstathiou, Garcia, and Seguin's (2020) edited volume,
Routledge Handbook of the Olympic and Paralympic Games, for more
complete analysis).

SPECIAL OLYMPICS

Eunice Kennedy Shriver, sister of US President John F. Kennedy, inspired by their sister, who was living with a mental illness, embarked on a campaign to address this issue. Research funded by the Kennedy Foundation surmised that physical activity provided substantial physical and psychological benefits to people with a mental illness. In 1968, she organized an international athletic competition in Chicago, modeled on the Olympic Games. The initial competitors came from Canada and the United States; but the movement soon expanded to international proportions with competitions held every two years, administered by volunteers. The Special Olympics prioritizes participants achieving their personal best efforts rather than obtaining the prize (Special Olympics n.d.).

GAY GAMES

The Gay Games are an international athletic competition modeled on the Olympic Games. Founded in San Francisco in 1982 by Dr. Tom Waddell, a decathlete in the 1968 Olympic Games, and Rikki Streicher, a lesbian activist, the event stressed inclusivity and required no qualifying standards. The quadrennial festival included Master's Athletes by 1990. The 1994 Games, held in New York City, exceeded the number of Olympic participants. In 1998, the Netherlands hosted the Games, with more than 13,000 taking part. The 2018 Games, held in Paris, attracted participants from 91 countries to take part in 36 sports and 14 cultural events (Federation of Gay Games n.d.).

WORLD MASTERS GAMES

The Masters Games originated in Toronto in 1975 under the organization of Don Farquharson. Initial track and field events expanded to include a wide variety of sports in later years. The International Masters Games Association assumed direction of multisport operations in 1985, and winter sports events began in 2010. There are no qualifying standards for participants other than age classifications in five-year intervals, generally starting at age 35. No team events are contested. Regional festivals limit expenses and travel for many, but the international championships are publicized the most. Age group world records increasingly gain public notice, such as Ed Whitlock's marathon run at the age of 73, completed in 2 hours, 54 minutes, and 48 seconds.

SOCCER WORLD CUP

Soccer greatly expanded beyond England in the latter nineteenth century. After 1900, more international matches occurred, and the 1900 Olympic Games included soccer as a demonstration sport. It would continue as an Olympic exhibit until official recognition by the IOC in 1908. Olympic soccer, however, only admitted amateur teams. FIFA, established in 1904, assumed governance of international play. The first World Cup championship appeared in 1930, hosted and won by Uruguay before 93,000 fans, a harbinger of the future fervor of World Cup play. By 2018, it had become a global sports behemoth, generating more than $3 billion in broadcast revenues (Parrish, Li, and Nauright 2020; O' Brien 2016). Media attention to World Cup play paralleled that of the Olympic Games, and the relationship between individual World Cups and the media requires further attention by sport historians. This will be of greater importance with the ascendance of digitalization.

WOMEN'S WORLD CUP

Women had engaged in football matches as early as the eighteenth century in Scotland, where they played against men in an annual affair. Interest spread in the late nineteenth century, and women formed their own club in 1895. During World War I, women's industrial teams flourished, and Dick, Kerr & Company fielded a prominent team. The male Football Association (FA) banned women's play in 1921; but the Dick, Kerr Ladies persisted, playing women's teams in France and men's teams in the United States. Women eventually established their own association in 1969, and the men's FA lifted their ban on the use of their pitch in 1971 (Weeks 2017).

Women's international team play was initiated in 1970 at an Italian tournament. Such events grew slowly and sporadically. The initial Women's World Cup did not come to fruition until 1991, in China, and was held quadrennially thereafter.

After the passage of Title IX in 1972, women's soccer bloomed in the United States, particularly in schools and colleges. A women's national team formed in 1983 and began play two years later. It would dominate the Women's World Cup and Olympic matches, capturing the first Women's World Cup and drawing more than 93,000 fans when the United States hosted the 1999 World Cup. The success of the women's team spurred the rapid growth of soccer in the United States after the turn of the twentieth century.

CRICKET WORLD CUP

The first women's international cricket test match occurred when the English team traveled to Australia in 1934. The team played New Zealand soon afterward. South Africa joined the fray in 1960 The International Cricket Council (commonly known as the ICC) organized the first Women's Cricket World Cup in 1973, two years before the inaugural men's competition. The women's initial tournament, held in England, included teams from Jamaica as well as from Trinidad and Tobago. The Women's World Cup was held sporadically until 2005 when it assumed a quadrennial schedule. The Australian team has won more than any other side.

England spread cricket throughout its colonial domains, and the game became a means for the indigenous populace to challenge its subordinate status, as detailed in C. L. R. James's (1963) *Beyond a Boundary*. Test matches began as early as 1877 when the English team traveled to Melbourne, Australia, only to be beaten by their hosts. After an 1882 English loss to the Aussies in England the media lamented the death of national cricket by proclaiming it burnt to ashes, commemorated with an ash-filled urn. The urn became the trophy awarded to future victors in the nationalistic struggle.

Although test matches continued over the next century, the men Cricket World Cup did not initiate play until 1975 in England, which continued on a quadrennial basis. The West Indies team captured the first two competitions, and the Australians eventually won three. India has two victories, while Pakistan, Sri Lanka, and England have managed one apiece, as the former colonies have conquered their previous master on the cricket pitch. The competition has become one of the most watched sports events, attracting an international audience (Browning 1999).

RUGBY WORLD CUP

The notion that William Webb Ellis, a student at Rugby School, picked up the ball and ran with it in 1823 and thus became the progenitor of rugby is apocryphal. Nevertheless, the rugby World Cup trophy retains his name. Several English schools were playing the game by the mid-nineteenth century. When the rugby clubs would not agree to the FA's disallowance of running with the ball in 1863, they left the organization. They formed the Rugby Union in 1871. A series of matches with Scotland soon followed, and the game was exported to Canada, France, Germany, Argentina, Australia, New Zealand, and South Africa. By 1883, a home nations tournament included England, Scotland, Wales, and Ireland, the first being won by England. In 1895, the Rugby Union split over the issue of professionalism. The modern Olympic Games included rugby from 1900 to 1924, with the exception of the 1912 Games. New Zealand, South Africa, and Australia each sent teams to engage in international play with the English in the first decade of the twentieth century, and France joined the annual nations championship in 1910. Rugby spread through Europe in the 1930s. The first Rugby World Cup, established in 1987, was captured by New Zealand (Nauright and Chandler 1996; Dunning and Sheard 2005; Collins 2009).

The political significance of sport proved apparent in the 1995 Rugby World Cup, hosted by South Africa. The country had finally abolished the long-standing policy of apartheid and resumed international athletic competition. President Nelson Mandela utilized rugby as a means to promote reconciliation in the racially divided country in the transition from apartheid to democracy. The South African victory moved the nation toward healing and full acceptance of its disparate population (Carlin 2008).

Administered by the World Rugby organization, the championship is held every four years. It has drawn more than a million spectators since 1991 and an increasing amount of media coverage. The women's championship, hosted by Wales, first occurred in 1991, and was won by the United States. The growth of women's rugby was evident by the entrance of 12 teams in the competition. After 1994, the women's tournament assumed the same four-year cycle as the men's championship. New Zealand dominated the competition with five titles through 2017. The increasing interest in women's rugby is discernible in the nearly three dozen teams that have participated in the World Cup competition.

Rugby sevens, a variant of the 15-a-side game, first appeared in Scotland. The game consisted of shorter seven-minute halves. In 1993, Scotland hosted the first championship for men. By 2009, a World Cup championship for women was added. Rugby sevens became an Olympic event in 2016.

WORLD BASEBALL CLASSIC

The United States and Japan had been playing international baseball games since the late nineteenth century. By the 1930s, Japan suggested a true World Series (the American championship), presumed to determine the best team in the world (Gems 2006). Baseball had appeared as a demonstration sport in the Olympic Games throughout the twentieth century, and it became an official event from 1992 to 2008. When the IOC decided to discontinue baseball in 2005, Major League Baseball (the governing body for American professional teams) joined with the International Baseball Federation to initiate the World Baseball Classic to promote the sport on a wider international basis.

Modeled after FIFA's World Cup competition, the World Baseball Classic, which debuted in 2006, consisted of professional national teams. Subsequent tournaments ensued in 2009, 2013, and 2017. The first two championships were played among invited teams; thereafter the increasing interest required qualification rounds. Japan has been the most successful team and its tournament games are nationally televised. The ability of smaller nations to showcase their abilities and the political benefits are yet to be analyzed by sport historians.

REGIONAL GAMES

COMMONWEALTH GAMES

In 1911, the British celebrated the coronation of King George V with the Festival of Empire in London. Part of the affair included the Inter-Empire Games, an athletic competition between the United Kingdom, Australia, Canada, and South Africa. Athletes competed in track and field, boxing, wrestling, and swimming. The Games served as a precursor to the Commonwealth Games (originally known as the British Empire Games), which commenced in Canada in 1930 as a multisport event to be conducted on a quadrennial schedule. World War II interrupted the festival, which resumed in 1950. The 1954 Games, held in Vancouver, Canada, featured a race between Roger Bannister and John Landy, the first two men to break the four-minute-mile barrier: the race was won by Bannister, but both beat the four-minute mark, considered to be impossible only a short time earlier. The Commonwealth Games include events for women and disabled athletes. A Winter Games was offered in 1958, but this was not continued after 1966. A separate Paraplegic Games ran from1962 to 1974 before inclusion in the Commonwealth Games (Groom 2017).

ASIAN GAMES

The Asian Games were first birthed through the auspices of the YMCA in the Philippines in 1913 (see Chapter 5). The Games continued through 1934 until the second Sino-Japanese War curtailed the festival. The Asian Games Federation resurrected the assemblage as the Pan-Asian Games, with the first Games hosted in 1951 in New Delhi, India. The Games are held every four years as a multisport competition for both men and women, and they are followed by a Para Games for disabled athletes (Huebner 2016; Tsutsui and Baskett 2011).

The history of the Asian Games is one of turmoil, often marred by political and religious differences. In 1962, Indonesia, the host country, refused admittance to Israel, which was opposed by the Arab nations, and Taiwan, opposed by China. As a consequence, the Asian Football Association, the International Amateur Athletic Federation, and the International Weightlifting Federation withdrew their recognition of the Games and the IOC censured Indonesia. The Indonesian President Sukarno responded, with an anti-imperialist motive, by organizing the Games of the New Emerging Forces (GANEFO) in Jakarta in 1963 as an alternative to the Olympic Games for socialist countries. The initial venture attracted widespread participation, including an Arab team from Palestine. A second GANEFO took place in Phnom Penh, Cambodia, in 1966; but participation was limited to Asian countries and the movement faltered (Field 2011; Shuman, 2013).

In 1970, South Korea proved unable to host the Asian Games, and in 1978, Pakistan also withdrew as hosts. In both instances, Thailand stepped in to rescue the Games. After 1982, the Olympic Council of Asia assumed the administration of the event, but Israel remained in exile. By 1990, Taipei had been readmitted under the designation of Chinese Taipei; but Iraq was suspended over the Persian Gulf War, and North Korea boycotted the event. The Asian republics of the former Soviet Union joined the Asian Games in 1994, marking greater stability in the organization.

SOUTHEAST ASIAN GAMES

At a 1958 meeting of the Asian Games representatives in Tokyo, delegates from the southeast Asian peninsula decided to form their own association with the intent of fostering greater understanding and cooperation. The next year, Bangkok hosted the first Southeast Asian Games with teams from Burma (now Myanmar), Cambodia, South Vietnam, Laos, Malaysia, and Thailand. The multisport festival was intended to be staged every two years; but the 1963 competition had to be cancelled due to political upheaval in Cambodia, which had been designated as the host country. By 1977, the association had attracted 11 members. In addition to the traditional Olympic sports the Southeast Asian Games may include those specific to the region such as the martial arts of arnis, pencak silat, sambo, wushu, and kurash. Underwater hockey and sepak takraw (see Chapter 5) have also appeared on the schedule of activities (Fédération Équestre Internationale n.d.).

SOUTH ASIAN GAMES

The South Asian Olympic Council formed in 1983 and initiated the South Asian Games in Kathmandu, Nepal, the following year as a means to promote cultural exchange between its eight members. The Games are scheduled to be conducted every two years, but there have been several lapses. In addition to the Olympic sports, regional activities such as kabbadi (see Chapter 5) and kho-kho, an Indian tag game, have also been included. In the 2011 version, beach games and winter events were added, but were not continued in subsequent festivals (South Asia Olympic Council n.d.).

EAST ASIAN GAMES

The East Asian Games first appeared in 1993 under the auspices of the Olympic Council of Asia. In addition to the eight members, the island of Guam, a US territory, joined the competition. The festival was conducted every four years until 2013 when it was disbanded (Sohu n.d.).

CENTRAL ASIAN GAMES

The Central Asian Games were organized by the Olympic Council of Asia, starting in 1995 in Tashkent, Uzbekistan. Five former Soviet republics joined with Iran for competitions every two years, but the 2001 festival to be hosted by Kyrgyzstan was cancelled, and no meetings occurred after 2005 (Bell 2003).

WEST ASIAN GAMES

The initial West Asian Games were organized by the West Asian Games Federation in 1997 and hosted by Tehran, Iran. Only male athletes were allowed to participate. A second version of the Games was hosted by Kuwait in 2002, and the final event occurred in Doha, Qatar, in 2005. Fifteen countries had participated in the Games, but due to continual political turmoil in the region among the group members, further meetings did not take place (Topend Sports n.d.).

AMERICAN SPORT SPECTACLES

SUPER BOWL

American football surpassed baseball as the national sport in the 1960s. The popularity of the NFL spawned a second American Football League (known as the AFL), founded in 1959. The success of the new venture resulted in a national championship challenge in 1967, which became known as the Super Bowl. The two leagues merged in 1970, but retained separate divisions with their own champions that continue to meet for the annual national title. The two weeks preceding the Super Bowl amount to a national holiday and a media frenzy. Massive amounts of money are bet on the result. Thirty-second television commercials cost millions of dollars, as the Super Bowl draws the largest audience annually (nearly 100 million viewers on average in 2020; Syracuse.com 2020). The game is broadcast to over 200 countries. Bars, restaurants, and family homes host elaborate Super Bowl parties. The game and its accompanying events and rituals have provided the material for a multitude of analyses by sport scholars (Gems and Pfister 2019b).

WORLD SERIES

The rapid spread of baseball after the American Civil War in the 1860s marked it as the national game, and it remained so for another century. A National League (or the NL) of professional teams was founded in 1876, with numerous other smaller leagues appearing throughout the country. A second professional American League (AL) was established in 1901, and the two rivals agreed to a national championship series in 1903. Although other countries had adopted the sport by that time, Americans assumed their athletic superiority in the game and termed the contest the 'World' Series. There was no championship match in 1904, and in 1994 the World Series was cancelled due to a labor strike by players. The series of games usually seven, are split between the urban venues of the two league champions and televised nationally. They have provided some of th most heroic exploits in American sport as well as some of the greates tragedies, including the Black Sox scandal of 1919 when the Chicago AL champion team accepted bribes from gamblers to purposel lose. Such events have attracted the attention of a multitude of sport history scholars (see, for example, Nathan (2005) *Saying It's So: A Cultural History of the Black Sox Scandal*).

NATIONAL BASKETBALL ASSOCIATION CHAMPIONSHIP

James Naismith, a YMCA instructor, invented the game of basketball in 1891. Basketball soon gained popularity among men and women, and it appeared in the 1904 Olympics tournament. Professional teams barnstormed throughout the United States thereafter, and professional leagues ensued by the 1920s. A national professional tournament sponsored by the *Chicago Herald American* newspaper sought to determine a national champion in 1939. A black team, the New York Rens, emerged as the winner. The following year, the all-black Harlem Globetrotters captured the title. The tournament continued through 1948. Two competing professional leagues, the Basketball Association of America and the National Basketball League, merged in 1949 to form the current NBA. The league championship has been played annually and has become a global event with a Canadian franchise and international rosters, challenging soccer as the most popular sport in the world.

STANLEY CUP

In 1892, Lord Stanley, the Governor General of Canada, donated a trophy for the best amateur ice hockey team in Canada, to be won via challenge matches. By 1907, professional teams contended for the prize, and American teams later became eligible. In 1917, the National Hockey League was formed, and both Canadian and US teams would join the competition for the cup. Over the course of the century, ice hockey would become a primary sport in Canada and a popular one in the United States and throughout much of Europe. Such developments led to the accumulation of international rosters in the NHL and increased global interest in the sport (Roarke 2017).

PAN AMERICAN GAMES

The Greater Texas and Pan-American Exposition of 1937 in the United States served as a predecessor to the Pan American Games. It included athletic competition among white, black, and Latin athletes at a time when racial segregation still ruled in the American South. Such events presaged the power of sport to effect social change (Dyreson 2016).

Buenos Aires was scheduled to host the original Pan American Games in 1942, but the outbreak of World War II delayed the event until 1951. The 'Pan Am' Games operate according to the Olympic Charter and include similar organization, rituals, symbols, and ceremonies. They are held every four years, in the year preceding the Olympic Games, and are open to all nations within the Americas, including territories. Relative to the latter condition, both Bermuda and Puerto Rico enter teams in the events. A winter version of the Games occurred only once, in 1990. The Pan American Games include some non-Olympic sports, such as water skiing, bowling and pelota. See Bruce Kidd and Cesar Torres's (2018) *Historicizing the Pan-American Games* for more complete coverage.

PAN ARAB GAMES

The Pan Arab Games are among the oldest of the regional competitions, originating as the brainchild of Abdul Rahman Hassan Azzam, General Secretary of the Arab League in 1947; but they did not become a reality until 1953 when Alexandria, Egypt, hosted the initial competition. Such athletic ventures are meant to bring a more cohesive Arab identity and favorable relationships to the Arab nations of Africa and Asia. The Games are organized by the Union of Arab National Olympic Committees.

The Arab Games continued through 2011 as a multisport competition, but the Arab Spring that followed, with political uprising throughout Northern Africa and the Middle East, curtailed such international cooperation. Sport historians are only beginning to assess the ramifications of political, religious, and ethnic difference and the effect on sport in the region. The IOC has tried to address the issue of gender representation on some national teams, but without significant success. See Fan Hong's (2015) edited volume, *Sport in the Middle East: Power, Politics, Ideology and Religion*, for a discussion of women in the Pan Arab and Olympic Games and sport as a means of emancipation.

PAN AFRICAN GAMES

The Pan African Games are similar to the other regional festivals in that they are in accord with the Olympic Charter, offering multisport competition every four years, one year before the Olympic Games. Initial attempts to organize intercontinental athletic meets started as early as the 1920s, without continued success. The first official Games opened in Brazzaville, Congo, in 1965. Like the Arab Games, political events disrupted the continuous flow of the festival, intended to bring greater unity among the nations on the continent; but a regular schedule has been maintained since 1987. All continental nations are eligible for participation, but some have been banned in the past, such as South Africa during its apartheid period. An African version of the Special Olympics to meet the needs of the intellectually disabled was added in 1999.

PACIFIC GAMES

Originally labeled the South Pacific Games at their advent in 1963, the multisport festival attracted mostly island nations, some of which were still European colonies at the time. The Games were scheduled at two- or three-year intervals, but assumed a quadrennial schedule after 1971. Australia and New Zealand joined the competition in 2015, but these two countries were limited to four sports (rugby sevens, weightlifting, taekwondo, and sailing) so as not to overwhelm the smaller nations.

While the Games are intended to promote a sense of unity and friendship, some issues relative to religious differences have occurred. Some countries adhere to the strict Protestant Sabbath, a remnant of their colonial history. Such sabbatarianism prohibits sport on Sunday, which has presented scheduling difficulties. Also, conservative beliefs required athletic sportswear to adequately cover the body. Such remnants of the past, and the Games in general, await thorough analysis by sport historians.

E-SPORTS

The impetus for e-sports began with the development of the *Spacewar* game in 1962, and it grew into simulated sports, fantasy leagues, and online gambling ventures by the 1990s. By 1990, the Nintendo World Championships appeared in the United States, and the World Cyber Games followed a decade later. South Korea provided a base for the growth of e-sports, and the Asian continent became a hotbed for the activity. Leagues spawned professionalization, and individual and team tournaments promised lucrative financial rewards. Players gained celebrity status and legions of followers online and as spectators in the tournaments, that featured battle games. In the United States and Australia, colleges formed e-sports teams for intercollegiate competition (Hindin, Howzen, Xue, Pu, and Newman 2020).

E-sports were included as a demonstration sport at the 2018 Asian Games, but an attempt to gain Olympic acceptance was denied. IOC president Thomas Bach stated that the violence inherent in the games conflicted with Olympic values. In addition to the violent nature of the e-sports games, there are not yet suitable accommodations for disabled players. Gender discrimination has been another concern, as most players are young men, and women often face discriminatory attitudes. Sport scholars have determined that e-sports face an indefinite future. Although wildly popular among youth, they may 'develop into an alternative counterculture' or 'become accepted as part of the mainstream hegemonic sports' or 'become the new hegemonic sports acting in concert within changing social conditions and the increasing importance of networked technologies' (Hindin, Howzen, Xue, Pu, and Newman 2020: 413).

FURTHER READING

Susan Brownell, ed. (2008) *The 1904 St. Louis Anthropology Days and Olympic Games: Sport, Race, and American Imperialism.* Lincoln: University of Nebraska Press.

Tony Collins (2009) *A Social History of English Rugby Union.* London: Routledge

Russell Field and Bruce Kidd (2016) 'Canada and the Pan American Games' International Journal of History of Sport 33:1–2, 217–239.

Stefan Huebner (2016) *Pan-Asian Sports and the Emergence of Modern Asia, 1913–1974.* Singapore: National University of Singapore Press.

Clemente A. Lisi (2015) *A History of the World Cup, 1930–2014.* London: Rowman & Littlefield.

J. A. Mangan, Marcus P. Chu, and Dong Jinxia (2015) *The Asian Games: Modern Metaphor for 'The Middle Kingdom' Reborn: Political Statement, Cultural Assertion, Social Symbol.* London: Routledge.

Andy Miah and Beatriz Garcia (2012) *The Olympics: The Basics.* London: Routledge.

Alan Tomlinson (2014) *FIFA: The Men, the Myths, and the Money.* London: Routledge.

Stephen Wagg (2018) *Cricket: A Political History of the Global Games, 1945–2017.* London: Routledge.

SPORT HISTORY AROUND THE WORLD

Sport history has struggled with its nomenclature. Vanessa Heggie, a medical historian, states that

> If the broadening of terms of reference seems like a loss of identity, then it is time to go back to the philosophical roots of the discipline and reconsider the meaning of sport in light of twenty-first century scholarship; it is clearly no longer about white, male, Anglo-centric competitive games and athletics.

> (2014: 220)

Jaime Schultz asserts that sport historians need to engage with 'questions of identity, coherence, and purpose. ... [T]here are gaps to fill, directions to take, theories to engage, disciplines to disrupt, and legitimacy to be claimed if sport history is to flourish' (2017: 25–26).

While a comprehensive review of sport historiography on a global scale is not possible in the brief assessment in this chapter, particular attention is focused on relatively recent works and areas in need of additional research. An assortment of representative works are presented from around the world.

NORTH AMERICA

UNITED STATES

Interest in social history grew in the 1970s, and American sport historians produced a plethora of studies over the remainder of the century that covered individual and team sports; school and professional sports; urban sport histories; racial, ethnic, social class, gender, and religious analyses; as well as regional, national, and colonial works. The economics and the business of sport was a growing interest by the turn of the century. The general public was attracted by a multitude of biographies. In the early decades of the twenty-first century, the topic of sport as a political and diplomatic tool has gained prominence.

Barbara Keys's (2006) *Globalizing Sport: National Rivalry and International Community in the 1930s* analyzes the role of sports officials in promoting nationalist causes at the Olympic Games and the World Cup. The Nazi Olympics of 1936 provide a good example of such a process. Nicholas Sarantakes's (2010) *Dropping the Torch: Jimmy Carter, the Olympic Boycott, and the Cold War* considers the overt politicizing of the Olympic Games by the American president as a diplomatic failure. Damion Thomas's (2012) *Globetrotting: African American Athletes and Cold War Politics* relates the use of athletes as agents of foreign policy to promote a favorable image of race relations in the United States. Heather Dichter and Andrew Johns's (2014) anthology *Diplomatic Games: Sport, Statecraft, and International Relations since 1945* is particularly useful in the post-World War II era, that saw independence granted to former colonies and ideological rivalries among the leading powers. Toby Rider's (2016) *Cold War Games: Propaganda, the Olympics, and U.S. Foreign Policy* examines the American use of Soviet bloc defectors as a means to promote favorable propaganda. T. C. Rider and Kevin Witherspoon (2018) edited an anthology, *Defending the American Way of Life: Sport, Culture, and the Cold War.* One reviewer claimed 'that these essays demonstrate how athletes were practically perfect diplomats in America's attempt to roll back communism across the globe' (Bass 2019: 817).

The globalization of sport has assumed greater proportions and scholars have embarked on ready analysis. Mark Dyreson's (2009)

Crafting Patriotism for Global Dominance offers an array of stories relative to such developments over the course of the twentieth century. A reviewer exclaimed that it can 'steer a generation of students to seize on historical writing of this quality as living, breathing, exciting analysis on issues and topics that are intriguing, fascinating, controversial, and made for the cut and thrust of seminar debate' (Crawford 2011: 319).

The globalization of sport can be traced to early colonization efforts and the role of sport in assimilation and acculturation processes (Gems 2006, 2016). Despite such limited forays, Malcolm MacLean charges that 'history-the-discipline retains major blind spots in relation to the perspectives of the colonized' (2014: 24). Some notable attempts to assuage that void are Antonio Sotomayor's '"Operation Sport": Puerto Rico's Recreational and Political Consolidation in the Age of Modernization and Decolonization, 1950s' (2015) and *The Sovereign Colony: Olympic Sport, National Identity, and International Politics in Puerto Rico* (2016). Rob Ruck's (2018) *The Tropic of Football: The Long and Perilous Journey of Samoans to the NFL* covers the outsized influence of American football in the small territory of American Samoa in the South Pacific.

The overwhelming and changing role of the media has drawn increasing interest from sport historians. John Dempsey's (2006) early anthology *Sports Talk Radio in America: Its Context and Culture* addresses the gendered nature of such programming. Travis Vogan has been a prolific scholar of sport media in its various forms; see his *Keepers of the Flame: NFL Films and the Rise of Sports Media* (2014), *ESPN: The Making of a Sports Media Empire* (2015), and *ABC Sports: The Rise and Fall of Network Sports Television* (2018). With the rapid development of technology and the increasing influence of social media, sport historians will have a wealth of material to diagnose and analyze in the future.

Other areas in need of greater research include sport arenas, sport for the disabled, and programs and activities of migrant populations. There is very limited information on rural sport or sport in border lands areas, where populations and cultures merge to produce hybrid societies (Dyreson 2010; Schultz 2017). The global Black Lives Matter crusade has the potential to bring significant change to sport administration, fan relationships, team cohesion, and the economics and business of sport, which will require documentation by sport historians.

CANADA

Canadian sport historians were among the founders of sport history in North America, and their students have continued to make significant contributions to the literature (see Schweinbenz 2010). Hockey is a major sport in Canada, and John Wong's (2005) *Lords of the Rinks: The Emergence of the National Hockey League, 1875–1935* uncovers the early history of the professionalization of the sport. Andrew Holman's (2009) anthology *Canada's Game: Hockey and Identity* covers the multiple factors in the creation of national, regional, class, and ethnic cohesion, or lack thereof. Craig Greenham (2019) offers a recent history of the Canadian version of football and its divergence from the American variety. Karen Wall's (2012) *Game Plan: A Social History of Sport in Alberta* provides a regional study in a land split by linguistic and territorial differences. John Reid and Robert Reid (2015) address the developmental differences in two popular sports in 'Diffusion and Discursive Stabilization: Sports Historiography and the Contrasting Fortunes of Cricket and Ice Hockey in Canada's Maritime Provinces.' Nancy Bouchier and Ken Cruikshank's (2016) *The People of the Bay: A Social and Environmental History of Hamilton Harbour* is an interdisciplinary urban study that merges environmental and recreational history. PearlAnn Rechwein's (2014) *Climber's Paradise: Making Canada's Mountain Parks, 1906–1974* is also interdisciplinary in nature, covering the sport of alpinism and the politics inherent in the activity.

M. Ann Hall's (2002) *The Girl and the Game: A History of Women's Sport in Canada* is the first extensive historical coverage of sport and gender in Canada. The new edition provides additional material on indigenous peoples. A number of Canadian scholars who contribute to gender studies are also activists for indigenous peoples. See the special edition of the *Journal of Sport History* on 'Indigenous Resurgence, Regeneration, and Decolonization through Sport History' (2019).

MEXICO AND CENTRAL AMERICA

Archeological evidence points to the existence of ball courts throughout Mexico and Central America (Scarborough and Wilcox 1991).
Mexican indigenous tribes, especially the Tarahumara, are well known
for their endurance running capabilities. Indigenous sports, such as
bullfights, cockfighting, and rodeo are still prevalent in Mexico. By
the twentieth century, foreigners brought the modern sports of soccer, baseball, basketball, and boxing to the region. Jai alai remains a
vestige of Spanish influence. A Guatemalan soccer team competed in
the first Central American Games in 1921, and the Catholic Church
supported clubs in Costa Rica. Mexico, Nicaragua, and Panama all
adopted the American game of baseball, while West Indian migrants
brought cricket to Costa Rica. The YMCA promoted basketball
and volleyball in the region, and women took readily to the games.
The upper class gravitated toward sailing, polo, golf, and tennis and
formed their own clubs. Indoor pools and natural lakes provided
swimming and diving activities, and both Mexico and Costa Rica
produced Olympic medalists. Professional boxers appeared by the
very early twentieth century, and they remain among the world's
best. Female boxers fought in Nicaragua as early as 1926. Mexicans
took up American football in the 1920s and continue to be among
the sport's most ardent supporters. Mexican college players compete
against an American all-star team annually in the postseason. Despite
this knowledge, mostly gleaned from newspapers and magazines,
there is relatively little formal sport history of the region in English
(McGehee 2010; Arbena 1988).

Mexico City hosted the 1968 Olympics and the 1970 World Cup.
There is considerable research on the former, but mostly written
from an American perspective. See Douglas Hartmann's (2003) *Race,
Culture, and the Revolt of the Black Athlete: The 1968 Olympic Protest
and Their Aftermath*, Kevin Witherspoon's (2014) *Before the Eyes of the
World: Mexico and the 1968 Olympic Games*, and Claire Brewster and
Keith Brewster's (2016) *Representing the Nation: Sport and Spectacle in
Post-revolutionary Mexico*.

Alan Klein (1994) produced an early history of the Mexican professional baseball league. A host of baseball players from Mexico,
Nicaragua, and Venezuela have attained stardom in the American

professional leagues, but their histories are generally recorded in popular biographies. Jorge Iber (2019) provides a recent comprehensive history of American football in Latin America. In the southern state of Oaxaca, basketball has a long history. Town plazas become basketball courts with social, religious, and cultural significance. Youth teams start as young as age six and compete barefoot in regional tournaments for prize money. At international tournaments, they often beat teams in the United States (Springwood 2006; Bermudez 2013; Gonzalez 2013). Such activities adopt and adapt sporting practices and change meanings as they cross borders, a process that requires greater scholarly attention and analysis.

Joseph Arbena (1991) covers the development of sport in Mexico during the twentieth century, and Richard McGehee published several articles (in 1992, 1994, 1998, 2000, 2002, and 2005) on Mexico and Central American countries; but a void remains relative to most countries in Central America. The merger of sport, politics, and war did receive greater attention in the soccer war of 1969 between El Salvador and Honduras in which violence erupted at the World Cup qualifying matches between the two neighboring countries. El Salvadorans were irate over the treatment of their countrymen, who had migrated to Honduras and composed 20 percent of its population. They were dispossessed of their land and expelled. At the conclusion of the qualifying matches, won by El Salvador, the latter's military invaded Honduras in a four-day attack that took a decade to resolve (Dunham 1979).

There is still much work to be done for sport historians. Indigenous games, women's sports, working-class clubs, the role of religious sponsorship, school sports, and external organizations such as the YMCA all provide topics in need of scholars (McGehee 2010).

CARIBBEAN

The Caribbean region is an assemblage of island nations and imperial territories ruled by the English, French, Spanish, Dutch, and Americans. British colonialists brought cricket to the region, played in upper-class clubs before the game filtered down to the middle and working classes. By the 1950s, black West Indians could claim the game as their own. C. L. R. James asserts that

> I haven't the slightest doubt that the clash of race, caste and class did not retard but stimulated West Indian cricket. I am equally certain that in those years social and political passions, denied normal outlets, expressed themselves so fiercely in cricket (and other games) precisely because they were games.
>
> (Quoted in Cobley 2010)

From 1975 to 1995, the West Indian teams dominated their former colonial masters. 'The Caribbean people basked in the reflected glory of their cricketers who gave them a stronger sense of pride and identity than they had ever known before. It strengthened their faith in themselves and vindicated their claims to self-determination (Sandiford 2004: 132). The power of sport to promote national identity, cultural competence, and social capital reasserted itself when male and female Jamaican sprinters gained world dominance after the turn of the twenty-first century (Cobley 2010).

The Jamaicans also excelled at soccer, sending many players to England and the United States. In the former Spanish colonies Cuba, Puerto Rico, and the Dominican Republic produced world-class boxers, but the American game of baseball had particular influence. Cubans began competing with American teams as early as 1860, and Cuba sent its first player to an American professional team by 1870. Cubans established their own professional league in 1873. They then introduced the sport to Puerto Rico and the Dominican Republic. Both would excel at the game, sending hundreds of players to the American professional leagues (Gems 2006). After the Cuban Revolution of the 1950s and its political turn to communism, Cuban sport officials exported their successful athletic system to developing countries around the world.

There is considerable literature on Cuban sport history. Paul Pettavino and Geralyne Pye's (1994) *Sport in Cuba* first analyzed the Cuban phenomenon; this was followed by Roberto González Echeverría's (1999) history of Cuban baseball and Milton Jamail (2000) inside look at the particular aspects of the Cuban influence. Similarly, Alan Klein's (1991) *Sugarball: The American Game, the Dominican Dream* and Rob Ruck's (1999) *The Tropic of Baseball: Baseball in the Dominican Republic* initiated studies of the sport in that country. Klein's (2014) *Dominican Baseball: New Pride, Old Prejudice* provide an in-depth analysis of the recruitment of Dominican athletes. (For Puerto Rico, see Chapter 5.) An abundance of biographical studies exist for Caribbean athletes, but most are directed at a general audience.

Outside of the English-speaking countries of the Caribbean, there is little historical research. While baseball is thoroughly documented, indigenous sports such as cockfighting are not. There is a need for updated studies of the baseball academies throughout the Dominican Republic and the lives of Caribbean athletes relative to race, social class, gender, and religion, as such factors from their colonial pasts continue to linger within a context of hegemonic masculinity.

SOUTH AMERICA

Indigenous peoples in South America engaged in a variety of physical activities long before the arrival of the European explorers. They boxed and wrestled, swam, ran races for speed and endurance, and danced at communal festivals. Archery was a necessity. Ball games might be played by individuals or with teams. Some Brazilian natives tested their endurance in the *corrida de tora*, which required them to carry heavy logs over varying distances. They also played a ball game called xikunahity, similar to volleyball without a net, in which teams tried to propel a ball with their head into the opponent's territory where it could not be returned (Torres 2010; van Mele and Renson, 1992).

The Spanish conquerors introduced bullfights in the sixteenth century in the northern areas of the continent. The introduction of horses spawned horse racing and the gaucho culture that eventually produced rodeos. In Argentina, the upper classes eventually adopted polo; while the Basque immigrants brought their game of jai alai to the southern countries. By the twentieth century, sport clubs proliferated for soccer, boxing, swimming, golf, field hockey, and cycling. The YMCA introduced basketball and volleyball. Auto racing became a passion for some (Torres 2010; Laffaye 2014).

Scholars began to take notice in the 1980s as anthropologist Roberto Da Matta began to assess the soccer fever in Brazil. A host of soccer studies in South America soon followed (Lever 1983; Stein 1988; Mason 1995; Curi 2014; Fontes and Buarque de Hollenda

2014; Bocketti 2016). Capoeira, the martial art of slave culture that evolved into a dance form, also drew attention (Assuncao 2005), as it has migrated to foreign shores. There is a considerable output on Brazilian sport history, mostly in Portuguese; but there is a need for greater attention to matters of class, race, ethnicity, gender, and imperialism (Booth 2013).

Eduardo Archetti (1999) analyzed the Argentinian pastimes of soccer, tango, and polo and their influence on gender identity. A host of soccer studies in South America soon followed (Lever 1983; Stein 1988; Mason 1995). South America was the first to establish a continental championship, the Copa America tournament, established in 1916. Uruguay won the first World Cup title in 1930, and South American teams are perennial contenders.

Cesar Torres (2001, 2006) has published works on Argentinian sport, particularly its Olympic endeavors. Yet other countries lack documentation and analysis. National histories for most countries other than Brazil and Argentina are lacking. Given the continental enthusiasm for soccer, why is American baseball the major sport in Venezuela? Given the prominence of Argentinian soccer, its boxers who have become world-class competitors are overshadowed. The machismo culture inherited from Europeans remains strong throughout the continent and has retarded the study of women's sport, an oversight which has only begun to be rectified.

EUROPE

It is not possible to present a comprehensive review of sport scholarship in all European countries. This chapter concentrates on English language sources. A somewhat dated but useful sport historiography of Europe is covered in a special issue of the *Journal of Sport History* (see Forum: European Sport and the Challenges of Its Recent Historiography 2011).

UNITED KINGDOM

British sport historians have been among the most prolific scholars. Early works focused largely on sport and social class (see Chapter 2; Collins 2009). As a class-based social structure, the upper classes' enforcement of amateurism became a prominent fixture of British sport, and professionalism became a contentious issue. Commercialization became a characteristic of modern sport, thoroughly analyzed by Wray Vamplew (1976, 1988) and Mike Huggins (2000).

Soccer hooliganism became a popular topic during the 1980s and thereafter (Dunning, Murphy, and Williams 1988; Johnes 2000). Jean Williams (2002) has made strides in her series on women's sport. National histories have been complemented by imperial studies (see Chapter 5) and community investigations (Jarvie and Walker 1994; Jarvie 1999; Jarvie and Barnett 2000; Johnes 2002, 2005; Metcalfe 2006). There are a multitude of studies on soccer, cricket, and rugby, but a surprising lack of research on boxing. Despite the promise of some early studies (Hill 2002; Borsay 2006), leisure activities before the Industrial Revolution have not been fully explored. Other areas of need include greater insight into gender and race issues, as well as the historical role of sport in Northern Ireland, where religion and politics have great bearing on the society (Johnes 2010).

IRELAND

During the nineteenth century, Irish Catholics brought their sporting pastimes with them as they emigrated, particularly to the United States (Darby and Hassan 2008). The Gaelic Athletic Association maintained an Irish Catholic identity in its programs both at home and abroad, while the English sports of rugby and cricket gained some adherents in Ireland during an ongoing period of cultural transition (Hassan and O'Kane 2010).

As in England, Irish historians adopted Marxism in the 1960s, and class analysis and the economy became prominent. With the later turn toward cultural history, sport assumed greater importance. The relationship of sport to the political conflict between the Protestant and Catholic communities within Northern Ireland, as well as the majority-Catholic Republic of Ireland's influence on sport across the whole of Ireland, gathered attention by the 1990s (Sugden and Bairner 1993; Cronin 1999; Bairner 2005), a period that saw a measure of amelioration in the tensions within Northern Ireland.

Despite the wealth of material on Irish sport, there is a lack of material on Irish boxers, who challenged the English in nationalistic encounters. Irish women also took up the sport, evidenced by Katie Taylor's Olympic title in 2012 and her professional championships thereafter. The dominance of male sport has greatly overshadowed that of women in Irish sport historiography. Greater attention to folk games should also be undertaken. As the impressive growth of the Irish economy has drawn a significant number of international migrants to the country and the ongoing resolution of differences within Northern Ireland play out, there is sure to be an effect on sporting practices, which will provide sufficient material for future studies (Hassan and O'Kane 2010).

SPAIN

Sport history developed late in Spain, with concentration on bull-fights, soccer, and the Olympics in the 1990s (Mitchell 1991; Pink 1997). Regional identity has been featured in the Catalan independence movement (Murtha 2017). Soccer teams have provided outlet for national and regional identities and instilled national pride as a World Cup champion.

While soccer is covered comprehensively, there are numerous lacunae in the history of Spanish sport for future researchers. There is very limited information on the role of sport under the regime of General Francisco Franco and the civil war that he initiated. Traditional games, such as Basque pelota require greater attention. The rise of the Spanish professional basketball league, tennis star Rafael Nadal, Spanish cyclists, female athletes, and the beach culture are little known. The IOC presidency of Juan Antonio Samaranch begs for scholarly analysis too (McFarland 2011).

FRANCE

Roger Caillois (1961) pioneered French sport history with *Man, Play, and Games*. French historians of the Annales School favored the *longue durée*, an approach that takes a long-term perspective and focuses on the slow evolution of events. By the late twentieth century, French scholars such as Pierre Bourdieu, Michel Foucault, and

Jacques Derrida would have a great impact on historical analysis. French sport historians focused on accounts of soccer, rugby, and cycling as well as physical education. Pierre Arnaud's (1991) *Le militaire, l'ecolier, le gymnast* provides a political history of gymnastics, and Andre Guonot (2002) wrote on the merger of sport and politics for an English readership. Authors focused on local, national, and international studies as well as on the role of religion, particularly the Catholic influence. Gender studies had to wait until the turn of the twentieth century (Arnaud and Terret 1996). French colonial studies followed (Combeau-Mari 1998). Thierry Terret (1996) greatly expanded the scope of sport studies with his *Histoire des sports*. A prolific author, Terret's many works in English broadened the audience for French sport history. Despite the relative health of the field in France, there is a need for more comparative studies as well as the religious influences of Judaism and Islam, particularly relevant to the large migrant populations in the country (Terret 2010).

GERMANY

There is an abundance of sport history research in Germany, which can be traced back to Jahn's advocacy in the early nineteenth century. The history of his Turner movement has figured prominently over the past two centuries. Carl Diem (1960) published a world sport history, followed by Horst Ueberhorst's massive six-volume follow-up (1972–1989). Arnd Kruger, Michael Kruger, Gertrud Pfister, and Annette Hofmann, among others, have produced prodigious scholarship in English. Topics such as workers' sport, Nazi sport (Margolick 2005; Erenburg 2007), Jewish sport, soccer (Tomlinson and Young 2006), the Olympics (Mandell 1987; Kruger and Murray 2003: Large 2007), and gender have been well covered. The political split of East and West Germany during the Cold War and its sporting ramifications have garnered considerable attention in German publications (Kruger 2010).

AUSTRIA

Equestrian sports, gymnastics, ice skating, and alpinism featured prominently in nineteenth-century Austria, and soccer clubs formed after 1880. Vienna hosted the Second Workers Olympiad in 1931, but sport historians took little notice until the 1990s. Most of the literature since then is in the German language. Studies have concentrated on Vienna as the hub of activity, and soccer holds the greatest attraction for scholars, although greater interest in skiing has been generated since the turn of the twenty-first century. In his review of the state of sport history in Austria, Matthias Marschik states that 'the focus has broadened to embrace questions of nationalism, migration, masculinity and gender, body politics, and space as well as other forms of sport and the nature of sporting cultures in general' (2011: 189).

ITALY

While there have been substantial studies of ancient sport in Rome (see Chapter 1), modern sport history is generally lacking in Italy. Sport historians have been greatly overshadowed by cultural historians, who have neglected the role and influence of sport. Sport studies have concentrated on the Fascist period (De Grazia 1981; Koon 1985), with a few exceptions. Adolfo Noto and Lauro Rossi (1992) present a comprehensive anthology of the historical growth of sport, but similar works are wanting. Simon Martin's *Football and Fascism: The National Game under Mussolini* (2004) and his *Sport Italia: The Italian Love Affair with Sport* (2011) are worthwhile English additions, as is Gigliola Gori's (2004) gender study *Female Bodies, Sport, Italian Fascism: Submissive Women and Strong Mothers*. Alessio Ponzio's (2015) *Shaping the New Man: Youth Training Regimes in Fascist Italy and Nazi Germany* offers a comparative study of physical education programs in both countries.

There is still abundant need for English works on sport in Italy. The modernization of sport in the country after unification in 1861 begs for coverage, as does the period after World War II. Sport in southern Italy and Sicily is relatively virgin territory for researchers. Sport festivals, such as the Palio horse race in Siena, have a long history without adequate analysis. The wider topic of leisure is little studied, especially given the importance of tourism and beach culture in the country. Given Italy's geographical location and its historic role as a cultural crossroads, there is much to be done in terms of comparative studies (Martin 2011a, 2011b).

SCANDINAVIA

Distinct gymnastics systems developed in both Denmark and Sweden by the early nineteenth century (Trangbæk and Kirmanen 1995; Hartmann-Tews and Pfister 2003; Bonde 2006). The Swedes exported their system internationally. Soccer clubs appeared by the 1870s to rival the practice of gymnastics. Danes invented the game of team handball in 1897, and this was soon exported to neighboring countries. Skiing competitions began in Finland in 1886, and Norwegians brought their passion for skiing to the United States. In a reverse cultural flow, Canadians brought ice hockey to Scandinavia, which the Swedes and Finns quickly adopted as their own. Finns dominated long-distance track events during the early decades of the twentieth century (Nielsen and Bale 2011).

Henrik Meinander and J. A. Mangan (1998) made an early comparative study of the physical education systems in the Nordic countries. During the latter decades of the twentieth century, sport historians published works in their native languages. Leea Virtanen and Thomas DuBois (2000) studied Finnish folklore with its peasant pastimes. Sport clubs provided a means to build a local sense of community (Nielsen and Bale 2011). That sense of cohesion was fractured by the Nazi invasion in World War II, captured by Hans Bonde's (2008) *Football with the Foe: Danish Sport under the Swastika*. Nordic scholars increasingly publish their works in English, making their rich cultures accessible to a wider audience.

SLAVIC COUNTRIES

RUSSIA

Traditional Russian folk games included games played with sticks thrown at targets and bat and ball games, which might still be seen in some areas (Ivanova 2014). Sport became a more important political tool during the Cold War era after World War II (Wagg and Andrews 2007). With the Soviet entry into the Olympics in 1952, sport offered a means to demonstrate presumed cultural superiority. After the fall of the Soviet Union in 1991, sport remained a public demonstration in the Russian resurgence. President Vladimir Putin spared no expense in hosting the 2014 Winter Olympics in Sochi, in which

Russia topped all competitors in the medal count (Orttung and Zhemukhov 2017). Subsequent inquiries revealed a state-sponsored doping scandal among Russian athletes, that resulted in a four-year ban from international competitions.

British scholar James Riordan was a pioneer in Russian studies (see Riordan 1977, 1978, 1980). As a Russian speaker, Riordan had access to sources unavailable to most western scholars. He showed the development of modern sport under the tsars. Russia became a founding member of the IOC, but the Bolshevik Revolution of 1917 changed the role of sport, which became a means to nation-building (Riordan 2010). Robert Edelman (1993) produced a study of Russian fandom in the newly commercialized state and followed this in 2012 with a history of the Spartak Moscow soccer team. William Frank (2013) published a study on skiing, and Jenifer Parks (2017) analyzed the Soviet sports bureaucracy and the Olympic Games. Manfred Zeller (2018) contributed a relatively recent work on the politics of soccer but little else has followed from western scholars.

CENTRAL AND EASTERN EUROPE

Gymnastics promoted nationalistic movements in mid-nineteenth century Europe. Both the Polish Falcons and the Czech Sokols copied the German Turners in their organization and intentions when they were established in the 1860s (Nolte 2003). Both groups later formed immigrant clubs in the United States that supported European independence movements. The gymnastic festivals, known as *slets*, became international with Czechs, Slovaks, Ukrainians, Yugoslavians, and Americans joining in the camaraderie (Gems 1997). Independence however, was not achieved until the cessation of World War I and the dismantling of the Austrian Empire. In the postwar era, soccer and ice hockey gained in popularity (Waic and Zwicker 2010).

Eastern European countries were subsumed within the Soviet bloc after World War II. Frantisek Kratky established the International Committee of Physical Education and Sport, which promoted sport history. Jiri Kossl published the *History of the Czechoslovak Olympic Movement* in 1977. Such works are not accessible in English, however.

With Polish independence in 1918, the Catholic Church assumed greater influence in the gymnastic clubs; but with Nazi occupation in World War II, sports were banned, to be resurrected under the communists in the Cold War era. Sport historians in Poland have concentrated on the influence of ethnic minorities, such as Bernard Woltman's (1980) *Polish Physical Culture in the German Eastern Poland* (see Waic and Zwicker 2010). German scholar Diethelm Blecking (2008) provides a study of Jewish sport in Poland before World War II, and Anke Hilbrenner and Britta Lenz (2011) offer a multiethnic analysis of soccer in Poland; but English language sources are limited (see Kossakowski, Nosal, and Wozniak 2020). There is a need and an opportunity for sport historians to examine the religious influence on sport in Poland as well as a need for comparative and transnational studies of central and eastern European nations (Lenz 2011).

BALKAN COUNTRIES

Slovenia and Croatia had been part of the Hapsburg Empire since the sixteenth century, while Serbia and Bulgaria remained within the Ottoman Empire until the nineteenth century. Sokol clubs in the region became bastions of nationalism. In 1929, King Aleksander managed to unite the Sokols under his regime (he was monarch from 1921 to 1934). In 1924, the Balkan Games (Kissoudi 2008) festival intended to bring some reconciliation to the ethnic and religious factions, which proved temporary (Rohdewald 2011). The king was assassinated in 1934. In the wake of World War II, the region was unified under the communist dictatorship of Josip Broz Tito from 1945 until his death in 1980. The dissolution of Yugoslavia in the 1990s resulted in the Balkan Wars among the disparate groups and the fracture of the country into several smaller nations.

In a violent region marked by ethnic and religious differences, sport can often serve as a surrogate form of war, as seen in soccer (Vrcan and Lalic 1999); Sack and Suster 2000; Mills 2009, 2018; Filipova-Kyurkchieva 2006) and basketball competitions (Perica 2001). Given the volatility, religious differences, and consistent transition in the region, there is much work to do for sport historians. The role of religion needs greater analysis. The influence of the former Ottoman Empire is little known, but Turkish wrestling remains popular in Bulgaria. Sport participation has produced a transformation in traditional gender roles that requires study; and the role of journalists who can incite or pacify is also in need of further research (see Starc 2007 for one such study).

GREECE

Greece is the home of both the ancient and modern Olympic Games (see Chapters 1 and 8), and there is abundant research on both (Sansone 1992; Miller 2004; Kyle 2007; Scanlon 2014; Mandell 2016; Papakonstantinou 2019). The International Olympic Academy provides an annual seminar for graduate students that promotes continued research. In comparison, there is a dearth of literature relative to modern Greek sport. The role of female athletes in Greece is in need of an update (Skiadas 1998).

AFRICA

Sport history in Africa remains largely in its infancy. Mahfoud Amara has charged that the Muslim nations of Northern Africa require a different lens for analysis, as the modernity and postmodernity theories employed by western researchers may not fit the region; this is because such concepts reach other nations and other cultures at different times and carry different meanings (Amana 2010). Arab nationalist history is often a response to European colonialism. Different interpretations of Islam further exemplify cultural differences. Northern Africa also witnessed the transverse of Mediterranean trade routes, bringing cross-cultural influences. As a result, the nature of traditional pastimes in the region is still seeking edification. The Pan Arab Games are a modern attempt to bring a semblance of unity to disparate political entities based on a western model of sport. Recent anthologies such as that from Nauright and Amara (2018), *Sport in the African World*, and Cleveland, Kaur, and Akindes (2020), *Sports in Africa: Past and Present*, address some of these issues.

Soccer has drawn the most attention from sport historians (Alegi 2004, 2010; Armstrong and Giulianotti 2008; Alegi and Bolsmann 2013; Deets 2015). The ascendance of Kenyan runners in the last half century has elicited several studies (Bale and Sang 1996; Bale 2012; Sikes 2019). Martial sports have been examined by a few researchers. Gems (2014a) covered early forms of fighting and African boxers while Ranger (1987) was an early study of boxers in Rhodesia. Paul (1987) and Carotenuto (2013) explored wrestling. More general studies were conducted by Phyllis Martin (see *Leisure and Society in Colonial Brazzaville* (1995)) and Laura Fair (see *Pastimes and Politics: Culture, Community, and Identity in Post-Abolition Urban Zanzibar, 1890–1945* (2001)). European powers divided up the African continent among themselves at a Berlin conference in 1884–1885, and they introduced their own leisure and sporting practices thereafter. There is still much to be known about such colonial societies as well as the influence of Christian missionaries in the adoption or adaptation of western sport forms (see Allen 2008; Nauright 2010).

SOUTH AFRICA

South Africa has long drawn the interest of sport historians due to its policy of apartheid (Lapchick 1975; Nauright 1997; Booth 1998; Black and Nauright 1998). Sport, literally and figuratively, remained a political football throughout the twentieth century, resulting in the country's banishment from the Olympic Games from 1964 until 1992. One can trace the sporting history of the country through numerous works (Van der Merwe 1986, 2009; Cleophas 2018). Despite the wealth of studies on soccer (Alegi and Bolsmann 2013), cricket (Allen 2015), and rugby (Nauright and Black 1998), there remain gaps in the literature relative to other sports and the role of women in South African sport (Nauright 2010).

NORTHEAST ASIA

CHINA

China has a robust sport history, recorded for more than 5,000 years (see Chapter 1). Its modern sport history began with the revolution of 1911 and the resultant westernization of physical education and sport. Guo Xifen published a *History of Sport in China* in 1919, which was followed by Hao Gengshen's *Of Chinese Physical Education and Sport* in 1926. Throughout the succeeding decades, several books were published on sport and the Olympics. With the communist victory in the civil war and the creation of the People's Republic of China in 1949, sports became of greater interest, taught in the schools and in publications. That interest waned with Mao Zedong's Cultural Revolution in the 1960s, to be resurrected with its collapse in the 1980s. The Chinese *Journal of Sport History and Culture* first appeared in 1983 and the Chinese Society for the History of Physical Education and Sport was founded a year later. Regular national and international conferences followed. By 2008, more than 100 sport history books had been published, covering ancient sport, politics (Brownell 1995), the Olympics, gender (Hong 1997; Dong 2002), provincial histories, and particular sport forms. Upon China's hosting of the Olympics in 2008, a flurry of Olympic studies (Hong, Mackay, and Christensen 2008; Jarvie, Hwang, and Brennan 2008; Brownell 2008a) were conducted and Olympic Studies research centers were established (Hong 2010). An increasing number of publications continue to appear in English, written by younger bilingual Chinese scholars as well as western scholars (Judkins and Nielson 2015; Liu and Hong 2017; Fuhua and Hong 2019).

Despite tenuous political relations, Taiwanese scholars have cooperated with their mainland counterparts in joint conference ventures and publications. By the 1990s, more than 20 books were published by Taiwanese sport historians, who continue to study Taiwan's own distinctive sporting history (Yu 2007; Harney 2019).

Such continued and comparative studies are a necessity to alleviate researchers' ethnocentric biases and lack of knowledge. Such cooperative ventures might unlock the influences of religious sport proselytizers, such as the YMCA in China and the role of sport among its ethnic minorities (Hong 2010).

JAPAN

Like China, Japan has a long sport history (see Chapter 1). Modern (western) sport practices came to Japan during the Meiji period (1868–1912). With the Japanese victory in the Russo-Japanese War of 1905, a greater sense of nationalism began to overtake the westernization movement. Martial arts won renewed interest, and baseball exchanges with American teams were meant as tests of cultural supremacy. In 1936, the Japanese instituted their own professional baseball league. After World War II, a national rugby league c company teams formed in 1949; but school teams garnered the most fan support. Soccer took hold in Japan in the 1990s, and the women's national team won the 2011 World Cup (Guttmann and Thompson 2001; Light 2010).

While Japan has a healthy contingent of sport historians, few publish in English due to linguistic barriers. Kawashima Kohei (2019) analyzed the growth of American football in his homeland, while Maguire and Nakayama, in *Japan, Sport and Society: Tradition and Change in a Globalizing World* (2006), took a broader scope in their coverage of sporting transitions in the country. Wolfram Manzenreiter and John Horne (2004) included Japan in their regional study of soccer. Dennis Frost's (2011) *Seeing Stars: Sports Celebrity, Identity, and Body Culture in Modern Japan* examines the important role of sport in the society. Manzenreiter followed with *Sport and Body Politics in Japan* (2014). Baseball has long been of interest to native Japanese and westerners alike. Robert Whiting's (1977) *The Chrysanthemum and the Bat: The Game Japanese Play* was the first in his ongoing series of studies (Keaveney 2018). In *Transpacific Field of Dreams: How Baseball Linked the United States and Japan in Peace and War*, Sayuri Guthrie-Shimizu (2015) analyzed the role baseball played in diplomacy. In *Japanese Women and Sport*, Robin Kietlinski (2013) researched a sorely needed topic in a male-dominated society. Thomas Havens's (2015) *Marathon Japan* covers female runners. There is still room for more English-language studies of sport in Japan. The invasion of foreign sumo wrestlers and the transnational nature of baseball, with Japanese and American players switching continents, require comprehensive analysis.

SOUTH KOREA

South Korea became a prominent participant in international sport as host of the 1988 Summer Olympics and cohost of the 2002 soccer World Cup and the 2018 Winter Olympics. The 1988 Games spurred economic development and fostered political reforms in the nation (Pound 1994). The 2018 Games engendered negotiations and a measure of cooperation with North Korea, including a combined women's ice hockey team (Joo, Bae, and Kassens-Noor 2017).

Few South Korean sport historians publish their work in English, and this has left gaps in the literature. Baseball is the most popular sport in the country, but little is known about its introduction by American missionaries or its growth under the Japanese occupation of the country after 1910. The martial art of taekwondo originated in South Korea (Moenig 2015) but awaits a definitive history. South Korean female golfers have been very successful on the international women's professional golf tour, but their success has generated little study (Shin and Nam 2004). Very little is known about sport in secretive North Korea, although its women boxers have enjoyed international success (Gems 2014a).

SOUTH ASIA

INDIA

India has a long history detailed in its indigenous games (see Chapter 1); but its modern sport history is deficient in western sources (Valiotis 2010). Ronojoy Sen's (2015) *Nation at Play: A History of Sport in India* is a heroic attempt to fill the void. There is considerable output relative to cricket, mostly relating to Bombay and Bengal (Docker 1977; Cashman 1980; Majumdar 2015), that addresses colonialism and nationalism. An inclusive anthology on soccer covers the political aspects of the game (Dimeo 2001). More recent analysis is provided by Bandyopadhyay and Majumdar (2016). Joseph Alter's (1992) *The Wrestler's Body: Identity and Ideology in North India* is an insightful study that covers the rituals and discipline of the sport relative to masculine identity.

Given the size of the country and its disparate population with differing religions and languages, there is a lack of community, ethnic, social class, and religious studies. Given the Olympic success of India's men's field hockey team with multiple gold medals, there is surprisingly little scholarly attention provided to its history (Chakraborty 2010). Work on women's sport is also lacking. The religious backgrounds of successful female boxers and the influence of this (Gems 2014a) awaits a thorough study.

OTHER COUNTRIES IN SOUTH ASIA

For India's neighbor Pakistan, sport history is almost nonexistent with nominal attention paid to cricket (Marqusee 1996; Osborn

2014). Most of the other countries in the South Asia region present virgin territory for sport historians.

SOUTHEAST ASIA

Similarly, sport history has been neglected in Southeast Asian countries, with a few exceptions (see Chapter 8). There is growing interest in sport in the Philippines (Gems 2006, 2016; Antolihao 2017). Simon Creak (2015) broke new ground with *Embodied Nation: Sport, Masculinity, and the Making of Modern Laos*. Clifford Geertz's (1972) path-breaking anthropological study of cockfighting in Indonesia remains a classic; but there has been limited research thereafter (see Chapter 8). Singapore has seen limited analysis (Mangan and Hong 2002). Malaysia also lacks recent study (Shennan 2000; DaCosta and Miragaya 2002), although Janice Brownfoot (1990; 2002) published a number of articles on girls and women's sport in the country.

Gender studies would be appropriate for all of the countries in the region. There is a need for national studies of Thailand, Vietnam, Cambodia, and Myanmar and colonial studies of all the nations previously under European rule. Both Cambodia and Thailand claim, without conclusion, the martial sport of Muay Thai. There is much work for sport historians in this region (Little 2010).

AUSTRALIA AND NEW ZEALAND

Although sport historians in both Australia and New Zealand have struggled to achieve academic respect, they have produced a wealth of material (Adair 2010; MacLean 2010). Disagreements over theory and epistemology have not hindered but, rather, increased productivity, and Australians Doug Booth (2005a, 2005b) and Murray Phillips (2001, 2006) have championed new approaches in sport history. Among early syntheses, see Richard Cashman's (1995) *Paradise of Sport: The Rise of Organized Sport in Australia*, Daryl Adair and Wray Vamplew's (1997) *Sport in Australian History*, and Doug Booth and Colin Tatz's (2000) *One-Eyed: A View of Australian Sport*. As a far-flung colony of England, sport provided a link to the settlers' homeland, as it also allowed for expressions of its own growing sense of nationalism (Nielsen 2014). Both Australia and New Zealand expressed their fidelity to the homeland through military service during wartime (Blackburn 2016; Crotty and Hess 2018).

The location and geography of Australia has fostered a particular attraction to individual sports such as swimming and surfing in ocean-side communities, duly explored by sport historians (Booth 2005b, 2016a, 2016b). Though sport has been a highly male-dominated activity, Australian women have outperformed their male counterparts on the Olympic stage (Adair 2010), and gender studies has been the focus for some sport historians (Burroughs and Nauright 2000). Studies of sport among the indigenous population has been more deficient, with some notable exceptions (Adair 2014; Osmond 2017, 2019). Celebrated Aboriginal athletes such as boxer Lionel Rose, tennis star Evonne Goolagong, and track sensation Cathy Freeman have drawn the attention of biographers. Despite the breadth of Australian sport history, some topics remain understudied. The women's game of netball has been subordinated to more popular male sports. The role of religion in Australian sport might offer new insights, and there has been limited analysis of economic factors, sport media, and the fan culture (Adair 2010).

New Zealand's close ties to England retarded the development of a national sport history; though sport historians have since rectified that lack (MacLean 2010; Ryan and Watson 2018). The role of rugby in enhancing a national identity has been significant and drawn considerable study (Sinclair 1986; Ryan 2005), and some attention has been given to cricket and netball. Within the country, the indigenous Maori culture has received earlier and more considerate study than that of Australian Aboriginals (Best 1925; Collins and Jackson 2007). New Zealand's sporting relationships with the apartheid government of South Africa have been given due diligence (Thompson 1975; Templeton 1998; Richards 1999).

The nationalist trope in New Zealand sport history might benefit from more comparative analysis relative to its similarities and differences with Australia as well other countries, moving beyond the assumed relationships and influences of Britain. Much of the sport history literature has focused on men and masculinity, and not enough attention has been accorded to women's sport (MacLean 2010). New Zealand's thriving sport tourism industry is also ripe for analysis.

This brief international survey of sport history indicates a plethora of opportunities for future sport historians. The multitude of stories to be told, dissected, analyzed, and argued will only increase annually as more sport history is made on a daily basis.

FURTHER READING

Tansin Benn, Gertrud Pfister, and Haifaa Jawad, eds. (2011) *Muslim Women and Sport*. New York: Routledge.

Dario Brentin and Dejan Zec, eds. (2018) *Sport in Socialist Yugoslavia*. London: Routledge.

Mauricio Drumond and Victor Andrade deMelo, eds. (2016) *Brazilian Sports History*. London: Routledge.

Mark Dyreson, ed. (2020) *Sport in the Americas: Local, Regional, and International Perspectives*. New York: Routledge.

Brenda Elsey and Joshua Nadel (2020) *Futbolera: A History of Women's Sport in Latin America*. Austin: University of Texas Press.

J. G. Michael and Shaheed Aderinto, eds. (2019) *Sports in African History, Politics and Identity Formation*. London: Routledge.

Ilse Hartmann-Tews and Gertrud Pfister, eds. (2003) *Sport and Women: Social Issues in International Perspective*. London: Routledge.

Annette Hofmann, ed. (2020) *Sport in Europe*. London: Routledge.

Fan Hong, ed. (2015) *Sport in the Middle East: Power, Politics, Ideology and Religion*. London: Routledge.

Fan Hong and Zhouxiang Lu, eds. (2020) *The Routledge Handbook of Sport in Asia*. London: Routledge.

Michael Kruger and Annette Hofmann, eds. (2020) *Sportgeschichte in Deutschland – Sport History in Germany*. Weisbaden: Springer.

Rosa Lopez de D'Amico, Tansin Benn, and Gertrud Pfister, eds. (2016) *Women and Sport in Latin America*. London: Routledge.

J. A. Mangan and L. P. DaCosta, eds. (2001) *Sport in Latin American Society: Past and Present*. London: Routledge.

Richard McElligott and David Hassan, eds. (2018) *A Social and Cultural History of Sport in Ireland*. London: Routledge.

Henrik Meinander and J. A. Mangan, eds. (1998) *The Nordic World: Sport in Society*. London: Frank Cass.

Gertrud Pfister and Stacey Pope, eds. (2018) *Female Football Players and Fans: Intruding into a Man's World*. London: Macmillan.

David Sheinin, ed. (2015) *Sports Culture in Latin American History*. Pittsburgh: University of Pittsburgh Press.

BIBLIOGRAPHY

_____ (1866) *Athletic Sports for Boys*. New York: Dick & Fitzgerald.

Adair, D. (2010) 'Australia,' in Pope, S. W. and Nauright, J., eds., *Routledge Companion to Sports History*. New York: Routledge, 330–349.

Adair, D. (2014) 'Indigenous Australians and Sport: Critical Reflections,' in Nauright, J., Cobley, A. G., and Wiggins, D. K., eds., *Beyond C.L.R. James: Shifting Boundaries of Race and Ethnicity in Sport*. Fayetteville: University of Arkansas Press, 63–76.

Adair, D. and Vamplew, W. (1997) *Sport in Australian History*. Melbourne: Oxford University Press.

Adams, M. L. (2011) *Artistic Impressions: Figure Skating, Masculinity and the Limit of Sport*. Toronto: University of Toronto Press.

Adelman, M. (1986) *A Sporting Time: New York City and the Rise of Modern Athletics, 1820–70*. Urbana: University of Illinois Press.

Alegi, P. (2004) *Laduma: Soccer, Politics, and Society in South Africa*. Scottsville, South Africa: KwaZulu-Natal Press.

Alegi, P. (2010) *African Soccerscapes: How a Continent Changed the World's Game*. Athens: Ohio University Press.

Alegi, P. and Bolsmann, C., eds. (2013) *South Africa and the Global Game: Football, Apartheid and Beyond*. London: Routledge.

Allen, D. (2008) 'South African Cricket, Imperial Cricketers and Imperial Expansion, 1850–1910,' *International Journal of the History of Sport* 25:4, 443–471.

Allen, D. (2015) *Empire, War, and Cricket in South Africa: Logan of Matjiesfontein*. Cape Town: Zebra.

Allen, T. W. (1998) *The Invention of the White Race: Racial Oppression and Social Control*. London: Verso.

Alter, J. (1992) *The Wrestler's Body: Identity and Ideology in North India*. Berkeley: University of California Press.

Altherr, T. L., ed. (1997) *Sports in North America: A Documentary History*, vol. 1 part II. Gulf Stream, FL: Academic International Press.

Amana, M. (2010) 'The Middle East and North Africa,' in Pope, S. W. and Nauright, J., eds., *Routledge Companion to Sports History*. New York: Routledge, 498–509.

American Battlefield Trust (2020) 'Women in the American Revolution,' at https://www.battlefields.org/learn/articles/women-american-revolution (accessed 16 April 2020).

Ancient Olympics (n.d.) 'Theagenes,' at http://ancientolympics.arts.kuleuven. be/eng/TP007EN.html (accessed 7 June 2020).

Anderson, B. (1993) *Imagined Communities: Reflections of the Origins and Spread of Nationalism*. New York: Verso.

Antolihao, L. (2017) *Playing with the Big Boys: Basketball, American Imperialism, and Subaltern Discourse in the Philippines*. Lincoln: University of Nebraska Press.

Arbena, J., ed. (1988) *Sport and Society in Latin America: Diffusionism, Dependency, and the Rise of Mass Culture*. New York: Greenwood.

Arbena, J. L. (1991) 'Sport, Development, and Mexican Nationalism, 1920–70,' *Journal of Sport History* 18:3, 350–364.

Archetti, E. (1999) *Masculinities: Football, Polo, and Tango in Argentina*. New York: Berg.

Armstrong, G. and Giulianotti, R., eds. (2008) *Football in Africa: Conflict, Conciliation, and Community*. Basingstoke: Palgrave Macmillan.

Arnaud, P. (1991) *Le militaire, l'ecolier, le gymnast*. Lyon: PUL.

Arnaud, P. and Terret, T. (1996) *Histoire du sport feminine*. Paris: L'Harmattan.

Asbridge, T. (2015) *The Greatest Knight: The Remarkable Life of William Marshal, the Power behind Five English Thrones*. New York: Simon & Schuster.

Ascham, R. (1545) *Toxophilus*. London: Edward Whytchurch.

Assuncao, M. R. (2005) *Capoeira: A History of an Afro-Brazilian Martial Art*. New York: Routledge.

Atwater, C. (2020) 'Climbing and mountaineering,' in Nauright, J. and Zipp, S., eds., *Routledge Handbook of Global Sport*. New York: Routledge, 429–445.

Austin, B. and Grundy, P., eds. (2019) *Teaching U.S. History through Sports*. Madison: University of Wisconsin Press.

Badran, M. (2009) *Feminism in Islam: Secular and Religious Convergences*. Oxford: Oxford University Press.

Bailey, P. (1978) *Leisure and Class in Victorian England: Rational Recreation and the Contest for Control, 1830–1885*. London: Methuen.

Bain-Selbo, E. (2009) *Game Day and God: Football, Faith, and Politics in the American South*. Macon, GA: Mercer University Press.

Bairner, A. (2001) *Sport, Nationalism and Globalisation*. New York: SUNY.

Bairner, A., ed. (2005) *Sport and the Irish: Histories, Identities, Issues*. Dublin: UCD Press.

Baker, W. J. (2007) *Playing with God: Religion and Modern Sport*. Cambridge, MA: Harvard University Press.

Baker, W. J. (2010) 'Religion,' in Pope, S. W. and Nauright, J., eds., *Routledge Companion to Sports History*. New York: Routledge, 216–228.

Bale, J. (2004) *Running Cultures: Racing in Time and Space*. London: Routledge.

Bale, J. (2013) *Kenyan Running: Movement Culture, Geography and Global Change*. London: Routledge.

Bale, J. and Bateman, A., eds. (2009) *Sporting Sounds: Relationships Between Sport and Music*. London: Routledge.

Bale, J. and Cronin, M. (2003) *Sport and Postcolonialism*. New York: Oxford.

Bale, J. and Sang, J. (1996) *Kenyan Running: Movement Culture, Geography and Global Change*. London: Routledge.

Bandy, S. J., ed. (2004) *Nordic Narratives of Sport and Physical Culture: Transdisciplinary Perspectives*. Aarhus: Aarhus University Press.

Bandy, S. J. (2010) 'Gender,' in Pope, S. W. and Nauright, J., eds., *Routledge Companion to Sports History*. New York: Routledge, 129–147.

Bandyopadhyay, K. and Majumdar, B. (2016) *A Social History of Indian Football*. London: Routledge.

Bass, A. (2014) 'State of the Field: Sports History and the "Cultural Turn,"' *Journal of American History* 101:1, 148–172.

Bass, A. (2019) [Review of the Book *Defending the American Way of Life: Sport, Culture, and the Cold War*, ed. by Toby C. Rider and Kevin B. Witherspoon] *Journal of American History* 106:3, 817–818.

BBC Radio 4 (n.d.) 'Whiteness,' at https://www.bbc.co.uk/programmes. m0008wv1 (accessed 3 May 2020).

Beal, B. (2007) 'Skateboarding,' in Booth, D. and Thorpe, H., eds., *Berkshire Encyclopedia of Extreme Sports*. Grand Barrington, MA: Berkshire Publishing, 271–276.

Beckles, H. and Stoddart, B. (1995) *Liberation Cricket: West Indies Cricket Culture*. Manchester: Manchester University Press.

Bederman, G. (1995) *Manliness and Civilization: A Cultural History of Gender and Race in the United States*. Chicago: University of Chicago Press.

Bell, D. (2003) *Encyclopedia of International Games*. Jefferson, NC: McFarland.

Bellis, M. (2020) 'The History of Water Skiing,' *ThoughtCo*, 20 January, at https://www.thoughtco.com/history-of-water-skiing-1992668 (accessed 1 June 2020).

Benn, T., Pfister, G., and Jawad, H., eds. (2011) *Muslim Women and Sport*. New York: Routledge.

Bermudez, E. (2013) 'Oaxacan Youth Basketball Team Competes on a Global Level,' *LA Times*, 21 December, at https://www.latimes.com/local/la-me-oaxaca-basketball-20131222-story.html (accessed 17 June 2020).

Besnier, N. and Brownell, S. (2012) 'Sport, Modernity and the Body,' *Annual Review of Anthropology* 41, 443–459.

Best, E. (1925) *Games and Pastimes of the Maori*. Wellington: Dominion Museum, Bulletin No. 8.

Betts, J. R. (1974) *America's Sporting Heritage, 1850–1950*. Reading, MA: Addison-Wesley.

Birrell, S. and Cole, C., eds. (1994) *Women, Sport and Culture*. Champaign, IL: Human Kinetics.

Black, D. and Nauright, J. (1998) *Rugby and the South African Nation*. Manchester: Manchester University Press.

Blackburn, K. (2016) *War, Sport, and the Anzac Tradition*. Basingstoke: Palgrave Macmillan.

Blecking, D. (2008) 'Jews and Sports in Poland before the Second World War,' in Mendelson, E., ed., *Jews and the Sporting Life*. Oxford: Oxford University Press, 17–35.

Bocketti, G. (2016) *The Invention of the Beautiful Game: Football and the Making of Modern Brazil*. Gainesville: University Press of Florida.

Boddy, K. (2008) *Boxing: A Cultural History*. London: Reaktion Books.

Bolton, H. E. (1921) *The Spanish Borderlands*. New Haven: Yale University Press.

Bonde, H. (2006) *Gymnastics and Politics: Neils Bukh and Male Aesthetics*. Copenhagen: Museum Tusculanum Press.

Bonde, H. (2008) *Football with the Foe: Danish Sport under the Swastika*. Odense: University of Southern Denmark.

Booth, D. (1998) *The Race Game: Sport and Politics in South Africa*. London: Frank Cass.

Booth, D. (2001) *Australian Beach Cultures: The History of Sun, Sand, and Surf*. London: Frank Cass.

Booth, D. (2005a) 'Searching for the Past: Sport Historiography in New Zealand,' *Sporting Traditions* 21:2, 1–28.

Booth, D. (2005b) *The Field: Truth and Fiction in Sport History*. London: Routledge.

Booth, D. (2007) 'Surfing,' in Booth, D. and Thorpe, H., eds., *Berkshire Encyclopedia of Extreme Sports*. Great Barrington, MA: Berkshire Publishing, 317–323.

Booth, D. (2013) 'Sport History in Brazil: Cementing Local Foundations, Strengthening a Subdiscipline,' *Journal of Sport History* 40:3, 371–383.

Booth, D. (2016a) 'Origins in History and Historiography: A Case Study of the First Swimmer at Bondi Beach,' *Journal of Sport History* 43:1, 21–36.

Booth, D. (2016b) 'The Bondi Surfer: An Underdeveloped History,' *Journal of Sport History* 43:3, 272–289.

Booth, D. and Nauright, J. (2014) 'Embodied Identities: Sport and Race in South Africa,' in Nauright, J., Cobley, A. G., and Wiggins, D. K., eds., *Beyond C.L.R. James: Shifting Boundaries of Race and Ethnicity in Sport.* Fayetteville: University of Arkansas Press, 41–62.

Booth, D. and Tatz, C. (2000) *One-Eyed: A View of Australian Sport.* Sydney: Allen & Unwin.

Booth, D. and Thorpe, H., eds. (2007) *Berkshire Encyclopedia of Extreme Sports.* Great Barrington, MA: Berkshire Publishing.

Borish, L. J., Wiggins, D. K. and Gems, G. R., eds. (2017) *The Routledge History of American Sport.* New York: Routledge.

Borsay, P. (2006) *A History of Leisure: The British Experience since 1500.* Basingstoke: Palgrave.

Bouchier, N. B. and Cruikshank, K. (2016) *The People of the Bay: A Social and Environmental History of Hamilton Harbour.* Vancouver: University of British Columbia Press.

Bourdieu, P. (1977) *Outline of a Theory of Practice.* Cambridge: Cambridge University Press.

Bourdieu, P. (1984) *Distinction: A Social Critique of the Judgment of Taste.* Cambridge MA: Harvard University Press.

Bowness, J. and Zipp, A. (2020) 'Highland Games,' in Nauright, J. and Zipp, S. eds., *Routledge Handbook of Global Sport.* New York: Routledge, 490–500.

Bradley, J. (2020) 'Gaelic Games,' in Nauright, J. and Zipp, S., eds., *Routledge Handbook of Global Sport.* New York: Routledge, 481–489.

Brailsford, D. (1969) *Sport and Society: Elizabeth to Anne.* Toronto: University of Toronto Press.

Brawley, S. (1995) *Vigilant and Victorious: A Community History of the Collaroy Surf Lifesaving Club 1911–1995.* Sidney: Collaroy Surf Life Saving Club.

Brawley, S. (1996) *Beach Beyond: History of the Palm Beach Surf Club 1921–1996.* Sydney: University of New South Wales Press.

Brawley, S. and Guoth, N., eds. (2015) *Australia's Asian Sporting Context, 1920s–30.* London: Routledge.

Breen, T. H. (1977) 'Horses and Gentlemen: The Cultural Significance of Gambling among the Gentry of Virginia,' *William and Mary Quarterly* 34:2, 239–257.

Brentin, D. and Zec, D., eds. (2018) *Sport in Socialist Yugoslavia.* London: Routledge.

Brewster, C. and Brewster, K. (2016) *Representing the Nation: Sport and Spectacle in Post-revolutionary Mexico*. London: Routledge.

Brodkin, K. (1998) *How Jews Became White Folks and What that Says About Race in America*. New Brunswick, NJ: Rutgers University Press.

Brownell, S. (1995) *Training the Body for China: Sports in the Moral Order of the People's Republic*. Chicago: University of Chicago Press.

Brownell, S. (2008a) *Beijing's Games: What the Olympics Mean to China*. Lanham, MD: Rowman & Littlefield.

Brownell, S., ed. (2008b) *The 1904 St. Louis Anthropology Days and Olympic Games: Sport, Race, and American Imperialism*. Lincoln: University of Nebraska Press.

Brownfoot, J. N. (1990) 'Emancipation, Exercise and Imperialism: Girls and the Games Ethic in Colonial Malaya,' *International Journal of the History of Sport* 7:1, 61–84.

Brownfoot, J. N. (2002) '"Healthy Bodies, Healthy Minds": Sport and Society in Colonial Malaya,' *The International Journal of the History of Sport*, 19, 129–156.

Browning, M. (1999) *A Complete History of World Cup Cricket*. New York: Simon & Schuster.

Bruce, H. A. (1910) 'The Psychology of Football,' *Outlook* 96, 541–545.

Bryson, L. (1987) 'Sport and the Maintenance of Masculine Hegemony,' *Women's Studies International Forum* 10:4, 349–360.

Buder, S. (1967) *Pullman: An Experiment in Industrial Order and Community Planning 1880–1930*. New York: Oxford University Press.

Burke, P. (1995) 'The Invention of Leisure in Early Modern Europe,' *Past and Present*, 146:1, 136–150.

Burroughs, A. and Nauright, J. (2000) 'Women's Sports and Embodiment in Australia and New Zealand,' in Mangan, J. A. and Nauright, J., eds., *Sport in Australasian Society: Past and Present*. London: Frank Cass, 188–205.

Butler, J. (1990) *Gender Trouble: Feminism and the Subversion of Identity*. New York: Routledge.

Butler, J. (1993) *Bodies That Matter: On the Discursive Limits of Sex*. London: Routledge.

Cahn, S. (1994) *Coming on Strong: Gender and Sexuality in Women's Sport*. Urbana: University of Illinois Press.

Caillois, R. (1961) *Man, Play and Games*. New York: Free Press of Glencoe.

Cameron, A. (1976) *Circus Factions: Blues and Greens at Rome and Byzantium*. Oxford: Clarendon.

Carlin, J. (2008) *Playing the Enemy: Nelson Mandela and the Game That Made a Nation*. New York: Penguin Press.

Carotenuto, M. (2013) 'Grappling with the Past: Wrestling and Performance Identity in Kenya,' *International Journal of the History of Sport* 30:16, 1889–1902.

Carrington, B. (2002) *'Race', Representation and the Sporting Body*, CUCR Occasional Papers Series. London: University of London.

Carrington, B. and McDonald, I. (2001) *Race, Sport and British Society*. London: Routledge.

Carrington, B. and McDonald, I. (2008) *Marxism, Cultural Studies and Sport*. London: Routledge.

Cashman, R. (1980) *Patrons, Players and the Crowd: The Phenomenon of Indian Cricket*. Delhi: Orient Longman.

Cashman, R. (1995) *Paradise of Sport: The Rise of Organized Sport in Australia*. Melbourne: Oxford University Press.

Castiglione, B. (1528) *Il Cortegiano* [The Courtier].Venice.

Caudwell, J., ed. (2006) *Sport, Sexualities and Queer Theory*. New York: Routledge.

Cavallo, D. (1981) *Muscles and Morals: Organized Playgrounds and Urban Reform*. Philadelphia: University of Pennsylvania Press.

Cavendish, R. (2009) 'Henry II of France dies of tournament wounds,' *History Today* 59:7, at https://www.historytoday.com/archive/henry-ii-france-dies-tournament-wounds (accessed 24 May 2020).

Chakraborty, S. R. (2010) *The Politics of Sport in South Asia*. London: Routledge.

Chapman, D. C. (1994) *Sandow the Magnificent: Eugen Sandow and the Beginnings of Bodybuilding*. Urbana: University of Illinoi Press.

Chatziefstathiou, D., Garcia, B. and Seguin, B., eds. (2020) *Routledge Handbook of the Olympic and Paralympic Games*. London: Routledge.

Chudacoff, H. P. (1999) *The Age of the Bachelor*. Princeton, NJ: Princeton University Press.

Claydon, J. (2019) 'Origin and History,' *World Lacrosse*, at https://worldlacrosse sport/worldlacrosse/origin-history/ (accessed 5 May 2020).

Cleophas, F. (2018) *Exploring Decolonizing Themes in South African Sport History: Issues and Challenges*. Stellenbosch, South Africa: African Sunmedia.

Cleveland, T., Kaur, T. and Akindes, G. (2020) *Sports in Africa: Past and Present*. Athens, OH: Ohio University Press.

Cobley, A. G. (2010) 'The Caribbean,' in Pope, S. W. and Nauright, J., eds *Routledge Companion to Sports History*. New York: Routledge, 375–390.

Collins, C. and Jackson, S., eds. (2007) *Sport in Aotearoa New Zealand Society*. Auckland: Thompson.

Collins, T. (2009) *A Social History of English Rugby Union*. London: Routledge.

Collins, T. (2013) *Sport in a Capitalist Society*. London: Routledge.

Colls, R. (2015) 'British Sports History,' *History Today* 65:4, at https://www.historytoday.com/archive/british-sports-history (accessed 24 March 2020).

Combeau-Mari, E. (1998) *Sport et decolonization a la Reunion*. Paris: L'Harmattan.

Connell, R. W. (1995) *Masculinities*. Berkeley, CA: University of California Press.

Cooper, J. and Laurendeau, J. (2007) 'BASE Jumping,' in Booth, D. and Thorpe, H., eds., *Berkshire Encyclopedia of Extreme Sports*. Great Barrington, MA: Berkshire Publishing, 20–26.

Cooper, P. (1998) *American Marathon*. Syracuse, NY: Syracuse University Press.

Crawford, S. A. G. M (2011) [Review of M. Dyreson, Crafting Patriotism for Global Dominance], *Journal of Sport History* 38:2, 319–320.

Creak, S. (2015) *Embodied Nation: Sport, Masculinity, and the Making of Modern Laos*. Honolulu: University of Hawai'i Press.

Cronin, M. (1999) *Sport and Nationalism in Ireland: Gaelic Games, Soccer, and Irish Identity since 1884*. Dublin: Four Courts Press.

Cronin, M. (2014) *Sport: A Very Short Introduction*. New York: Oxford.

Cronin, M., Murphy, W. and Rouse, P., eds. (2009) *The Gaelic Athletic Association, 1884–2009*. Dublin: Irish Academic Press.

Crotty, M. and Hess, R., eds. (2018) *Sport, War and Society in Australia and New Zealand*. London: Routledge.

Crowther, N. B. (2004) *Athletika: Studies in the Olympic Games and Greek Athletics*. Hildesheim: Weidmann.

Cunningham, H. (1980) *Leisure in the Industrial Revolution, c.1780–c.1880*. London: Croom Helm.

Curi, M. (2014) *Soccer in Brazil*. London: Routledge.

DaCosta, L. and Miragaya, A., eds. (2002) *Worldwide Experiences and Trends in Sport for All*. Oxford: Meyer and Meyer.

Daly, J. (1994) *Feminae Ludens*. Adelaide: Openbook Publishers.

Darby, P. and Hassan, D., eds. (2008) *Emigrants at Play: Sport and the Irish Diaspora*. London: Taylor & Francis.

Darnell, S. C., Nakamura, Y. and Joseph, J., eds. (2012) *Race and Sport in Canada: Intersecting Inequalities*. Toronto: Canadian Scholars' Press.

Darwin, C. (1859) *The Origin of Species by Means of Natural Selection*. London: John Murray.

Davis, R. C. (1998) *The War of the Fists: Popular Culture and Public Violence in Late Renaissance Venice*. New York: Oxford University Press.

Dawson, K. (2006) 'Enslaved Swimmers and Divers in the Atlantic World,' *Journal of American History* 92:4, 1327–1355.

Deathscapes: Mapping Race and Violence in Settler States (n.d.) [project web site] at https://www.deathscapes.org/about-project/#aboutdeathscapes

De Beauvoir, S. (1997) *The Second Sex*, translated by H. M. Parshley. New York: Vintage Books.

Decker, W. (1987) *Sports and Games of Ancient Egypt*. New Haven: Yale University Press.

Deets, M. (2015) '"Grown-ups on White Plastic Chairs": Soccer and Separatism in Senegal, 1969–2012,' *History in Africa* 43, 347–374.

De Grazia, V. (1981) *The Culture of Consent: Mass Organisation of Leisure in Fascist Italy*. Cambridge: Cambridge University Press.

Demas, L. (2004) 'The Brown Bomber's Dark Day: Louis-Schmeling I and America's Black Hero,' *Journal of Sport History* 31:3, 252–271.

deMenezes, J. (2018) 'Esports Will Not be Added to Olympics Because "Killer" Games are Too Violent,' *Independent*, 4 September, at https://www.independent.co.uk/sport/olympics/olympics-esports-wont-be-added-killer-games-too-violent-ioc-president-thomas-bach-a8522301.html (accessed 12 June 2020).

Dempsey, J. M., ed. (2006) *Sports Talk Radio in America: Its Context and Culture*. New York: Haworth Press.

de Wilde, A. (2017) 'Revisiting "Ghosts of the Garden": Sport History, Modernizing Technology, and the Promise and Perils of Digital Vizualization,' *Journal of Sport History* 44:2, 225–238.

Dichter, H. L. and Johnes, A. L., eds. (2014) *Diplomatic Games: Sport, Statecraft, and International Relations since 1945*. Lexington: University Press of Kentucky.

Diem, C. (1960) *Weltgeschichte des Sports*. Stuttgart: Cotta.

Dimeo, P. (2001) 'Football and Politics in Bengal,' in Dimeo, P. and Mills, J., eds., *Soccer in South Asia: Empire, Nation, Diaspora*. London: Frank Cass, 57–74.

Dimeo, P. and Mills, J., eds. (2001) *Soccer in South Asia: Empire, Nation, Diaspora*. London: Frank Cass.

Dinces, S. (2018) *Bulls Markets: Chicago's Basketball Business and the New Inequality*. Chicago: University of Chicago Press.

Docker, E. (1977) *History of Indian Cricket*. Delhi: Macmillan.

Dong, J. (2002) *Women, Sport, and Society in Modern China: Holding Up More than Half the Sky*. London: Routledge.

Dover, R. (1636) *Annalia Dubrensia: Upon the Yearly Celebration of Mr. Robert Dovers (sic) Olympick Games upon Cotswold Hills*. London: Robert Raworth for Matthew Walbancke.

Drumond, M., and deMelo, V. A., eds. (2018) *Brazilian Sports History*. London: Routledge.

Duis, P. (1983) *The Saloon: Public Drinking in Chicago and Boston, 1880–1920*. Urbana: University of Illinois Press.

Dulles, F. R. (1940) *America Learns to Play: A History of Popular Recreation 1607–1940*. New York: D. Appleton-Century.

Dunham, W. H. (1979) *Scarcity and Survival in Central America: Ecological Origins of the Football War*. Stanford, CA: Stanford University Press.

Dunlap, H. L. (1951) 'Games, Sports, Dancing and Other Vigorous Physical Activities and their Function in Samoan Culture,' *Research Quarterly* 22, 298–311.

Dunning, E. and Sheard, K. (2005) *Barbarians, Gentlemen and Players*. London: Routledge.

Dunning, E, Murphy, P. and Williams, J. (1988) *The Roots of Football Hooliganism: An Historical and Sociological Study*. London: Routledge.

Dyreson, M. (2004) 'The Foot Runners Conquer Mexico and Texas: Endurance Racing, "Indigenismo," and Nationalism,' *Journal of Sport History* 31:1, 1–31.

Dyreson, M. (2009) *Crafting Patriotism for Global Dominance*. Abingdon: Routledge.

Dyreson, M. (2010) 'The United States of America,' in Pope, S. W. and Nauright, J., eds., *Routledge Companion to Sports History*. New York: Routledge, 599–624.

Dyreson, M. (2016) 'The Original Pan-American Games? The 1937 Dallas Pan-American Olympics,' *The International Journal of the History of Sport*, 33:1–2, 6–28.

Dyreson, M. (2019) 'Looking Backward and Forward from the 24-Million-Word Mark: A Managing Editor's Perspective on *The International Journal of the History of Sport* in Transition,' *The International Journal of the History of Sport* 36:17–18, 1487–1500.

Dyreson, M., ed. (2020). *Sport in the Americas: Local, Regional, and International Perspectives*. New York: Routledge.

Dyreson, M., Mangan, J. A. and Park, R. J., eds. (2013) *Mapping an Empire of American Sport: Expansion, Assimilation, Adaptation and Resistance*. London: Routledge.

Edelman, R. (1993) *Serious Fun: A History of Spectator Sport in the USSR*. Oxford: Oxford University Press.

Edelman, R. (2012) *Spartak Moscow: A History of the Peoples' Team in the Workers' State*. Ithaca, NY: Cornell University Press.

Egan, P. (1997) *Boxiana I* [reprint, orig. 1813]. Toronto: Nicol Island Publishing.

Eichberg, H. (2004) *The People of Democracy: Understanding Self-Determination on the Basis of Body and Movement*. Aarhus: Klim.

Eichberg, H. (2010) 'Body Culture,' in Pope, S. W. and Nauright, J., eds., *Routledge Companion to Sports History*. New York: Routledge, 162–181.

Elias, N. (2000) *The Civilizing Process* [reprint]. Malden, MA: Blackwell.

Elyot, T. (1531) *The Boke Named the Governour* [1907, London: Dent].

Elsey, B. and Nadel, J. (2020) *Futbolera: A History of Women's Sport in Latin America*. Austin: University of Texas Press.

Engelmann, L. (1988) *The Goddess and the American Girl: The Story of Suzanne Lenglen and Helen Wills*. New York: Oxford University Press.

Erenburg. L. A. (2007) *The Greatest Fight of Our Generation: Louis vs. Schmeling*. New York: Oxford University Press.

Ernst, R. (2004) *Weakness Is a Crime: The Life of Bernarr Macfadden*. Syracuse, NY: Syracuse University Press.

Fair, L. (2001) *Pastimes and Politics: Culture, Community, and Identity in Post-Abolition Urban Zanzibar, 1890–1945*. Athens: Ohio University Press.

Fédération Équestre Internationale (n.d.) 'South East Asian Games,' at https://inside.fei.org/fei/games/cont-regional/sea (accessed 12 June 2020).

Federation of Gay Games (n.d.) 'History of the Gay Games,' at https://gaygames.org/History (accessed 8 June 2020).

Field, R. and Kidd, B. (2016) 'Canada and the Pan American Games,' *International Journal of History of Sport*, 33:1–2, 217–239.

Fields, S. K. (2005) *Female Gladiators: Gender, Law, and Contact Sport in America*. Urbana: University of Illinois Press.

Filipova-Kyurkchieva, I. (2006) 'Football and Political Symbolism in Bulgaria in the 1980s and 1990s,' *Ethnologia Balkanica* 10, 345–362.

Fishpool, M. (2018) 'Miles and Laps: Women's Cycle Races in Great Britain at the Turn of the 19th Century – Part 1,' *Playing Pasts*, at https://www.play-ingpasts.co.uk/articles/gender-and-sport/miles-and-laps-womens-cycle-racing-in-great-britain-at-the-turn-of-the-19th-century-part-i/ (accessed 20 April 2020).

Fletcher, R. (2008) 'Living on the Edge: The Appeal of Risk Sports For the Professional Middle Class,' *Sociology of Sport Journal* 25:3, 310–330.

Flowers, B. (2011) 'Stadiums: Architecture and the Iconography of the Beautiful Game,' *International Journal of the History of Sport*, 28:8–9, 1174–1185.

Fontes, P. and Buarque de Hollanda, B., eds. (2014) *The Country of Football: Politics, Popular Culture and the Beautiful Game in Brazil*. New York: Oxford University Press.

Ford, B., Chilton, K., Endy, C., Henderson, M., Jones, B., and Son, J. Y. (2020) 'Beyond Big Data: Teaching Introductory U.S. History in the Age of Student Success,' *Journal of American History* 106:4, 989–1011.

Forsyth, J. and Giles, A. R., eds. (2013) *Aboriginal Peoples and Sport in Canada: Historical Foundations and Contemporary Issues*. Vancouver: University of British Columbia Press.

Forum: European Sport and the Challenges of Its Recent Historiography (2011) [Special issue], *Journal of Sport History* 38:2, 211–372.

Field, R. (2011) *The Olympic Movement's Response to the Challenge of the Emerging Nationalism in Sport: An Historical Consideration of GANEFO*. Winnipeg: University of Manitoba Press.

Frank, W. D. (2013) *Everyone to Skis! Skiing in Russia and the Rise of Soviet Biathlon*. DeKalb: University of Northern Illinois Press.

Friedan, B. (1963) *Feminine Mystique*. Harmondsworth: Penguin Books.

Frost, D. (2011) *Seeing Stars: Sports Celebrity, Identity, and Body Culture in Modern Japan*. Cambridge, MA: Harvard University Asia Center.

Fuhua, H. and Hong, F., eds. (2019) *A History of Chinese Martial Arts*. New York: Routledge.

Futrell, A. (2009) *The Roman Games: Historical Sources in Translation*. Oxford: Blackwell.

Galily, Y. and Ben-Porat, A., eds. (2016) *Politics and Society in the Land of Israel: Past and Present.* London: Routledge.

Gardiner, E. N. (1910) *Greek Athletic Sports and Festivals.* London: Macmillan.

Geertz, C. (1972) 'Deep Play: Notes on the Balinese Cockfight,' *Daedalus* 101: 27, 1–37.

Geertz, C. (1973) *The Interpretation of Cultures.* New York: Basic Books.

Gems, G. R. (1980) *Physical Activity in Sixteenth Century England as Influenced by the Works of Elyot, Ascham, and Mulcaster.* MS thesis, University of Arizona.

Gems, G. R., ed. (1996a) *Sports in North America: A Documentary History: Sports Organized, 1880–1900,* Vol. 5. Gulf Breeze, FL: Academic International Press.

Gems, G. R. (1996b) 'The Prep Bowl: Sport, Religion, and Americanization in Chicago,' *Journal of Sport History* 23:3, 284–302.

Gems, G. R. (1997) *Windy City Wars: Labor, Leisure, and Sport in the Making of Chicago.* Lanham, MD: Scarecrow Press.

Gems, G. R. (2000) *For Pride, Profit & Patriarchy: Football and the Incorporation of American Cultural Values.* Lanham, MD: Scarecrow Press.

Gems, G. R. (2006) *The Athletic Crusade: Sport and American Cultural Imperialism.* Lincoln: University of Nebraska Press.

Gems, G. R. (2010) 'The city,' in Pope, S. W. and Nauright, J., eds., *Routledge Companion to Sport History.* London: Routledge, 51–70.

Gems, G. R. (2013) *Sport and the Shaping of Italian American Identity.* Syracuse, NY: University of Syracuse Press.

Gems, G. R. (2014a) *Boxing: A Concise History of the Sweet Science.* Lanham, MD: Rowman & Littlefield.

Gems, G. R. (2014b) *Blood and Guts to Glory: A History of Sports* [e-book]. Oslo: Total Health Publications.

Gems, G. R. (2014c) 'Historians Take on Ethnicity, Race, and Sport,' in Riess, Steven A. ed., *A Companion to American Sport History.* DeKalb, IL: John Wiley & Sons, 404–433.

Gems, G. R. (2016) *Sport and the American Occupation of the Philippines: Bats, Balls, and Bayonets.* Lanham, MD: Lexington Books.

Gems, G. R. (2017) 'Women and the Advent of American Sport Tourism: The Feminine Invasion of Male Space,' *International Journal of the History of Sport,* 34:14, 1468–1482.

Gems, G. R. (2020) *Sport and the Shaping of Civic Identity in Chicago.* Lanham, MD: Lexington Books.

Gems, G. R. and Pfister, G. (2019a) 'Gender and the Sportification of Mountaineering: Case studies,' *Stadion* 43:2, 234–249.

Gems, G. R. and Pfister, G., eds. (2019b) *Touchdown: An American Obsession.* Great Barrington, MA: Berkshire.

Gems, G. R. and Pfister, G. (2009) *Understanding American Sports.* New York: Routledge.

Gems, G. R., Borish, L. J. and Pfister, G. (2017) *Sports in American History: From Colonization to Globalization*. Champaign, IL: Human Kinetics.

Gengshen, H. (1926) *Of Chinese Physical Education and Sport*. Shanghai: Commercial Press.

Gennaro, M. J. and Aderinto, S., eds. (2019) *Sports in African History, Politics and Identity Formation*. London: Routledge.

Georgiadis, K. (2003) *Olympic Revival: The Revival of the Olympic Games in Modern Times*. Athens: Ekdotike Athenon S. A.

Goellner, W. A. (1953) 'The Court Ball Game of the Original Mayas,' *Research Quarterly* 24, 147–168.

Goksoyr, M. E. (2007) 'Ski Jumping,' in Booth, D. and Thorpe, H., eds., *Berkshire Encyclopedia of Extreme Sports*. Great Barrington, MA: Berkshire Publishing, 276–278.

Gonzalez, D. (2013) 'Hoop Dreams in Oaxaca's Hills,' *LA Times*, 25 June, at https://lens.blogs.nytimes.com/2013/06/25/hoop-dreams-in-oaxacas-hills/ (accessed 17 June 2020).

González Echevarría, R. (1999) *The Pride of Havana: A History of Cuban Baseball*. New York: Oxford University Press.

Goodman, C. (1979) *Choosing Sides: Playground and Street Life on the Lower East Side*. New York: Schocken Books.

Goodman, R. (2018) *How to Behave Badly in Elizabethan England*. New York: Liveright.

Gori, G. (2004) *Female Bodies, Sport, Italian Fascism: Submissive Women and Strong Mothers*. London: Frank Cass.

Gorn, E. (1985) '"Gouge and Bite, Pull Hair and Scratch": The Social Significance of Fighting in the Southern Backcountry,' *American Historical Review* 90, 18–43.

Gorn, E. (1986) *The Manly Art: Bare-Knuckle Prize Fighting in America*. Ithaca, NY: Cornell University Press.

Gorn, E. and Goldstein, W. (1993) *A Brief History of American Sports*. New York: Hill and Wang.

Gould, S. J. (1981) *The Mismeasure of Man*. New York: W. W. Norton.

Grant, M. (1916) *The Passing of the Great Race*. New York: Charles Scribner's Sons.

Greenham, C. (2019) 'Canadian Football,' in Gems, G. R. and Pfister, G., eds., *Touchdown: An American Obsession*. Great Barrington, MA: Berkshire Publishing, 237–251.

Greer, G. (1970) *The Female Eunuch*. London: MacGibbon & Kee.

Groom, G. (2017) *The Complete Book of the Commonwealth Games*. Morrisville, NC: Lulu Press.

Guedes, C. (2020) *Mulheres a Cesta* [documentary film], at https://www.youtube.co/watch?v=oJ-YTxlobVk and with subtitles at https://www.youtube.com/watch?v=PeLhfrBQ6xc&feature=youtu.be

Gullion, L. (2007) 'Whitewater Kayaking and Canoeing,' in Booth, D. and Thorpe, H., eds., *Berkshire Encyclopedia of Extreme Sports*. Grand Barrington, MA: Berkshire Publishing, 362–368.

Guglielmo, J. and Salerno, S., eds. (2003) *Are Italians White? How Race Is Made in America*. New York: Routledge.

Guonot, A. (2002) 'Sport or Political Organization? Structures and Characteristics of the Red Sport International, 1921–1937,' *Journal of Sport History* 28:1, 23–39.

Gurock, J. S. (2005) *Judaism's Encounter with American Sports*. Bloomington: Indiana University Press.

Guterl, M. P. (2001) *The Color of Race in America, 1900–1940*. Cambridge, MA: Harvard University Press.

Guthrie-Shimizu, S. (2015) *Transpacific Field of Dreams: How Baseball Linked the United States and Japan in Peace and War*. Chapel Hill: University of North Carolina Press.

Guttmann, A. (1978) *From Ritual to Record: The Nature of Modern Sports*. New York: Columbia University Press.

Guttmann, A. (1991) *Women's Sports: A History*. New York: Columbia University Press.

Guttmann, A. (1994) *Games and Empires: Modern Sports and Cultural Imperialism*. New York: Columbia University Press.

Guttmann, A. (2004) *Sports: The First Five Millennia*. Amherst: University of Massachusetts Press.

Guttmann, A. and Thompson, L. (2001) *Japanese Sports*. Honolulu: University of Hawaii Press.

Hall, M. A. (1978) *Sport and Gender: A Feminist Perspective on the Sociology of Sport*. Vanier City, Ottawa: Canadian Association for Health, Physical Education, and Recreation.

Hall, M. A. (2002) *The Girl and the Game: A History of Women's Sport in Canada*. Peterborough, Ontario: Broadview Press.

Hall, M. A. (2018) *Muscle on Wheels: Louise Armaindo and the High-Wheel Racers of Nineteenth-Century America*. Montreal: McGill-Queens University Press.

Hallinan, C. (1991) 'Aborigines and Positional Segregation in Australian Rugby League,' *International Review for the Sociology of Sport* 26:2, 69–79.

Hallinan, C. and Judd, B. (2016) *Indigenous People, Race Relations and Australian Sport*. London: Routledge.

Hanna, E. (2015) 'Young Men's Christian Association (YMCA),' in Daniel, U., Gatrell, P., Janz, O., Jones, H., Keene, J., Kramer, A. and Nasson, B., eds., *International Encyclopedia of the First World War*. Berlin: Freie Universität, at https://encyclopedia.1914–1918 online.net/article/young_mens_christian_association_ymca (accessed 15 May 2020).

Hardy, S. (1982) *How Boston Played: Sport Recreation, and Community, 1865–1915.* Boston: Northeastern University Press.

Hardy, S. (1990) 'Entrepreneurs, Structures, and the Sportgeist: Old Tensions in a Modern Industry,' in D. G. Kyle and G. Stark, eds., *Essays in Sport History and Sport Mythology.* College Station: Texas A&M University Press, 45–82.

Hardy, S. (2014) 'Counting the Ways: Wray Vamplew's *Pay Up and Play the Game* and Its Importance to Sport History,' *Journal of Sport History*, 41:1, 117–128.

Hargreaves, J. (1985) 'Playing Like Gentlemen While Behaving Like Ladies: Contradictory Features of the Formative Years of Women's Sports,' *British Journal of Sport History* 2, 40–52.

Hargreaves, J. (1986a) *Sport, Power, and Culture: A Social and Historical Analysis of Popular Sports in Britain.* Cambridge: Polity.

Hargreaves, J. (1986b) 'Where's the Virtue? Where's the Grace? A Discussion of the Social Production of Gender Relations in and Through Sport,' *Theory, Culture, and Society* 3, 109–121.

Hargreaves, J. (1994) *Sporting Females: Critical Issues in the History and Sociology of Women's Sports.* London: Routledge.

Hargreaves, J. (1998) *Freedom for Catalonia? Catalan Nationalism, Spanish Identity and the Barcelona Olympic Games.* Cambridge: Cambridge University Press.

Hargeaves, J. (2001) 'Women's Boxing and Related Activities: Introducing Images and Meanings,' *In Yo: Journal of Alternative Perspectives*, at https://ejmas com/jalt/jaltart_hargreaves_0901.htm

Hargreaves, J. and Anderson, E., eds. (2014) *Routledge Handbook of Sport, Gender and Sexuality.* London: Routledge.

Hargreaves, J. and Vertinsky, P., eds. (2006) *Physical Culture, Power and the Body.* London: Routledge.

Harney, J. J. (2019) *Empire of Infields: Baseball in Taiwan and Cultural Identity, 1895–1968.* Lincoln: University of Nebraska Press.

Harris, H. A. (1964) *Greek Athletes and Athletics.* London: Hutchinson.

Hartmann, D. (2003) *Race, Culture, and the Revolt of the Black Athlete: The 1968 Olympic Protests and Their Aftermath.* Chicago: University of Chicago Press.

Hartmann-Tews, I. and Pfister, G., eds. (2003) *Sport and Women: Social Issues in International Perspective.* London: Routledge.

Hassan, D. and O'Kane, P. (2010) 'Ireland,' in Pope, S. W. and Nauright, J., eds. *Routledge Companion to Sports History.* New York: Routledge, 461–471.

Havens, T. R. H. (2015) *Marathon Japan: Distance Racing and Civic Culture.* Honolulu: University of Hawaii Press.

Hedenborg, S. and Pfister, G., eds. (2018) *Extraordinary Sportswomen.* New York: Routledge.

Heggie, V. (2014) 'Making Histories: Sport, Science, Medicine,' in Delheye, P., ed., *Making Sport History: Disciplines, Identity and the Historiography of Sport.* Abingdon: Routledge, 216–223.

Heywood, L. and Dworkin, S. L. (2003) *Built to Win: The Female Athlete as Cultural Icon*. Minneapolis: University of Minnesota Press.

Higgs, R. J. (1995) *God in the Stadium: Sport and Religion in America*. Lexington: University Press of Kentucky.

Higginson, T. W. (1858) 'Saints and Their Bodies,' *Atlantic Monthly* 1:5, 582–595.

Hilbrenner, A. and Lenz, B. (2011) 'Looking at European Sport from an Eastern European Perspective: Football in the Multi-ethnical Polish Territories,' *European Review* 19:4, 595–610.

Hill, J. (1996) 'British Sport History: A Postmodern Future?' *Journal of Sport History* 23:1, 1–19.

Hill, J. (2002) *Sport, Leisure, and Culture in Twentieth Century Britain*. New York: Palgrave.

Hill, J. (2003) 'Introduction: Sport and Politics,' *Journal of Contemporary History* 38:3, 355–361.

Hill, J. (2006) *Sport and the Literary Tradition: Essays in History, Literature, and Sport*. Oxford: Peter Lang.

Hindin, J., Howzen, M., Xue, H., Pu, H. and Newman, J. (2020) 'E-sports,' in Nauright, J. and Zipp, S., eds., *Routledge Handbook of Global Sport*. New York: Routledge, 405–415.

Hoare, Q. and Smith, G. N., eds. (1971) *Selections from the Prison Notebooks of Antonio Gramsci*. New York: International Publishers.

Hobsbawm, E. (1987) *The Age of Empire: 1875–1914*. London: George Weidenfeld and Nicolson.

Hobsbawm, E. and Ranger, T., eds. (1983) *The Invention of Tradition*. Cambridge: Cambridge University Press.

Hoffman, S. J., ed. (1992) *Sport and Religion*. Champaign, IL: Human Kinetics.

Hoffman, S. J. (2010) *Good Game: Christianity and the Culture of Sports*. Waco, TX: Baylor University Press.

Hofmann, A. R. (2001) *The American Turner Movement: A History from its Beginnings to 2000*. Indianapolis, IN: Max Kade German-American Center at Indiana-Purdue University and Indiana German Heritage Society.

Hofmann, A., ed. (2020) *Sport in Europe*. London: Routledge.

Holland, B. (2003) *Gentlemen's Blood: A History of Dueling from Swords at Dawn to Pistols at Dusk*. New York: Bloomsbury.

Holliman, J. (1931) *American Sports, 1785–1835*. Durham, NC: Seeman.

Holman, A., ed. (2009) *Canada's Game: Hockey and Identity*. Montreal: McGill-Queen's University Press.

Holt, R. (1989) *Sport and the British: A Modern History*. Oxford: Clarendon Press.

Holt, R. (2014) 'Historians and the History of Sport,' *Sport in History* 34:1, 1–33.

Hong, F. (1997) *Footbinding, Feminism, and Freedom: The Liberation of Women's Bodies in Modern China*. London: Frank Cass.

Hong, F. (2010) 'China,' in Pope, S. W. and Nauright, J., eds., *Routledge Companion to Sports History*. New York: Routledge, 405–419.

Hong, F., ed. (2015) *Sport in the Middle East: Power, Politics, Ideology and Religion*. London: Routledge.

Hong, F. and Lu, Z., eds. (2020) *The Routledge Handbook of Sport in Asia*. London: Routledge.

Hong, F., Mackay, D. and Christensen, K., eds. (2008) *China Gold: China's Quest for Global Power and Olympic Glory*. Great Barrington, MA: Berkshire Publishing.

hooks, bell (1981) *Ain't I a Woman? Black Women and Feminism*. Boston: South End Press.

Howard, J. (2018) 'On Sport, Public History, and Public Sport History,' *Journal of Sport History* 45:1, 24–40.

Howell, C. (2007) 'Assessing Sport History and the Cultural and Linguistic Turn,' *Journal of Sport History* 34:3, 459–465.

Howell, C. and Leeworthy, D. (2010) 'Borderlands,' in S. W. Pope and J. Nauright, eds., *Routledge Companion to Sport History*. New York: Routledge, 71–84.

Huebner, S. (2016) *Pan-Asian Sports and the Emergence of Modern Asia, 1913–1974*. Singapore: National University of Singapore Press.

Huggins, M. (2000) *Flat Racing and British Society 1790–1914: A Social and Economic History*. London: Frank Cass.

Huggins, M. (2008) 'Sport and the British Upper Classes *c*.1500–2000: A Historiographic Overview,' *Sport in History*, 28:3, 364–388.

Huggins, M. (2020) 'Associativity, Gambling, and the Rise of Protomodern British Sport, 1660–1800,' *Journal of Sport History* 47:1, 1–17.

Hughes, T. (1857) *Tom Brown's Schooldays*. Cambridge: Macmillan and Co.

Huizinga, J. (1938) *Homo ludens: Proeve eener bepaling van het spel-element der cultuur* [Homo Ludens: A Study of the Play-element in Culture]. Haarlem: Tjeenk Willink.

Iber, J. (2019) 'American Football in Latin America,' in Gems, G. R. and Pfister, G., eds., *Touchdown: An American Obsession*. Great Barrington, MA: Berkshire.

Ignatiev, N. (1995) *How the Irish Became White*. New York: Routledge.

Ingham, A. G. and Hardy, S. (1993) 'Introduction: Sport Studies Through the Lens of Raymond Williams,' in Ingham, A. and Loy, J., eds., *Sport in Social Development: Traditions, Transitions and Transformations*, Champaign, IL: Human Kinetics, 1–19.

International Committee of the Mediterranean Games (n.d.) 'Mediterranean Games,' at https://cijm.org.gr/mediterranean-games/ (accessed 11 June 2020).

Isenberg, N. (2016) *White Trash: The 400-Year Untold History of Class in America*. New York: Penguin Books.

Ismond, P. (2003) *Black and Asian Athletes in British Sport and Society: A Sporting Choice?* Basingstoke: Palgrave Macmillan.

Ivanova, V. (2014) 'Traditional Russian Sports,' *Russia IC*, at http://russia-ic.com/sport/in_depth/2041/#.XvH5j9iSmyI (accessed 23 June 2020).

Jacobson, M. F. (1998) *Whiteness of a Different Color: European Immigrants and the Alchemy of Race*. Cambridge, MA: Harvard University Press.

Jaggard, E. (2002) 'Writing Australian Lifesaving's History,' *Journal of Sport History* 29:1, 15–23.

Jamail, M. H. (2000) *Full Count: Inside Cuban Baseball: Writing Baseball*. Carbondale: Southern Illinois University Press.

James, C. L. R. (1963) *Beyond a Boundary*. London: Stanley Paul.

Jarvie, G., ed. (1991) *Sport, Racism and Ethnicity*. London: Falmer.

Jarvie, G., ed. (1999) *Sport in the Making of Celtic Cultures*. Leicester: Leicester University Press.

Jarvie, G. and Burnett, J., eds. (2000) *Sport, Scotland, and the Scots*. Phantassie: Tuckwell Press.

Jarvie, G. and Walker, G. eds. (1994) *Scottish Sport in the Making of the Nation: Ninety Minute Patriots?* Leicester: Leicester University Press.

Jarvie, G., Hwang, D. and Brennan, M., eds. (2008) *Sport, Revolution and the Beijing Olympics*. Oxford: Berg.

Jensen, E. N. (2010) *Body by Weimar: Athletes, Gender and German Modernity*, Oxford: Oxford University Press.

Johnes, M. (2000) 'Hooligans and Barrackers: Crowd Disorder and Soccer in South Wales, 1906–39,' *Soccer in Society* 1:2, 19–35.

Johnes, M. (2002) *Soccer and Society: South Wales, 1900–39*. Cardiff: University of Wales Press.

Johnes, M. (2004) 'Putting the History into Sport: On Sport History and Sport Studies in the U.K.,' *Journal of Sport History* 31:2, 145–160.

Johnes, M. (2005) *History of Sport in Wales*. Cardiff: University of Wales Press.

Johnes, M. (2010) '*Great Britain*,' in Pope, S. W. and Nauright, J., eds., *Routledge Companion to Sports History*. New York: Routledge, 444–460.

Johnson, B. (n.d.) 'William Marshal, a Knight's Tale,' at https://www.historic-uk.com/HistoryUK/HistoryofEngland/William-Marshal-Knights-Tale/ (accessed 26 March, 2020).

Jones, G. S. (1974) 'Working Class Culture and Working Class Politics in London, 1870–1900,' *Journal of Social History* 7, 460–508.

Jones, S. (1986) *Workers at Play: a Social and Economic History of Leisure, 1918–1939*. London: Routledge and Kegan Paul.

Joo, Y., Bae, Y. and Kassens-Noor, E. (2017) *Mega-Events and Mega-Ambitions: South Korea's Rise and the Strategic Use of the Big Four Events*. London: Palgrave Macmillan.

Judkins, B. N. and Nielson, J. (2015) *The Creation of Wing Chun: A Social History of the Southern Chinese Martial Arts*. Albany: State University of New York Press.

Kaplan, R. (2015) *The Jewish Olympics: The History of the Maccabiah Games.* New York: Skyhorse Publishing.

Keaveney, C. T. (2018) *Contesting the Myths of Samurai Baseball: Cultural Representations of Japan's National Pastime.* Hong Kong: Hong Kong University Press.

Keys, B. J. (2006) *Globalizing Sport: National Rivalry and International Community in the 1930s.* Cambridge, MA: Harvard University Press.

Kidd, B. (1987) 'Sports and Masculinity,' *Queens Quarterly* 94, 116–131.

Kidd, B. and Torres, C. (2018) *Historicizing the Pan-American Games.* London: Routledge.

Kietlinski, R. (2013) *Japanese Women and Sport: Beyond Baseball and Sumo.* London: Bloomsbury.

Kimball, R. I. (2009) *Sports in Zion: Mormon Recreation, 1890–1940.* Urbana: University of Illinois Press.

Kimmel, M. S. (1996) *Manhood in America: A Cultural History.* New York: Free Press

King, C. R., ed. (2015) *Asian American Athletes in Sport and Society.* New York: Routledge.

Kissoudi, P., ed. (2008) 'The Balkan Games and Balkan Politics in the Inter-war Years (1929–1939): Politicians in Pursuit of Peace,' *International Journal of the History of Sport* 25:13 [special issue].

Klein, A. (1991) *Sugarball: The American Game, the Dominican Dream.* New Haven, CT: Yale University Press.

Klein, A. M. (1994) 'Baseball Wars: The Mexican Baseball League and Nationalism in 1946,' *Studies in Latin American Popular Culture* 13, 33–56.

Klein, A. M. (2014) *Dominican Baseball: New Pride, Old Prejudice.* Philadelphia: Temple University Press.

Koch, N., ed. (2017) *Critical Geographies of Sport: Space, Power and Sport in Global Perspective.* New York: Routledge.

Kohei, K. (2019) 'American Football in Japan,' in Gems, G. R. and Pfister, G., eds., *Touchdown: An American Obsession.* Great Barrington, MA: Berkshire Publishing, 315–329.

Koon, T. (1985) *Believe, Obey, Fight: Political Socialization of Youth in Fascist Italy 1922–1943.* Chapel Hill: North Carolina University Press.

Korsgaard, O. (1990) 'Sport as a Practice of Religion: The Record as Ritual,' in Carter, J. M. and Kruger, A., eds., *Ritual and Record: Sports Records and Quantification in Pre-Modern Societies.* Westport, CT: Greenwood Press, 115–12.

Kossakowski, R., Nosal, P. and Wozniak, W. (2020) *Politics, Ideology and Football Fandom: The Transformation of Modern Poland.* London: Routledge.

Kossl, J. (1977) *History of the Czechoslovak Olympic Movement (Dejiny ceskoslovensk kopane).* Prague: Olympia.

Krout, J. A. (1929) *Annals of American Sport.* New Haven, CT: Yale University Pres

Kruger, A. (2010) 'Germany,' in Pope, S. W. and Nauright, J., eds., *Routledge Companion to Sports History*. New York: Routledge, 432–443.

Kruger, M. and Hofmann, A., eds. (2020) *Sportgeschichte in Deutschland – Sport History in Germany*. Weisbaden: Springer.

Kruger, A. and Murray, W., eds. (2003) *The Nazi Olympics: Sport, Politics and Appeasement in the 1930s*. Champaign: University of Illinois Press.

Kusz, K. (2007) 'Whiteness and Extreme Sports,' in Booth, D. and Thorpe, H., eds., *Berkshire Encyclopedia of Extreme Sports*. Grand Barrington, MA: Berkshire Publishing, 357–361.

Kwak, D. H., Ko, J. Y., Kang, I., and Rosentraub, M., eds. (2019) *Sport in Korea: History, Development, Management*. London: Routledge.

Kyle, D. G. (2007) *Sport and Spectacle in the Ancient World*. Oxford: Blackwell.

Laffaye, H. A. (2014) *Polo in Argentina: A History*. Jefferson, NC: McFarland.

Lapchick, R. E. (1975) *The Politics of Race and International Sport: The Case of South Africa*. Westport, CT: Greenwood.

Large, D. C. (2007) *Nazi Games: The Olympics of 1936*. New York: W. W. Norton.

Laurendeau, J. (2007) 'Skydiving/Skysurfing,' in Booth, D. and Thorpe, H., eds., *Berkshire Encyclopedia of Extreme Sports*. Great Barrington, MA: Berkshire Publishing, 281–286.

Lenz, B. (2011) 'Polish Sport and the Challenges of Its Recent Historiography,' *Journal of Sport History* 38:3, 349–360.

Lever, J. (1983) *Soccer Madness: Brazil's Passion for the World's Most Popular Sport*. Chicago: University of Chicago Press.

Light, R. L. (2010) 'Japan,' in Pope, S. W. and Nauright, J., eds., *Routledge Companion to Sports History*. New York: Routledge, 472–486.

Lisi, C. A. (2015) *A History of the World Cup, 1930–2014*. London: Rowman & Littlefield.

Little, C. (2010) 'South-East Asia,' in Pope, S.W. and Nauright, J., eds., *Routledge Companion to Sports History*. New York: Routledge.

Liu, L. and Hong, F. (2017) *The National Games and National Identity in China: A History*. New York: Routledge.

Lomax, M. (2003) *Black Baseball Entrepreneurs, 1860–1901: Operating By Any Means Necessary*. Syracuse, NY: Syracuse University Press.

Lopez de D'Amico, R., Benn, T. and Pfister, G., eds. (2016) *Women and Sport in Latin America*. London: Routledge.

Lorber, J. (1994) *Paradoxes of Gender*. New Haven, CT: Yale University Press.

Love, C., ed. (2008) *A Social History of Swimming in England 1800–1918: Splashing in the Serpentine*. New York: Routledge.

MacAloon, J.J. (1981) *This Great Symbol: Pierre de Coubertin and the Origins of the Modern Olympic Games*. Chicago: University of Chicago Press.

MacLean, M. (2010) 'New Zealand (Aotearoa),' in Pope, S. W. and Nauright, J., eds., *Routledge Companion to Sports History*. New York: Routledge, 510–525.

MacLean, M. (2014) 'Ambiguity within the Boundary: Rereading C.L.R. James's Beyond a Boundary,' in Nauright, J., Cobley, A. G. and Wiggins, D. K., eds., *Beyond C.L.R. James: Shifting Boundaries of Race and Ethnicity in Sport*. Fayetteville: University of Arkansas Press, 17–39.

Magdalinski, T. and Chandler, T. J. L., eds. (2002) *With God on Their Side: Sport in the Service of Religion*. London: Routledge.

Magrath, R., Cleland, J. and Anderson, E., eds. (2020) *Palgrave Handbook of Masculinity and Sport*. Cham: Palgrave Macmillan.

Maguire, J. (1995) 'Common Ground? Links Between Sports History, Sports Geography, and the Sociology of Sport,' *Sporting Traditions* 12:1, 3–25.

Maguire, J. A. and Nakayama, M., eds. (2006) *Japan, Sport and Society: Tradition and Change in a Globalizing World*. New York: Routledge.

Majumdar, B. (2015) *Cricket in Colonial India, 1780–1947*. London: Routledge.

Malcolm, D., Gemmell, J. and Mehta, N., eds. (2010) *The Changing Face of Cricket: From Imperial to Global Game*. London: Routledge.

Malcolmson, R. W. (1973) *Popular Recreations in English Society*. Cambridge: Cambridge University Press.

Mallon, B. and Buchanan, I. (1999) 'To No Earthly King.....,' *Journal of Olympic History* 7:3, 21–28.

Mandell, R. (1987) *The Nazi Olympics*. Champaign: University of Illinois Press.

Mandell, R. (2016) *The First Modern Olympic Games*. London: Endeavour Press.

Mangan, J. A. (1981) *Athleticism in the Victorian and Edwardian Public School: The Emergence and Consolidation of an Educational Ideology*. Cambridge: Cambridge University Press.

Mangan, J. A. (1986) *The Games Ethic and Imperialism: Aspects of the Diffusion of an Ideal*. London: Frank Cass.

Mangan, J. A., ed. (1996) *Tribal Identities: Sport, Nationalism, Identity*. London: Frank Cass.

Mangan, J. A., ed. (1999) *Shaping the Superman, Fascist Body as Icon – Aryan Fascism*. London: Frank Cass.

Mangan, J. A., ed. (2000) *Superman Supreme, Fascist Body as Political Icon – Global Fascism*. London: Frank Cass.

Mangan, J. A. (2011) *'Manufactured' Masculinity-Making Imperial Manliness, Morality and Militarism*. Abingdon: Routledge.

Mangan, J. A. and DaCosta, L. P., eds. (2001) *Sport in Latin American Society: Past and Present*. London: Routledge.

Mangan, J. A. and Hong, F., eds. (2002) *Sport in Asian Society: Past and Present*. London: Frank Cass.

Mangan, J. A. and Ndee, H. S. (2003) 'Military Drill – Rather more than "Brief and Basic": English Elementary Schools and English Militarism,' in Mangan, J. A., ed., *Militarism, Sport, Europe: War without Weapons*. London: Frank Cass, 65–96.

Mangan, J. A. and Park, R. J., eds. (1986) *From 'Fair Sex' to Feminism: Sport and the Socialization of Women in the Industrial and Post-Industrial Eras*. London: Frank Cass.

Mangan, J. A. and Walvin, J. (1987) *Masculinity and Morality: Middle-class Masculinity in Britain and America, 1800–1940*. Manchester: Manchester University Press.

Mangan, J. A., Chu, M. P. and Jinxia, D. (2015) *The Asian Games: Modern Metaphor for 'The Middle Kingdom' Reborn: Political Statement, Cultural Assertion, Social Symbol*. London: *Routledge*.

Mansfield, L. and Malcolm, D. (2010) 'Sociology,' in Pope, S. W. and Nauright, J., eds., *Routledge Companion to Sports History*. London: Routledge, 99–113.

Manzenreiter, W. (2014) *Sport and Body Politics in Japan*. New York: Routledge.

Manzenreiter, W. and Horne, J. (2004) *Football Goes East: Business, Culture and the People's Game in China, Japan, and Korea*. London: Routledge.

Margolick, D. (2005) *Beyond Glory: Joe Louis vs. Max Schmeling and a World on the Brink*: New York: Alfred A. Knopf.

MarineBio (n.d.) 'Scuba Diving,' at https://marinebio.org/creatures/tools/scuba-diving/ (accessed 1 June 2020).

Marqusee, M. (1996) *War Minus the Shooting: A Journey through South Asia during Cricket's World Cup*. London: Heineman.

Marschik, M. (2011) 'Austrian Sport and the Challenges of Its Recent Historiography,' *Journal of Sport History* 38:2, 189–198.

Martel, J.-P. (2019) 'Origins of Ice Hockey,' at https://thecanadianencyclopedia.ca/en/article/origins-of-ice-hockey (accessed 5 May 2020).

Martin, P. (1995) *Leisure and Society in Colonial Brazzaville*. Cambridge: Cambridge University Press.

Martin, S. (2004) *Football and Fascism: The National Game under Mussolini*. Oxford: Berg.

Martin, S. (2011a) *Sport Italia: The Italian Love Affair with Sport*. London: I. B. Tauris.

Martin, S. (2011b) 'Italian Sport and the Challenges of Its Recent Historiography,' *Journal of Sport History* 38:2, 199–209.

Mason, T. (1980) *Association Football and English Society, 1863–1915*. Brighton: Harvester Press.

Mason, T. (1995) *Passion of the People? Football in South America*. London: Verso.

Mathews, G. R. (1980) 'The Controversial Olympic Games of 1908 as Viewed by the New York Times and Times of London,' *Journal of Sport History* 7:2, 40–53.

McConnell, R. C. (2007) 'Bungee Jumping,' in Booth, D. and Thorpe, H., eds., *Berkshire Encyclopedia of Extreme Sports*. Great Barrington, MA: Berkshire Publishing, 54–57.

McCrone, K. E. (1988) *Playing the Game: Sport and the Physical Emancipation of English Women, 1870–1940*. University Press of Kentucky.

McCrone, K. E. (1988) *Sport and the Physical Emancipation of Women, 1870–1914*. Lexington: University Press of Kentucky.

McElligott, R. and Hassan, D., eds. (2018) *A Social and Cultural History of Sport in Ireland*. London: Routledge.

McFarland, A. (2011) 'Spanish Sport and the Challenges of Its Recent Historiography,' *Journal of Sport History* 38:2, 211–221.

McGehee, R. V. (1992) 'The Rise of Sport in Guatemala and the First Central American Games,' *International Journal of the History of Sport* 9, 132–140.

McGehee, R. V. (1994) 'Sports and Recreational Activities in Mexico and Guatemala, Late 1800s to 1926,' *Studies in Latin American Popular Culture* 13, 7–32.

McGehee, R. V. (1998) 'Carreras, Patrias y Caudillos: Sport/Spectacle in Mexico and Guatemala, 1926–43,' *South Eastern Latin Americanist* 41, 19–32.

McGehee, R. V. (2000) 'The Impact of Imported Sports on the Popular Culture of Nineteenth and Early Twentieth Century Mexico and Central America,' in Fey, I. E. and Racine, K., eds., *Strange Pilgrimages: Exile, Travel, and National Identity in Latin America, 1800–1990s*. Wilmington, DE: Scholarly Resources, 95–111.

McGehee, R. V. (2002) 'Sport in Nicaragua, 1889–1926,' in Arbena, J. L. and LaFrance, D. G., eds., *Sport in Latin American and the Caribbean*. Wilmington, DE: Scholarly Resources, 350–364.

McGehee, R. V. (2005) 'Early Development of Modern Sport in Costa Rica, 1890s to 1926,' *Journal of ICHPER* 41, 57–63.

McGehee, R. V. (2010) 'Mexico and Central America,' in Pope, S. W. and Nauright, J., eds., *Routledge Companion to Sports History*. New York: Routledge, 487–497.

McIntosh, P. (1963) *Sport in Society*. London: C. A. Watts.

McKibbin, R. (2011) 'Sports History: Status, Definitions and Meanings,' *Sport in History* 31:2, 167–174.

Meinander, H. and Mangan, J. A. (1998) *The Nordic World: Sport in Society*. London: Frank Cass.

Messner, M. and Sabo, D. (1990) *Sport, Men, and the Gender Order: Critical Feminist Perspectives*. Champaign, IL: Human Kinetics.

Metcalfe, A. (1976) 'Organized Sport and Social Stratification in Montreal,' in Gruneau, R. S. and Albinson, J. G., eds., *Canadian Sport: Sociological Perspective*. Don Mills: Addison-Wesley.

Metcalfe, A. (1978) 'The Evolution of Organized Physical Recreation in Montreal, 1840–1895,' *Histoire Social – Social History* 11:2, 144–166.

Metcalfe, A. (2006) *Leisure and Recreation in a Victorian Mining Community: The Social Economy of Leisure in North-East England, 1820–1914*. London: Routledge.

Miah, A. and Garcia, B. (2012) *The Olympics: The Basics*. London: Routledge.

Miller, P. and Wiggins, D. K., eds. (2004) *Sport and the Color Line: Black Athletes and Race Relations in Twentieth-Century America*. New York: Routledge.

Miller, S. G. (2004) *Ancient Greek Athletics*. New Haven: Yale University Press.

Mills, R. (2009) "'It All Ended in an Unsporting Way": Serbian Football and the Disintegration of Yugoslavia, 1989–2006,' *International Journal of the History of Sport* 26, 1187–1217.

Mills, R. (2018) *The Politics of Football in Yugoslavia: Sport, Nationalism and the State*. London: I. B. Tauris.

Mitchell, T. (1991) *Blood Sport: A Social History of Spanish Bullfighting*. Philadelphia: University of Pennsylvania Press.

Moenig, U. (2015) *Taekwondo: From a Martial Art to a Martial Sport*. New York: Routledge.

Morelli, J. (1990) *Mujeres Deportistas*. Buenos Aires: El Planeta.

Morrison, T. (1992) *Playing in the Dark: Whiteness and the Literary Imagination*. New York: Vintage Books.

Morrow, D. and Wamsley, K. (2017) *Sport in Canada: A History*. Don Mills, Ontario: Oxford.

Murtha, R. (2017) 'A History of International Sport in Catalonia,' *World News*, 20 October, at https://intpolicydigest.org/2017/10/20/a-history-of-international-sport-in-catalonia/#:~:text=Ryan%20Murtha%20A%20History%20of%20International%20Sport%20in,region%20located%20in%20the%20northeast%20corner%20of%20Spain (accessed 2 November 2020).

Naess-Holm, A. (2008) *Batting for Peace: A Study of Cricket Diplomacy between India and Pakistan*. Saarbrucken: VDM Verlag.

Nasaw, D. (1993) *Going Out: The Rise and Fall of Public Amusements*. New York: Basic Books.

Nathan, D. A. (2003) *Saying It's So: A Cultural History of the Black Sox Scandal*. Urbana: University of Illinois Press.

National Geographic (n.d.) 'NG Live! Free Soloing with Alex Hammond' [video], https://video.nationalgeographic.com/video/00000144-0a3d-d3cb-a96c-7b3da3db0000 (accessed 27 May 2020).

Nauright, J. (1997) *Sport, Cultures and Identity in South Africa*. Leicester: Leicester University Press.

Nauright, L. (2010) 'Africa (sub-Saharan),' in Pope, S. W. and Nauright, J., eds., *Routledge Companion to Sports History*. New York: Routledge, 319–329.

Nauright, J. and Amara, M., eds. (2018) *Sport in the African World*. London: Routledge.

Nauright, J. and Black, D. (1998) 'Sport at the Center of Power: Rugby in South Africa During Apartheid,' *Sport History Review*, 29:2, 192–211.

Nauright, J. and Chandler, T., eds. (1996) *Making Men: Rugby and Masculine Identity*. London: Frank Cass.

Nauright, J. and Wiggins, D. K., eds. (2019) *Routledge Handbook of Sport, Race and Ethnicity*. London: Routledge.

Nicholson, R. (2019) *Ladies and Lords: A History of Women's Cricket in Britain.* Oxford: Peter Lang.

Niehaus, A. and Tagsold, C. (2017) *Sport, Memory and Nationhood in Japan: Remembering the Glory Days.* London: Routledge.

Nielsen, E. (2014) *Sport and the British World, 1900–1930: Amateurism and National Identity in Australasia and Beyond.* New York: Palgrave Macmillan.

Nielsen, N. K. and Bale, J. (2011) 'The Contribution of Sport to the Nordic Way,' *Journal of Sport History* 38:2, 223–236.

Nolte, C. E. (2003) *The Sokol in the Czech Lands until 1914: Training for the Nation.* Basingstoke: Palgrave.

Nossov, K. (2009) *Gladiator: Rome's Bloody Spectacle.* Westminster, MD: Osprey.

Noto, A. and Rossi, L., eds. (1992) *Coroginnica: saggi sulla ginnastica, lo sport e la cultura del corpo, 1861–1991.* Rome: La Meridiana.

Nyren, J. (1933) *The Cricketeers of My Time* [in *The Young Cricketer's Tutor*]. London.

O'Brien, J. (2016) 'A Brief History of Olympic Soccer,' *Paste Magazine*, 4 August at https://www.pastemagazine.com/soccer/a-brief-history-of-olympic-soccer/ (accessed 6 June 2020).

Oliver, J. (2007) 'Inline Skating/Rollerblading,' in Booth, D. and Thorpe, H., eds., *Berkshire Encyclopedia of Extreme Sports.* Grand Barrington, MA: Berkshire Publishing, 145–151.

Olivova, V. (1984) *Sports and Games in the Ancient World.* New York: St. Martin's Press.

Oriard, M. (1993) *Reading Football: How the Popular Press Created an American Spectacle.* Chapel Hill, NC: University of North Carolina Press.

Orttung, R. W. and Zhemukhov, S. N. (2017) *Putin's Olympics: The Sochi Game and the Evolution of Twenty-First Century Russia.* London: Routledge.

Osborne, P. (2014) *Wounded Tiger: A History of Cricket in Pakistan.* London: Simon & Schuster.

Osmond, G. (2017) 'Indigenous Sporting Pasts: Resuscitating Aboriginal Swimming History,' *Australian Aboriginal Studies* 2, 43–55.

Osmond, G. (2019) 'Decolonizing Dialogues: Sport, Resistance, and Australian Aboriginal Settlements,' *Journal of Sport History* 46:2, 288–301.

Osmond, G. and Phillips, M. G. (2010) 'Sources,' in Pope, S. W. and Nauright, J., eds., *Routledge Companion to Sports History.* London: Routledge, 34–50.

Osmond, G. and Phillips, M. G., eds. (2015) *Sport History in the Digital Er.* Urbana: University of Illinois Press.

Oxendine, J. B. (1988) *American Indian Sports Heritage.* Champaign, IL: Human Kinetics.

Painter, N. I. (2010) *The History of White People.* New York: W. W. Norton.

Papakonstantinou, Z. (2019) *Sport and Identity in Ancient Greece.* London: Routledge.

Paralympic Games (n.d.) 'History of the Paralympic Movement,' https://www.paralympic.org/ipc/history (accessed 6 June 2020).

Park, R. (1985) 'Sport, Gender, and Society in a Transatlantic Victorian Perspective,' *British Journal of Sports History* 2, 5–28.

Park, R. J. (2012) 'Contesting the Norm: Women and Professional Sports in Late Nineteenth-Century America,' *International Journal of the History of Sport* 29:5, 730–749.

Parks, J. (2017) *The Olympic Games, the Soviet Sports Bureaucracy, and the Cold War: Red Sport, Red Tape.* Lanham, MD: Lexington Books.

Parratt, C. (2001) *More Than Mere Amusement: Working Class Women's Leisure in England, 1750–1914.* Boston: Northeastern University Press.

Parrish, C., Li, H. and Nauright, J. (2020) 'Association Football,' in Nauright, J. and Zipp, S., eds., *Routledge Handbook of Global Sport.* New York: Routledge, 18–28.

Parsons, T. H. (2020) *The British Imperial Century, 1815–1914.* Lanham, MD: Rowman & Littlefield.

Paul, S. (1987) 'The Wrestling Traditions and Its Social Functions,' in Baker, W. J. and Mangan, J. A., eds., *Sport in Africa: Essays in Social History.* New York: Africana Publishing Co., 23–46.

Paxson, F. (1917) 'The Rise of Sport,' *Mississippi Valley Historical Review*, 4, 143–168.

Perica, V. (2001) 'United they Stood, Divided they Fell: Nationalism and the Yugoslav School of Basketball, 1968–2000,' *Nationalities Papers* 29, 267–291.

Pettavino, P. J. and Pye, G. (1994) *Sport in Cuba: The Diamond in the Rough.* Pittsburgh: University of Pittsburg Press.

Pfister, G. (1996) 'Physical Activity in the Name of the Fatherland: Turnen and the National Movement, (1810–1820),' *Sporting Heritage* 1, 14–36.

Pfister, G. and Gems, G. R. (2018) 'The Shady Past of Female Boxers: What Case Studies in the USA reveal,' in Hedenborg, S. and Pfister, G., eds., *Extraordinary Sportswomen.* New York: Routledge, 4–18.

Pfister, G. and Gems, G. R. (2019) 'Gender and the Sportification of Mountaineering: Case Studies,' *Stadion* 43, 234–249.

Pfister, G. and Peyton, C. (1989) *Frauen-sport in Europa.* Hamburg: Czwalina.

Pfister, G. and Pope, S., eds. (2018) *Female Football Players and Fans: Intruding into a Man's World.* London: Macmillan.

Pfister, G. and Sisjord, M. K., eds. (2013) *Gender and Sport: Changes and Challenges.* Munster: Waxman.

Phillips, M. G. (2001) 'Deconstructing Sport History: The Postmodern Challenge,' *Journal of Sport History* 28:3, 327–343.

Phillips, M. G., ed. (2006) *Deconstructing Sport History: A Postmodern Analysis.* Albany, NY: SUNY Press.

Phillips, M. G., ed. (2012) *Representing the Sporting Past in Museums and Halls of Fame.* New York: Routledge.

Phillips, M. G. and Osmond, G (2018) 'Marching for Assimilation: Indigenous Identity, Sport, and Politics,' *Australian Journal of Politics and History* 64:4, 544–560.

Piccione, P. A. (2010) 'Book Review of Joyce Tyldesley, Egyptian Games and Sports,' *American Journal of Archaeology* 114:2, at https://www.ajaonline.org/book-review/670 (accessed 12 May 2020).

Piess, K. (1986) *Cheap Amusements: Working Women and Leisure in Turn-of-the-Century New York*. Philadelphia: Temple University Press.

Pink, S. (1997) *Women and Bullfighting: Gender, Sex and the Consumption of Tradition* Oxford: Berg.

Poliakoff, M. P. (1987) *Combat Sports in the Ancient World: Competition, Violence and Culture*. New Haven: Yale University Press.

Polley, M. (2007) *Sports History: A Practical Guide*. New York: Palgrave Macmillan.

Ponzio, A. (2015) *Shaping the New Man: Youth Training Regimes in Fascist Italy and Nazi Germany*. Madison: University of Wisconsin Press.

Pope, S. W. (1997) *The New American Sport History: Recent Approaches and Perspectives*. Urbana: University of Illinois Press.

Pope, S. W. (2006) 'Decentering "Race" and (Re)presenting "Black" Performance in Sport History: Basketball and Jazz in American Culture, 1920–50,' in Phillips, M., ed., *Deconstructing Sport History: A Postmodern Analysis*. Albany NY: SUNY Press, 147–180.

Porter, P. E. B. (1905) '"Ann Glanville," Saltash History and Heritage,' at https://saltash.org/saltash-people/ann-glanville.html (accessed 19 April 2010).

Pound, R. W. (1994) *Five Rings over Korea*. Boston: Little, Brown.

Powers, M. (1998) *Faces along the Bar: Lore and Order in the Workingman's Saloon 1870–1920*. Chicago: University of Chicago Press.

Prebish, C. S. (1993) *Religion and Sport: The Meeting of Sacred and Profane*. Westport CT: Greenwood Press.

Pronger, B. (1990) *The Arena of Masculinity: Sports, Homosexuality, and the Meaning of Sex*. New York: St. Martin's Press.

Putney, C. (2001) *Muscular Christianity: Manhood and Sports in Protestant America 1880–1920*. Cambridge, MA: Harvard University Press.

Radford, P. (2017) 'Was the Long Eighteenth Century a Golden Age for Women in Sport? The Case of Madame Bunel and Alicia Thornton,' *Early Modern Women: An Interdisciplinary Journal* 12:1, 183–194.

Rampersad, A. (2014) 'Ethnicity, National Identity, and Cricket in Contemporary Trinidad and Tobago,' in Nauright, J., Cobley, A. G. and Wiggins, D. K eds., *Beyond C.L.R. James: Shifting Boundaries of Race and Ethnicity in Sport* Fayetteville: University of Arkansas Press, 239–252.

Ranger, T. (1987) 'Pugilism and Pathology: African Boxing and the Black Urban Experience in Southern Rhodesia,' in Baker, W. J. and Mangan, J. A., ed.

Sport in Africa: Essays in Social History. New York: Africana Publishing Co., 196–213.

Rechwein, P. (2014) *Climber's Paradise: Making Canada's Mountain Parks, 1906–1974.* Edmonton: University of Alberta Press.

Regalado, S. O. (2013) *Nikkei Baseball: Japanese American Players from Immigration and Internment to the Major Leagues.* Urbana: University of Illinois Press.

Regalado, S. O. and Fields, S. K., eds. (2014) *Sport and the Law: Historical and Cultural Intersections.* Fayetteville: University of Arkansas Press.

Reid, J. G. and Reid, R. (2015) 'Diffusion and Discursive Stabilization: Sports Historiography and the Contrasting Fortunes of Cricket and Ice Hockey in Canada's Maritime Provinces,' *Journal of Sport History* 42:1, 87–113.

Reisler, J. (2015) *Walk of Ages: Edward Payson Weston's Extraordinary 1909 Trek Across America.* Lincoln: University of Nebraska Press.

Richards, T. (1999) *Dancing on Our Bones: New Zealand, South Africa, Ruby and Racism.* Wellington: Bridget Williams Books.

Rider, T. C. (2016) *Cold War Games: Propaganda, the Olympics, and U.S. Foreign Policy.* Urbana: University of Illinois Press.

Rider, T. C. and Witherspoon, K. B., eds. (2018) *Defending the American Way of Life: Sport, Culture, and the Cold War.* Fayetteville: University of Arkansas Press.

Riess, S. A. (1989) *City Games: The Evolution of American Urban Society and the Rise of Sports.* Urbana: University of Illinois Press.

Riess, S. A. (1991) 'Sport and the Redefinition of American Middle-Class Masculinity,' *International Journal of the History of Sport* 8, 5–27.

Rinehart, R. E. (2007) 'Alternative Sports,' in Booth, D. and Thorpe, H., eds., *Berkshire Encyclopedia of Extreme Sports.* Great Barrington, MA: Berkshire Publishing, 295–316.

Rinehart, R. E. and Sydnor, S. S., eds. (2003) *To the Extreme: Alternative Sports, Inside and Out.* Albany: State University of New York Press.

Riordan, J. (1977) *Sport in Soviet Society: Development of Sport and Physical Education in Russia and the USSR.* Cambridge: Cambridge University Press.

Riordan, J., ed. (1978) *Sport under Communism.* Montreal: McGill-Queens University Press.

Riordan, J. (1980) *Soviet Sport: Background to the Olympics.* Oxford: Blackwell.

Riordan, J. (2010) 'Russia/The Soviet Union,' in Pope, S. W. and Nauright, J., eds., *Routledge Companion to Sports History.* New York: Routledge, 541–552.

Roarke, S. (2017) 'Stanley Cup has Incredible History,' *NHL News*, 13 March, at https://www.nhl.com/news/stanley-cup-has-incredible-125-years-of-history/c-287633638 (accessed 12 June 2020).

Roberts, R. (2010) *Joe Louis: Hard Times Man.* New Haven, CT: Yale University Press.

Roberts, R. (2014) 'The Two-Fisted Testing Ground of Manhood: Boxing and the Academy,' *Journal of American History* 101:1, 188–191.

Roden, D. (2001) 'Baseball and the Quest for National Dignity in Meiji Japan,' in Dreifort, J. E., ed., *Baseball History from Outside the Lines: A Reader*. Lincoln: University of Nebraska Press, 280–303.

Roediger, D. R. (1991) *The Wages of Whiteness: Race and the Making of the American Working Class*. New York: Verso.

Roediger, D. R., ed. (1998) *Black on White: Black Writers on What It Means to Be White*. New York: Schocken Books.

Rohdewald, S. (2011) 'Yugoslavian Sport and the Challenges of Its Recent Historiography,' *Journal of Sport History* 38:3, 387–395.

Rosenzweig, R. (1983) *Eight Hours for What We Will: Workers and Leisure in an Industrial City, 1870–1920*. Cambridge: Cambridge University Press.

Ross, E. E. (1914) *The Old World in the New*. New York: Century.

Rotundo, E. A. (1993) *American Manhood: Transformations in Masculinity from the Revolution to the Modern Era*. New York: Basic Books.

Ruck, R. (1999) *The Tropic of Baseball: Baseball in the Dominican Republic*. Lincoln: University of Nebraska Press.

Ruck, R. (2014) 'The Field of Sports History at Critical Mass,' *Journal of American History* 101:1, 192–194.

Ruck, R. (2018) *The Tropic of Football: The Long and Perilous Journey of Samoans to the NFL*. New York: New Press.

Ryan, G., ed. (2005) *Tackling Rugby Myths: Rugby and New Zealand Society 1854–2004*. Dunedin: Otago University Press.

Ryan, G. and Watson, G. (2018) *Sport and the New Zealanders: A History*. Auckland: Auckland University Press.

Ryba, T. V. and Wright, H. K. (2005) 'From Mental Game to Cultural Praxis: A Cultural Studies Model's Implications for the Future of Sport Psychology,' *Quest* 57:2, 192–212.

Sack, A. L. and Suster, Z. (2000) 'Soccer and Croatian Nationalism: A Prelude to War,' *Journal of Sport and Social Issues* 24, 305–320.

Sandiford, K. (2004) 'Cricket and a Crisis of Identity in the Anglophone Caribbean,' in Smith, A. and Porter, D., eds., *Sport and National Identity in the Post-War World*. London: Routledge, 128–144.

Sansone, D. (1992) *Greek Athletic and the Genesis of Sport*. Berkeley: University of California Press.

Sarantakes, N. E. (2010) *Dropping the Torch: Jimmy Carter, the Olympic Boycott, and the Cold War*. New York: Cambridge University Press.

Scanlon, T. F. (2014) *Sport in Greek and Roman Worlds*. Oxford: Oxford University Press.

Scarborough, V. L. and Wilcox, D. R., eds. (1991) *The Mesoamerican Ballgame*. Tucson: University of Arizona Press.

Schultz, J. (2014) *Qualifying Times: Points of Change in U.S. Women's Sport*. Urbana: University of Illinois Press.

Schultz, J. (2017) 'New Directions and Future Considerations in American Sport History,' in Borish, Linda J., Wiggins, David K. and Gems, Gerald R., eds., *The Routledge History of American Sport*. New York: Routledge, 17–29.

Schultz, J., O'Reilly, J. and Cahn, S. (2018) *Women and Sports in the United States: A Documentary Reader*. Chicago: University of Chicago Press.

Schweinbenz, A. (2010) 'Canada,' in Pope, S. W. and Nauright, J., eds., *Routledge Companion to Sports History*. New York: Routledge, 360–374.

Sclar, A. (2014) 'Redefining Jewish Athleticism: New Approaches and Research Directions,' in Rei, R. and Sheinin, D. M. K., eds., *Muscling in on New Worlds: Jews, Sport, and the Making of the Americas*. Leiden, Netherlands: Brill, 160–178.

Seecharan, C. (2006) *Muscular Learning: Cricket and Education in the Making of the British West Indies at the End of the 19th Century*. Kingston, Jamaica: Ian Randle.

Sen, R. (2015) *Nation at Play: A History of Sport in India*. New York: Columbia University Press.

Sheinin, D., ed. (2015) *Sports Culture in Latin American History*. Pittsburgh: University of Pittsburgh Press.

Shennan, M. (2000) *Out in the Midday Sun: The British in Malaya, 1880–1960*. London: John Murray.

Shin, E. H. and Nam, E. A. (2004) 'Culture, Gender Roles, and Sport: The Case of Korean Players on the LPGA Tour,' *Journal of Sport and Social Issues* 28:3, 223–244.

Shuman, A. (2013) 'Elite Competitive Sport in the People's Republic of China, 1958–966: The Games of the New Emerging Forces (GANEFO),' *Journal of Sport History* 40:2, 258–283.

Shurley, J. R., Todd, J. and Todd. T. (2019) *Strength Coaching in America: A History of the Innovation That Transformed Sports*. Austin: University of Texas Press.

Shuster, R. (2020) 'The Aquatic Neanderthal: They Could Swim and Dive for Clams,' *Archaeology Magazine*, 15 January, at https://www.haaretz.com/archae-ology/.premium.MAGAZINE-the-aquatic-neanderthal-they-could-swim-and-dive-for-clams-1.8403830 (accessed 1 June 2020).

Sikes, M. (2019) 'Enduring Legacies and Convergent Identities: The Male-Dominated Origins of the Kenyan Running Explosion,' *Journal of Sport History* 46:2, 273–287.

Silk, M., Andrews, D. and Thorpe, H., eds. (2017) *Routledge Handbook of Physical Culture Studies*. London: Routledge.

Sinclair, K. (1986) *A Destiny Apart: New Zealand's Search for National Identity*. Wellington: Allen & Unwin.

Skiadas, E. G., ed. (1998) *Women's Sport in Modern Greece*. Athens: Labyrinth.

Smith, E. B., Grant, J. C. and Starkey, H. M. (1898) *Historical Sketch of the Young Men's Christian Association, 1858–1898*. Chicago: YMCA.

Smith, M., ed. (2019) 'Special Edition: Indigenous Resurgence, Regeneration, and Decolonization through Sport History,' *Journal of Sport History* 46:2, 143–324.

Sohu (n.d.) 'Fok Hails 6th EAG as Most Successful,' https://sports.sohu.com/20131015/n388203384.shtml (accessed 12 June 2020).

Somers, D. (1972) *The Rise of Sport in New Orleans, 1850–1900*. Baton Rouge: Louisiana State University Press.

Sotomayor, A. (2015) '"Operation Sport": Puerto Rico's Recreational and Political Consolidation in the Age of Modernization and Decolonization 1950s,' *Journal of Sport History* 42:1, 59–86.

Sotomayor, A. (2016) *The Sovereign Colony: Olympic Sport, National Identity, and International Politics in Puerto Rico*. Lincoln: University of Nebraska Press.

South Asia Olympic Council (n.d.) 'History of South Asia Olympic Council,' https://web.archive.org/web/20130603133706/http://www.southasiangames.org/ (accessed 12 June 2020).

Special Olympics (n.d.) 'History,' https://www.specialolympics.org/about/history (accessed 6 June 2020).

Sporting and Theatrical Journal (1884) 3:26, 10 May.

Sporting and Theatrical Journal (1887) 11:7, 24 December.

Springwood, C. F. (2006) 'Basketball, Zapatistas, and Other Racial Subjects,' *Journal of Sport and Social Issues* 30:4, 364–373.

Staley, S. C. (1962) 'Notes Regarding the History and Scope of Sport and the Need for Training Sport Historians,' *Proceedings of National College Physical Education Association, 66th Annual Meeting*.

Starc, G. (2007) 'Bad Game, Good Game, Whose Game? A History of Soccer through Slovenian Press Coverage,' *Journal of Sport History* 34:3, 439–458.

Stearns, P. (2010) 'Foreword,' in Pope, S. W. and Nauright, J., eds., *Routledge Companion to Sports History*. New York: Routledge, x–xv.

Stein, S. J. (1988) 'The Case of Soccer in Early Twentieth-century Lima,' in Arbena J. L., ed., *Sport and Society in Latin America*. New York: Greenwood, 63–84.

Sterling, J., Phillips, M. G. and McDonald, M. (2017) 'Doing Sport History in the Digital Present,' *Journal of Sport History* 44:2, 135–145.

Stone, D., Hughson, J. and Ellis, R. (2017) *New Directions in Sport History*. London: Routledge.

Struna, N. (1984) 'Beyond Mapping Experience: The Need for Understanding the History of American Sporting Women,' *Journal of Sport History* 11:1, 120–133.

Struna, N. (1996) *People of Prowess: Sport, Leisure, and Labor in Early Anglo-America*. Urbana: University of Illinois Press.

Strutt, J. (1801) *The Sports and Pastimes of the People of England*. London: Methuen & Co.

Stuart, W. (1854) *Sketches of the Life of William Stuart, the First and Most Celebrated Counterfeiter of Connecticut.* Bridgeport, CT: privately printed.

Stumpf, F. and Cozens, F. W. (1947) 'Some Aspects of the Role of Games, Sports, and Recreational Activities in the Culture of Modern Primitive Peoples: The New Zealand Maoris,' *Research Quarterly* 18, 198–218.

Stumpf, F. and Cozens, F. W. (1949) 'Some Aspects of the Role of Games, Sports, and Recreational Activities in the Culture of Modern Primitive Peoples II: The Fijians,' *Research Quarterly* 20, 2–20.

Sugden, J. and Bairner, A. (1993) *Sport, Sectarianism and Society in a Divided Ireland.* Leicester: Leicester University Press.

Swanson, R. (2017) 'The Wild West of Pedagogy: Thoughts on Teaching American Sport History,' in Borish, L. J., Wiggins, D. K., and Gems, G. R., eds., *The Routledge History of American Sport.* New York: Routledge, 30–41.

Sydnor, S. (1998) 'A History of Synchronized Swimming,' *Journal of Sport History* 25:2, 252–267.

Syracuse.com (2020) '2020 Super Bowl Ratings: 102 Million Viewers, Up from Last Year,' 3 February, at https://www.syracuse.com/sports/2020/02/2020-super-bowl-ratings-102-million-viewers-up-from-last-year.html (accessed 3 November 2020).

Szymanski, S. (2008) 'A Theory of the Evolution of Modern Sport,' *Journal of Sport History*, 35:1, 1–32.

Tatz, C. (1995) *Obstacle Race: Aborigines in Sport.* Sydney: University of New South Wales Press.

Templeton, M. (1998) *Human Rights and Sporting Contacts: New Zealand's Attitudes to Race Relations in South Africa 1921–94.* Auckland: Auckland University Press.

Terret, T. (1996) *Histoire des sports.* Paris: L'Harmattan.

Terret, T. (2008) 'The Future of Sport History: ISHPES, Potential, and Limits,' *Journal of Sport History* 35:2, 303–309.

Terret, T. (2010) 'France,' in Pope, S. W. and Nauright, J., eds., *Routledge Companion to Sports History.* New York: Routledge, 420–431.

Thomas, D. (2012) *Globetrotting: African American Athletes and Cold War Politics.* Urbana: University of Illinois Press.

Thomas, K. (1964) 'Work and Leisure in Pre-Industrial Society,' *Past and Present* 29, 50–66.

Thompson, E. P. (1963) *The Making of the English Working Class.* New York: Vantage Books.

Thompson, R. (1975) *Retreat from Apartheid: New Zealand's Sporting Contacts with South Africa.* Wellington: Oxford University Press.

Thorpe, H. (2007) 'Snowboarding,' in Booth, D. and Thorpe, H., eds., *Berkshire Encyclopedia of Extreme Sports.* Great Barrington, MA: Berkshire Publishing, 286–294.

Todd, J. (1990) 'The Mystery of Minerva,' *Iron Game History*, 1, 14–17.

Tomlinson, A. (2014) *FIFA: The Men, the Myths, and the Money*. London: Routledge.

Tomlinson, A. and Young, C., eds. (2006) *German Football: History, Culture, Society*. London: Routledge.

Topend Sports (n.d.) 'The West Asian Games,' https://www.topendsports.com/events/games/asian-games/west-asian/index.htm (accessed 12 June 2020).

Torres, C. R. (2001) 'Tribulations and Achievements: The Early History of Olympism in Argentina,' *The International Journal of the History of Sport* 18:3, 59–92.

Torres, C. R. (2006) 'The Latin American "Olympic Explosion" of the 1920s: Causes and Consequences,' *The International Journal of the History of Sport* 23:7, 1088–1111.

Torres, C. R. (2010) 'South America,' in Pope, S. W. and Nauright, J., eds. *Routledge Companion to Sports History*. New York: Routledge, 553–570.

Townsend, S., Osmond, G. and Phillips, M. G. (2019) 'Clay vs. Ali: Distant Reading, Methodology, and Sport History,' *Journal of Sport History* 46:3, 380–395.

Trangbæk, E. and Kirmanen, A. (1995) *Gymnastikkens historie*. Copenhagen: Danmarks Hojskole for Legemsovelden.

Tranter, N. (1998) *Sport, Economy, and Society in Britain, 1750–1914*. Cambridge: Cambridge University Press.

Trueman, C. N. (2015) 'Tudor Sports and Pastimes,' *History Learning Site*, 17 May at https://www.historylearningsite.co.uk/tudor-england/tudor-sports-and-pastimes/ (accessed 13 May 2020).

Trumpbour, R. (2007) *The New Cathedrals: Politics and Media in the History of Stadium Construction*. Syracuse, NY: Syracuse University Press.

Trumpbour, R. and Womack, K. (2010) *The Eighth Wonder of the World: The Life of Houston's Iconic Astrodome*. Lincoln: University of Nebraska Press.

Tsutsui, W. and Baskett, M. (2011) *The East Asian Olympiads, 1934–2008: Building Bodies and Nations in Japan, Korea, and China*. Leiden: Brill.

Ueberhorst, H., ed. (1972–1989) *Geschicte der Leibesubungen* [6 vols.]. Berlin: Barte & Wernitz.

Vahed, G. (2004) 'Deconstructing "Indianness": Cricket and the Articulation of Indian Identities in Durban, 1900–32,' in Mangan, J. A. and Ritchie, A., eds. *Ethnicity, Sport, Identity: Struggles for Status*. London: Routledge, 115–134.

Valiotis, C. (2010) 'South Asia,' in Pope, S. W. and Nauright, J., eds., *Routledge Companion to Sports History*, 571–586.

Vamplew, W. (1976) *The Turf: A Social and Economic History of Horse Racing*. London: Allen Lane.

Vamplew, W. (1988) *Pay Up and Play the Game, 1863–1915*. Cambridge: Cambridge University Press.

Vamplew, W., ed. (2008) 'Forum: Indigenous Sport,' *Journal of Sport History* 35:2, 191–283.

Vamplew, W., ed. (2012) 'Forum: Britain and the Olympics,' *Journal of Sport History*, 39:1, 1–62.

Vamplew, W. (2017) *Numbers and Narratives: Sport, History and Economics*. London: Routledge.

Vamplew, W. and Day, D., eds. (2017) *Methodology in Sport History*. London: Routledge.

Vamplew, W. and Dyreson, M., eds. (2016) *Sports History*. London: Sage.

Van der Merwe, F. (1986) *A History of Sport and Physical Education in the Republic of South Africa*. Hatfield, Pretoria: SAASSPER.

Van der Merwe, F. (2009) *Essays on South African Sport History*. Stellenbosch, South Africa: FJG Publikasies.

van Hilvoorde, I. (2007) 'Buildering,' in Booth, D. and Thorpe, H., eds., *Berkshire Encyclopedia of Extreme Sports*. Great Barrington, MA: Berkshire Publishing, 50–53.

van Mele, V. and Renson, R. (1992) *Traditional Games in South America*. Shorndorf: Hofmann.

Vassort, C. (2007) 'Hang Gliding,' in Booth, D. and Thorpe, H., eds., *Berkshire Encyclopedia of Extreme Sports*. Great Barrington, MA: Berkshire Publishing, 121–123.

Veblen, T. (1899) *The Theory of the Leisure Class: An Economic Study of Institutions*. New York: Macmillan.

Vertinsky, P. (1990) *The Eternally Wounded Woman: Women, Doctors, and Exercise in the Nineteenth Century*. Manchester: Manchester University Press.

Vertinsky, P. and McKay, S., eds. (2004) *Disciplining Bodies in the Gymnasium*. London: Routledge.

Virtanen, L. and DuBois, T. A. (2000) *Finnish Folklore*. Seattle: University of Washington Press.

Vogan, T. (2014) *His Keepers of the Flame: NFL Films and the Rise of Sports Media*. Urbana: University of Illinois Press.

Vogan, T. (2015) *ESPN: The Making of a Sports Media Empire*. Urbana: University of Illinois Press.

Vogan. T. (2018) *ABC Sports: The Rise and Fall of Network Sports Television*. Oakland: University of California Press.

Vrcan, S. and Lalic, D. (1999) 'From Ends to Trenches and Back: Football in the Former Yugoslavia,' in Armstrong, G and Giulianotti, R., eds., *Football Cultures and Identities*. New York: Palgrave Macmillan, 176–185.

Wacquant, L. (2004) *Body and Soul: Notebooks of an Apprentice Boxer*. New York: Oxford.

Wagg, S. (2018) *Cricket: A Political History of the Global Games, 1945–2017*. London: Routledge.

Wagg, S. and Andrews, D., eds. (2007) *East Plays West: Sport and the Cold War*. London: Routledge.

Waic, M. and Zwicker, S. (2010) 'Central and Eastern Europe,' in Pope, S. W. and Nauright, J., eds., *Routledge Companion to Sports History*. New York: Routledge, 391–404.

Wall, K. L. (2012) *Game Plan: A Social History of Sport in Alberta*. Edmonton: University of Alberta Press.

Walvin, J. (1975) *The People's Game: The History of British Football*. London: Allen Lane.

Wassong, S. (2007) 'Climbing,' in Booth, D. and Thorpe, H., eds., *Berkshire Encyclopedia of Extreme Sports*. Great Barrington, MA: Berkshire Publishing, 67–71.

Weeks, J. (2017) '1921: The Year When Football Banned Women,' *History Extra*, at https://www.historyextra.com/period/first-world-war/1921-when-football-association-banned-women-soccer-dick-kerr-ladies-lily-parr/ (accessed 7 June 2020).

Wheaton, B. (2007) 'Windsurfing,' in Booth, D. and Thorpe, H., eds., *Berkshire Encyclopedia of Extreme Sports*. Great Barrington, MA: Berkshire Publishing, 368–373.

Whiting, R. (1977) *The Chrysanthemum and the Bat: The Game Japanese Play*. Tokyo: Permanent Press.

Wiggins, D. K. (1980) 'Sport and Popular Pastimes: Shadow of the Slavequarter,' *Canadian Journal of the History of Sport* 11, 61–88.

Wiggins, D. K. (2018) *More Than a Game: A History of the African American Experience in Sport*. Lanham, MD: Rowman & Littlefield.

Wiley (n.d.) 'Teaching Practices for Your Virtual Classroom,' at https://edservices.wiley.com/teaching-practice-for-virtual-classrooms/ (accessed 8 April 2020).

Williams, J. (2002) *A Game for Rough Girls? A History of Women's Football in Britain*. London: Routledge.

Williams, J. (2014) *A Contemporary History of Women's Sport, Part One, Sporting Women, 1850–1960*. London: Routledge.

Williams, R. (1977) *Marxism and Literature*. Oxford: Oxford University Press.

Wills, C. (2005) *Destination America: The People and Cultures that Created a Nation*. New York: DK Publishing.

Wiltse, J. (2009) *Contested Waters: A Social History of Swimming Pools in America*. Chapel Hill: University of North Carolina Press.

Witherspoon, K. (2014) *Before the Eyes of the World: Mexico and the 1968 Olympic Games*. DeKalb: Northern Illinois University Press.

Wollstonecraft, M. (1792) *A Vindication of the Rights of Woman*. London: Joseph Johnson.

Woltman, B. (1980) *Polish Physical Culture in the German Eastern Poland (Polska kultura fzyczna na wschodnim pograniczu niemieckim 1919–1939*. Poznan: AWF.

Wong, J. C. (2005) *Lords of the Rinks: The Emergence of the National Hockey League, 1875–1935*. Toronto: University of Toronto Press.

Wyatt-Brown, B. (1982) *Southern Honor: Ethics and Behavior in the Old South*. New York: Oxford University Press.

Xifen, G. (1919) *History of Sport in China*. Beijing: China Shangwu Press.

Yamamoto, E. (2016) 'Memories of the 1932 Olympics: A Page in Japanese American History,' *Discover Nikkei*, at www.discovernikkei.org/en/journal/2016/2/10/1932-olympics/ (accessed 9 May 2020).

Young, C. (1996) *Olympic Politics*. Manchester: Manchester University Press.

Young, D. C. (1984) *The Olympic Myth of Greek Amateur Athletics*. Chicago: Ares.

Yu, J. (2007) *Playing in Isolation: A History of Baseball in Taiwan*. Lincoln: University of Nebraska Press.

Zeller, M. (2018) *Sport and Society in the Soviet Union: The Politics of Football After Stalin*. London: I. B. Taurus.

INDEX

Printed in the United States
by Baker & Taylor Publisher Services